AF512569

A Handbook of Buddhism: Art, Architecture, Literature and Philosophy

A Handbook of Buddhism: Art, Architecture, Literature and Philosophy

Suraj Vashishth

CYBER TECH PUBLICATIONS
4264/3, Ansari Road, Daryaganj, New Delhi-110002 (India)
Ph.: 011-23244078. Fax: 011-23280028
E-Mail: cyberpublicationsdelhi@yahoo.com

A HANDBOOK OF BUDDHISM: ART, ARCHITECTURE, LITERATURE & PHILOSOPHY

Suraj Vashishth

© Reserved

First Edition 2009

All rights reserved. No part of this publication may be reproduced, stored in a retrieval system or transmitted, in any form or by any means, electronic, mechanical, photo copying, recording or otherwise, without the prior permission of the publisher.

Published by :

G.S. Rawat for **Cyber Tech Publications**
4264/3, Ansari Road, Daryaganj, New Delhi-110002 (India)
Ph.: 011-23244078. Fax: 011-23280028
E-Mail: cyberpublicationsdelhi@yahoo.com

Printed at :

Preface

Buddhism is one of the important religions of world. Albeit Lord Buddha was not born in Andhra Desa, but the contribution of Andhra Desa to Buddhism is not small. Famous Buddhist Stupas and Viharas as seen at Amaravati, Nagarjunakonda, Bhattiprolu, Guntupalli, Chandavaram are only a few to name in Andhra Desa. With the passing time, new discoveries on Buddhism are pouring in from different corners. Recent discoveries of Totlakonda, Bavikonda, Pavuralakonda etc. from Andhra Pradesh throw welcome light on the subject. This publication contains the papers presented at the seminar, "Contribution of Andhra Desa to Buddhism" organized by Birla Archaeological & Cultural Research Institute, Hyderabad a few years ago. The purpose of the seminar is to bring to light the new discoveries and throw further light on the already existing information on Buddhism from Andhra Desa in particular and India in general. Research is a never ending process and results of research will always be either finding out something new or updating the existing information with the new discoveries. This publication contains papers submitted by both seasoned and budding scholars covering almost all the aspects of Buddhism like art, architecture, philosophy, survey reports, excavation findings etc. As mentioned above, there are papers altogether with new discoveries and papers highlighting new points on the already existing information.

—Author

CONTENTS

1

Buddhist Architecture

The beginnings of the Buddhist school of architecture can be traced back to B.C. 255 when the Mauryan emperor Asoka established Buddhism as the state religion of his large empire. Buddhism spread rapidly throughout India and other parts of Asia. Buddhism was, as it were, a graphic creed, and correspondingly its expansion was accompanied by a distinctive style of architecture that expressed the teachings of the Buddha. In India this early Buddhist art was influenced to a large extent by Asoka. He was responsible for the construction of several stupas, which are sacred mounds of brick commemorative of the Buddha. Asoka also constructed stone pillars symbolizing his creed. These were lofty free-standing monolithic columns erected on sacred sites. The most famous of these is at Sarnath.

The Mauryan dynasty crumbled after Asoka's death in 232 B.C; in its wake came the Sungas, who in turn were succeeded by the Andhras. Both these Brahmanical dynasties treated the Buddhists with toleration. The initial steps of the new architectural movement involved enlarging Asoka's stupas. For instance, the stupa at Sanchi was enlarged to nearly twice its size and elaborate gateways were added.

At about the same time that the Buddhist communities were elaborating Asoka's stupas, an entirely different form of architecture was developing in western India. These structures were not, however, built of stone or wood, but carved out of living rock. It is therefore unfortunate that these structures are now referred to as "caves", as though they were natural grottoes in the mountainside, since they are actually large and well planned temples. Some of the finest specimens of this rock cut architecture are to be seen at Ajanta.

Under the reign of the 8th century ruler Lalitaditya, the central Kashmir valley became an important artistic site. A magnificent Surya temple was constructed at Martand. Though now ruined, this remains the masterpiece of Kashmiri architecture. Mahayana Buddhism flourished in the arid valleys of Ladakh, beyond the first high range of the Himalayas. The monasteries at Alchi, dating from the 11th century, have beautiful paintings depicting the Mahayana pantheon. Cave temples were constructed in the 13th to 15th centuries at Saspol and Karsha. The monasteries at Leh and Phiyang continue to be renovated even today, and the recent resurgence of Indian Buddhism, associated not only with the conversion of lower-caste Hindus to Buddhism under the influence of Ambedkar but with the establishment of Tibetan Buddhist communities, particularly in north India, has introduced a fresh chapter in the history of Buddhist architecture in India.

CONTRIBUTION OF BUDDHISM TO THE WORLD

All civilizations whether primitive, ancient, mediaeval or modem have in the course of their development produced cultures. In the name of Culture they have created art and architecture, language and literature, music and dance social customs, codes of ethics and behaviour, laws, philosophy and religion. It is by examining a civilization's cultural contributions to the world that we can gain some idea and appreciation of its achievements. This becomes more visible when we look into different periods of the art and architecture from around the world.

Every civilization's religion too, in the course of its history contributes something to the world in general and in particular to the world of art and architecture. Religious beliefs, ideas and ideals are sometimes given visual expression and sometimes form the subject matter of art and architecture. In a sense art and architecture provide mirrors to reflect a civilization's religion. In this respect Buddhism is no exception.

To contribute means to give. What Buddhism has given to the world is not only a profound analysis of, and a practical solution for the problem of human suffering but also a monumental and rich legacy to the world of art and architecture. Much of this legacy is visible even today in its homeland of India and in much of the eastern world. Today, I would like to give all of you gathered here, a glimpse at what is in a way Buddhism's fourth jewel, its art and architecture.

The very earliest examples of Buddhist art are not iconic but aniconic images and were popular in India after the death of the Buddha. This is because the Buddha, himself did not sanction personal worship or the making of images of the Tathagata, as to have done so would have contradicted his message to mankind. He taught and encouraged people to heed his example and be self-reliant in striving to put an end to human suffering and endless rebirth in Samsara and realise Nibbana for themselves. He was the living proof that this was possible and promised this was attainable by anyone through renouncing worldly and ego-centric desires and by making earnest efforts at mental development and purification as this would help one to eradicate the causes of suffering, greed, hatred and delusion and ultimately result in the attainment of Arahatship and Nibbana. Siddhatha Gotama was a Buddha, a self-perfected, self-enlightened human being and not a saviour of men. He was a human role-model to be followed but not idolized. Of himself he said, 'Buddha's only point the way'. So this is why the earliest artistic tributes to the Buddha Gotama are abstract symbols indicative of major events and achievements in his last life and in some cases his previous lives. They also serve as reminders of his teachings and provide inspiration. Some of these early aniconic representations of the Buddha include:

1. The Buddha's footprints which were often created at a place where he was know to have walked or was the scene of one of the Jataka Tales which recount his lifetimes as the Bodhisatta, striving to fulfil the perfections necessary in order to become a Buddha in the future. Such an image exists at Swat in Pakistan

and indicates what is believed to have been the scene of the Deer or Migara Jataka Story. Another example of this type of narrative imagery are the depictions of the Jataka Tales at Barhut in India.

2. The Bodhi-tree which is symbolic of Gotama's enlightenment at the age of thirty-five. A cutting of a tree, believed to have been taken from the original Bodhi Tree is enshrined at Bodh Gaya in the grounds of the Mahabodhi Temple. The Bodhi-tree image was retained and used in many later examples of Buddhist art.

3. The Lotus Flower which symbolizes both purity and enlightenment and is a popular motif in much Buddhist art and architecture and is very widely used in Tibetan Buddhist Art.

4. The Wheel which is a reminder of the Buddha's First Sermon. 'The Turning of the Wheel of the Law" delivered at Sarnath in Northern India and where stand the ruins of the ancient Dhamekh Stupa commemorating this major event. The wheel has also been adapted to symbolize the wheel of suffering in Samsara in Tibetan Buddhism and many examples of it are beautifully and skillfully depicted in Tibetan Buddhist Art on mandals, a type of meditation-aid and on the cloth paintings known as thankgas.

5. A riderless horse which recalls Prince Siddhattha's renunciation of worldly life for the ascetic life and the beginning of his search for the path to Enlightenment.

6. An empty throne which serves as a reminder of his passing away and attainment of Parinibbana.

After the Buddha's death out of deference to his wishes and devotion to his memory and his teachings, these symbols were widely used in the early days of Buddhist Art in India. Some still survive there and can be seen for example, at the Mahabodhi Temple built at Bodh Gaya, near the scene of the Buddha's Enlightenment. Some of them were also incorporated in later developments of Buddhist art and architecture and featured prominently in places as far afield as for example, the Temples of Thailand. Many of these symbols are used in contemporary Buddhist art and architecture in both the East and West.

To better appreciate Buddhism's contribution to art and architectural we have to take into account the two major schools of Buddhism, the Theravada or Hinayana and the Mahayana as these were to play significant roles in the creation and development of very different types of Buddhist art and architecture. The two schools arose as the result of a rift in the Sangha which had its cause in a dispute over the rule of life for monks. This occurred during the Second Buddhist Council, convened about a century after the first Council was called, in order that the Sangha Elders might recite and agree upon the Dhamma (doctrine) and Vinaya (discipline). This was necessary as the Buddha chose to name no successor. He explicitly stated that the Dhamma and Vinaya was to be his followers' only guide and teacher when he had gone. Later on this fundamental spilt caused the Dhamma itself to be interpreted differently and this brought about the rise of the two major schools of Buddhism with their different beliefs and ideals, which in turn were to have an important influence on Buddhist art and architecture. Despite the schism and the establishing of the two schools neither school's adherents abandoned the Buddha nor the ultimate goal of deliverance from suffering and rebirth culminating in the realisation of Nibbana or Nirvana. However, as the word, 'yana' implies, the vehicle used to reach that goal was different. It is this choice of vehicle which accounts for a difference in the beliefs and ideals which we see mirrored in the art and architecture created by Theravadins and Mahayanists throughout the history of Buddhism.

The Theravada School is the more orthodox and conservative of the two. Its adherents uphold the Dhamma and the ideal of the Arahat and look to the Buddha as the human role-model to imitate in their striving to attain deliverance from suffering and rebirth, and eventually Arahatship and Nibbana. Their vehicle to reach this goal is renunciation of all worldly attachments, the eradication of greed, hatred and delusion through following the Noble Eightfold Path and the cultivation of wisdom and insight. India is the birth-place of Theravada Buddhism and its art and architecture. There the artists and builders of Buddhist structures sought to portray the historical Buddha, and his disciples in the context of Theravadin beliefs and ideals. The chosen medium for this was the Buddha rupa or image and was developed in India. The earliest image we know of is actually a coin struck in the reign of King Kanishak. It shows a robed, standing Buddha. His head is surrounded by a halo, symbolizing his Enlightenment, and his hair is twisted into a top-knot, and one of his hands is raised in the gesture of blessing. The art of Buddhist sculpture and of Buddha images in particular, originated in India, and two distinct styles were created. One in the north, in Gandhara, where the image makers looked to the Greco-Roman tradition for inspiration.

The second style of Buddha image was directly influenced by the earlier Indian style of art peculiar to the south. The first images that we know of appeared in Mathura. The Mathura Buddha images had straight hair tied up in a top knot, and were garbed in the traditional Indian dhoti. The Mathura Buddhas are often shown, smiling peacefully. As these images were most commonly made of sandstone they are much softer in contour and more rounded and curved than those made in the north. Many early Indian Buddhist images show the Buddha as having the thirty-two marks of a Buddha and with his hands placed in various positions displaying gestures of blessing, meditation and teaching. The number of Buddha images and Buddhist architectural structures which survive in India is very great indeed, but in all of the faces of every image, and in the art and design of every stupa. and temple or rock-cave vihara traces of the Buddha-Dhamma are visible.

As Buddhist Art developed and spread outside India the two basic styles were imitated as for example in China where the Gandhara style was imitated in images made of bronze. Gradually the faces on these images were made to look more and more Chinese and are even dressed in long flowing, robes and shawls, after the Chinese fashion. In those countries where Sarvastivada or Theravada Buddhism took hold and remained, such as Afghanistan, Laos, and Sri Lanka, famous for its enormous reclining Buddha. and in Siam, modern Thailand, which is famous for its exquisite and graceful 'Walking Buddhas' or in the temples and shrines of the ancient capital city of Pagan in Burma now known as Myanmar with its many temples, and in the temples of Malaysia, too the Buddha images housed there, show the influence of the early types of Indian Buddha image.

Other notable surviving examples of Buddhist art which mirror the Theravada tradition are to be found at Lumbini in Nepal, the site of the Buddha's birth and in India at Bodh Gaya, Saranath. Kushinagara, Nalanda and at the Shwedagon Pagoda in Yangon, Myanmar, and also at the massive temple complex at Angkor Wat in Cambodia and the very simply, designed yet impressive Temple of the Sacred Tooth in Kandy, Sri Lanka.

The main difference between the Theravada and Mahayana Schools of Art is their subject matter. This difference was a direct reflection of the different ideals and beliefs held by the two schools. For the Theravadins the ideal is the Arahat, who like a Buddha seeks to eradicate suffering and rebirth in Samsara through renouncing the world, and through the eradication of greed, hatred and delusion. This achievement is made possible if one follows the Middle Way and the Noble Eightfold Path as taught by the Buddha Gotama. Nibbana is the Theravadin's final goal and is attainable through the practice of insight. These beliefs and ideals form the subject matter of Theravada Buddhist Art. On the other hand, although the followers of the Mahayana School of Buddhism uphold the goal of Nirvana also and deliverance from endless suffering and rebirth in Samsara, they have a different spiritual hero.

Their hero is not the Buddha Gotama, but the Bodhisattva. A Bodhisattva is a kind of divine saviour, whose role is to aid any being desirous of deliverance and Nirvana. In Mahayana Buddhism anyone can become enlightened and renunciation of the world in order to win Arahatship is not absolutely necessary, but the practice of specific rites and rituals and meditations and visualizations is. These spiritual practices will aid the practitioner in purifying the mind and will also attract the help of the Bodhisattva. The Mahayana School recognised the historical Buddha Gotama, the Shakyamuni, but raised him to the level of a god. He then became but one of many, many divine Buddhas and was eventually regarded as a powerful emanation of the Supreme Essence. It was these celestial Buddhas that were portrayed in Mahayanist Art and very beautifully too in countries such as China, Vietnam, Japan and Korea and of course Tibet where the Mahayana Tradition is followed.

As the Mahayanist school of thought evolved it developed many separate sects which attracted many followers such as the Zen sects of China and Japan. As has been said earlier, Mahayana Buddhism does not uphold the ideal of the Arahat but the Bodhisattva ideal and along with the Cosmic and celestial Buddhas form the subject matter of Mahayanist Art as well as the populous pantheon which surrounds the many Buddhas and Bodhisattvas that belong to the Mahayana Tradition. The word, Bodhisattva, means, 'a being of wisdom' and is a being whose perfections are fulfilled and who stands on the threshold of Nirvana but postpones the attainment of it out of compassion for all other unenlightened beings trapped in Samsara. The greatest virtue of the Bodhisattvas, and there are many, both male and female, is their compassion in contrast to the supreme wisdom of the historical Buddha. This boundless compassion it is what makes a Bodhisattva a saviour and not a human role-model as was the Buddha Gotama. It is also believed that anyone can become enlightened who asks for their help and who practises all the special mediation exercises and performs all the relevant rituals such as chanting.

Mahayana Buddhism is much more mystical than Theravada Buddhism, and therefore so is its art. The figures we see depicted in Mahayanist Art such as Maitreya, Avalokiteshvara, Chenrezig, Manjushri, Tara and Kuan Yin, are all Bodhisattvas. Their beauty and other-worldliness is inexpressable in words, but impressively and well conveyed through the medium of art. We can see them portrayed on wall paintings, on silk scrolls or their images delicately carved of wood, and also notably in the Buddhist caves of China such as those at Longmen, and in the surviving temples of Tibet and the Tibetan exile's place of refuge at Dharmasala in India and in the Mahayanist Buddhist holy places of Nepal, Vietnam, Mongolia and in the Buddhist places of Indonesia, in the east as well as in the many Tibetan centres which in recent times have been founded in the West, such as Samye-Ling, in Scotland.

Throughout the history of Buddhism the supporters of both these major schools have provided countless fine examples of Buddhist art and built magnificent stupas and temples. As one of the functions of Art is to mirror and another is to inspire then most certainly, the ideals and beliefs mirrored in both the major schools of Buddhist Art are a source of inspiration and encouragement to anyone wishing to follow the spiritual beliefs and ideals they reflect.

Both Buddhist Traditions made a huge and impressive contribution to mankind which can be chronicled for over two thousand years and follows the progress the Buddha-Dhamma made as it spread outwards from India in all directions. To better appreciate just how much Buddhism influenced the world and contributed to the world of art and architecture, it is necessary to understand how and why Buddhism spread as far as it did. Buddhism owes its success and its many converts to the catholicity of its appeal and its promise of deliverance from suffering. This is true of both traditions. It also was widely adopted and in some case fully integrated into an existing culture as was the case in Japan. And this success was possible because of the non-coercive approach of its missionaries. However, Buddhists did sometimes suffer persecution and even death and was the case in India, Tibet and China.

Buddhism was also successful because at various times in its history, it enjoyed royal patronage, as for example, that of the great Mauryan King Asoka and some of the later rulers of India including the Pala Kings, the last Buddhist Kings of India. Outside India it was embraced by King Tissa of Ceylon, in 247 B.C.E., the Mon ruler of Thaton. and later in 1056 by the Burmese King Anawrahta the founder of Pagan, in Siam in the eleventh century by King Rama Khamheng and in 1327 by Cambodia's King Jayavarman VII who ruled from his capital at Angkor. It was also adopted by the rulers of Laos and in the eight century in Indonesia by King Sailendra who sponsored the building of the largest Buddhist monument in the world, Borobodur. This devotion to Buddhism and the enthusiasm for Buddhist culture shown by these royal converts and most of their subjects was sincere and the world of art and architecture was all the richer for it.

Another significant factor to influence the spread of Buddhism and indirectly the development of Buddhist Art and Architecture was the tremendous volume of trade which existed in the ancient world most notably along the Silk Road, which was a trade route not only for goods but for ideas as well. The spread of Buddhism in its homeland of northern India began the day the Buddha and the first sixty Arahats went forth to preach the Dhamma. "For the gain of many, for the welfare of many, in compassion for the world." Although Buddhism in India was to die out as a result of the revival of Hinduism and in the aftermath of the Moslem invasions in the seventh century, it was able to spread, and evolve and survive in many other places since. The visible proof of this is to be see in the many examples of Buddhist Architecture.

The size of Buddhism's contribution to the world of architecture is enormous. There are two basic types of structure found in those places where Buddhism spread and developed and they are the Vihara and the Stupa. The word vihara, means "an abode", and its function was two-fold. It was intended to house Buddha images and art and also to serve as a dwelling place for monks. King Bimbisara donated the first Vihara, Veluvana at Rajagaha. to the Buddha himself and his disciples. This was a monastery sited in a Bamboo Grove. Much later on monks would dwell in the shelter of India's caves. One of the most famous cave complexes is the magnificently embellished caves at Ajanta, with its brightly coloured Buddhist murals. Another impressive cave complex is in Afghanistan. As the Vihara evolved in style it was adapted to the climate and terrain of the countries to which Buddhism spread and its design changed and evolved and eventually reflected the cultural characteristics of the lands where either Mahayana Buddhism or Theravada Buddhism had taken root and flourished. The more modern styles of Buddhist temple remain a type of vihara. These structures are made from a variety of materials such as stone in India and Sri Lanka, and from wood as can be see at Kyoto and Nara, in Japan. Brick was also used and some of the surviving temples of Pagan are made of brick. Sandstone is the material used in the building of Malaysian temples.

The second type of Buddhist structure is the Stupa and is itself an object of worship as it was intended to serve as a relic chamber for the Buddha's remains. The earliest examples of the Buddhist stupa were raised in India, as for example the dome shaped stupa at Sanchi, the ancient Dhamekh Stupa at Sarnath and those built inside the caves at Ellora and Ajanta. In time the basic Indian stupa-design evolved into the Dagoba in Sri Lanka, the Chorten in Tibet and the Pagodas of China, Korea and Japan. One of the finest examples of all is the splendid Shwedagon Pagoda in Yangon. As with Buddhist Art, the materials used in the building of viharas and temples and the various types of stupa and pagoda varied and depended on the materials available in the places where they were built. So we find some stupas are built of marble or other types of local stone or brick and even wood, as was the Goose Pagoda at Chagan in China. Happily in the west where Buddhism is becoming a very popular religion, the artists and architects who work on Buddhist building projects turn to the rich and varied legacy of Buddhist Art and Architecture for their inspiration.

All the Buddhist structures that were ever built by their very existence contributed something to the world and are holy places, places of learning and sanctuary for the people who were to use them and the repositories of some of the greatest treasures of Buddhist Art. They were and those that have survived continue to be a source of personal inspiration for all who saw them either in person long ago or even see them depicted in a drawing or a photograph these days. As was said, earlier Buddhist Art and Architecture mirrors the beliefs, ideas and ideals of both the Mahayana and Theravada traditions.

Buddhism in India together with its art and architecture reached its zenith during the Gupta dynasty which was established in northern India in 320 A.D. It was to last into the seventh century. The best known examples of Buddhist Art are from this period and were to form the standard of comparison for all subsequent Buddhist art and architecture both in India and in the rest of the Asian countries where it spread, took root and flourished. The Gupta period also saw the advent of Buddhism's decline in India. It slowly waned for three reasons. First was the rise of Mahayana Buddhism in India which was to bring Buddhism closer to Hinduism. The second reason was that Hinduism enjoyed the support of Kings and underwent a revival. This was so successful that in time it was to absorb the now strongly Mahayana influenced Buddhism. The third reason for Buddhism's decline was the various Moslem invasions, the last of which was waged in the seventh century A.D. and was directly responsible for Buddhism's slow decline and fall. However, at this time as we shall see Buddhism spread out of India to Nepal, later on to Sri Lanka and then eastwards to South East Asia and survived.

In short, Buddhism and its art and architecture was to spread geographically outwards from India in two directions. One was to the northwest into Afghanistan, Iran and then along the Silk Road to Central Asia and then further east to China, Korea and Japan. This development came about not only because of the activity of Buddhist Missionaries, but also because of the work of those Indian traders and the migration of those Indian emigres who settled in Central Asia. These people carried both Hinduism, and Buddhism and much of Indian culture with them wherever they went. This is obvious when we look at the wealth of Indian and Buddhist Art which was created there and can still be seen, today. However, in China, Korea and Japan Buddhism did not supplant the existing cultures but was totally integrated into them.

At the end of India's Gupta period Buddhism was taken to Nepal, Sri Lanka and to the South East Asian Mainland. As I said before, this outward movement was the direct result of the changes taking place in India at the time. Indian commerce also played a part, in Buddhism's spread to these places and were to be greatly influenced not only by Indian culture but also by the work of Indian merchants and monks, who brought with them not only religion but also their country's civilization-writing, art, architecture and methods of ruling as well. The influence of Hinduism was to touch these places before that of Buddhism did, but in time the two coexisted. In the end, however, Hinduism could not endure for long abroad because of the very rigid caste system it supported. Nevertheless, traces of Hindu culture have survived in these places and testify to the great contribution India made over the centuries to all of the Asian world and is still going on. Nowadays India's culture is being carried abroad by the large numbers of Asians emigrating to Australia, Europe, Africa and the United States of America and South America. They are the current carriers of Buddhism and its fourth jewel Buddhist Art and Architecture.

Now, I would like to tell you a true story. The late John Blofeld, a Buddhist scholar and writer of great repute once told the story of how he first became attracted to Buddhism when he was young. One day, he spied a strange statue in shop in Brighton. Sussex and his curiosity was awakened. When he asked what it was, the shop-keeper kindly told him it was a statue of a Buddha. Although, he could not afford to by it then and there, he very much wanted to. For days he could not get the image with its calm and peaceful expression out of his mind. As soon as he was able to afford it he bought it and it became his most treasured possession and kept it with him always. Seeing that statue, was for him a turning-point in his life. Later he began a life-long investigation into Buddhism.

Buddhism has been making contributions to the world's cultures through its teachings, its art and architecture for more than two millennium long. May this continue!

2

Buddhist Art and Architecture

Buddhist and Jain Art and Architecture have made substantial contribution to Indian Culture. These are in the form of:

STUPAS

Stupas were built of stones or bricks to commemorate important events or mark important places associated with Buddhism or to house important relics of Buddha. Ashok Maurya who laid the foundation of this group of monuments is said to have built 84,000 stupas, most of which have perished.

The best examples of stupas are those constructed at Amaravati, Sanchi, Barhut and Gaya. "One of the most striking architectural remains of ancient India" and the earliest and largest of the three stupas found in Sanchi was built by Ashoka (273-236 B.C.)

Sanchi in Raisen district of Madhya Pradesh is famous for its magnificent Buddhist monuments and edifices. Situated on a hill, these beautiful and well-preserved stupas depict the various stages of development of Buddhist art and arch1teeture over a period of thirteen hundred years from the third century B.C. to the twelfth century A.D. Inscriptions show that these monuments were maintained by the rich merchants of that region.

The stupa built by Ashoka was damaged during the break-up of the Maurya Empire. In the 2nd century B.C., during the. rule of the Sungas it was completely reconstructed. Religious activity led to the improvement and enlargement of the stupa and a stone railing was built around it. It was also embellished with the construction of heavily carved gateways.

The Great stupa has a large hemispherical dome which is flat at the top, and crowned by a triple umbrella or Chattra on a pedestal surrounded by a square railing or Karmika. Buddha's relics were placed in a casket chamber in the centre of the Dome. At the base of the dome is a high circular terrace probably meant for parikrama or circumambulation and an encircling balustrade. At the ground level is a stone-paved procession path and another stone Balustrade and two flights of steps leading to the circular terrace. Access to it is through four exquisitely carved gateways or Toranas in the North, South, East and West. The diameter of the stupa is 36.60 metres and its height is 16.46 metres. It is built of large burnt bricks and mud mortar. It is presumed that the elaborately carved Toranas were built by ivory or metal workers in the 1st Century BC during the reign of King Satakarni of the Satavahana Dynasty. The last addition to the stupa was made during the early 4th Century AD in the Gupta period when four images of Buddha sitting in the dhyana mudra or meditation were installed at the four entrances.

The first Torana gateway to be built is the one at the principal entrance on the South. Each gateway has two square pillars. Crowning each pillar on. all four sides are four elephants, four lions and four dwarfs. The four dwarfs support a superstructure of three architraves or carved panels one above the other. Between these are intricately carved elephants and riders on horseback. The lowest architrave is supported on exquisitely carved bracket figures. The panels are decorated with finely carved figures of men, women, yakshas, lions and elephants. The entire panel of the gateways is covered with sculptured scenes from the life of Buddha, the Jataka Tales, events of the Buddhist times and rows of floral or lotus motifs. The scenes from Buddha's life show Buddha represented by symbols-the lotus, wheel a riderless caparisoned horse, an umbrella held above a throne, foot prints and the triratnas which are symbolic of Buddha, Dharma and Sangha. The top panel has a Dharma chakra with two Yakshas on either side holding chamaras. South of the Scenes depicted from Buddha's life are the Enlightenment of Buddha (a throne beneath a peepul tree); the First Sermon (a Dharma chakra placed on a throne); The Great Departure (a riderless horse and an empty chariot with an umbrella above); Sujata's offering and the temptation and assault by Mara.

The big Stupa at Bharhut also in Madhya Pradesh was constructed in the 2nd century BC in the Sunga Period. It is a hemispherical dome built of brick and is surmounted by a shaft and an umbrella to represent the spiritual sovereignty of Buddhism. The railing surrounding it is of red sandstone. Scenes from the life of Buddha and the Jataka Tales are sculptured on the gateways, pillars, uprights and cross-bars of the railings.

During the same period, a number of stupas, chaityas, viharas and pillars were constructed in Sanchi, Bodh-Gaya, Mathura, Gandhara, Amaravati and Nagarjunakonda. Though most of these have not remained in their entirety, the ruins are of architectural interest.

The Stupas of Nagajunakonda and Amaravati, both in the Guntur District of Andhra Pradesh show that the Stupas of the Southern region differ in structure from those of the North. The architecture here is a shift from the usual Buddhist style, which reflected the two main divisions in Buddhism-Hinayana and Mahayana. Different trends and styles were incorporated here giving rise to new architectural forms, i.e. a quadrangular monastery, square and rectangular image shrine, pillared hall and a. small stupa on a square platform.

The stupas of Nagarjunakonda are in the form of a hemispherical dome resting on a low drum encased in panels sculptured with scenes of events depicting the life of Buddha. A notable feature of the stupas here is ayaka platforms in the four directions with five inscribed pillars on each of them. The five pillars symbolise the five important events in the life of Buddha-his Birth, Renunciation, Enlightenment, First Sermon and Parinirvana.

Some of the stupas are built on a square platform having an apsidal shrine on either side and a pillared hall within a quadrangular monastery. Some stupas were wheel-shaped having four to ten spokes and a two or three winged vihara. The earliest of the Nagarjunkonda stupas is the Maha Chaitya which contains the tooth relic of Buddha. The stupa is wheel-shaped with ayaka platforms surmounted by pillars. The smallest stupa here has only two cells and the Chaitya griha enshrines the image of Buddha.

Ruins of stupas have been found in Rajgriha or Rajgir (Bihar) where the First Buddhist Council was held; at Vaisali (Bihar) where the Second Buddhist Council was held and at Sravasti (U.P.) one of the eight places of Buddhist pilgrimage where Buddha is said to have performed the Great Miracle. To show his spiritual powers, he made a mango tree to sprout in a day and created numerous images of himself, sitting and standing on lotuses with fire and water emanating from his body. The conversion of King Prasenajit and the dacoit Angulimala is also said to have taken place here. Ruins of the main stupa in Kusinagara in U.P. where Buddha passed away and was cremated, is believed to contain the bodily remains of Buddha. Both Fa-hien and Hiuen-Tsang have recorded their visits to these places.

The Dhamekh Stupa and the Dharmarajika stupa at Sarnath are believed to have been built by Ashoka and later rebuilt in the Gupta period. These stupas contain the relics of Buddha and are therefore important places of Buddhist pilgrimage. Buddha gave his First Sermon in Sarnath and also founded the Sangha or Order of Monks here. The original Dhamekh Stupa built with mud or brick is a cylindrical structure 43.5 m. high. The stone basement has eight projecting faces with niches in them. Delicately carved with beautiful floral and geometrical patterns, it is believed to have been put up in the Gupta period.

VIHARAS

Viharas or monasteries constructed with brick or excavated from rocks are found in different parts of India. Usually built to a set plan, they have a hall meant for congregational prayer with a running verandah on three sides or an open courtyard surrounded by a row of cells and a pillared verandah in front. These cells served as dwelling places for the monks. These monastic buildings built of bricks were self-contained units and had a Chaitya hall or Chaitya mandir attached to a stupa-the chief object of worship.

Some of the important Buddhist viharas are those at Ajanta, Ellora. Nasik, Karle, Kanheri, Bagh and Badami. The Hinayana viharas found in these places have many interesting features which differentiate them from the Mahayana type in the same regions. Though plain from the point of view of architecture, they are large halls with cells excavated in the walls on three sides. The hall has one or more entrances. The small cells, each with a door have one or two stone platforms to serve as beds.

The excavations of viharas at Nagarjunakonda show large rectangular courtyards with stone-paved central halls. Around the courtyard, the row of cells, small and big, suggest residences and dining halls for monks.

Twenty-five of the rock-cut caves of Ajanta are viharas and are the finest of monasteries. Four of the viharas belong to the 2nd century BC. Later, other caves were excavated during the reign of the Vakataka rulers who were the contemporaries of the Gupta Rulers. Some of the most beautiful viharas belong to this period.

The finest of them. Cave 1, of the Mahayana type consists of a verandah, a hall, groups of cells and a sanctuary. It has a decorated facade. The portico is supported by exquisitely carved pillars. The columns have a square base with figures of dwarfs and elaborately carved brackets and capitals. Below the capital is a square abacus with finely carved makara motifs. The walls and the ceilings of the cave contain the most exquisite paintings.

The viharas of Ellora dated 400 AD to 7th century AD are of one, two, and three storeys and are the largest of the type. They contain sculptured figures and belong to both Hinayana and Mahayana Buddhism.

CHAITYAS

Chaitya grihas or halls of worship were built all over the country either of brick or excavated from rocks. Ruins of a large number of structural Buddhist chaity grihas are found in the eastern districts of Andhra Pradesh, in valleys, near rivers and lakes. The ruins located in the districts of Srikakulam at Salihundam, of Visahkapatnam at Kotturu, of West Godavari at Guntapalli, of Krishna at Vijayawada, of Guntur at Nagajunakonda and Amaravati belong to the 3rd century BC and later. The largest brick chaitya hall was excavated at Guntapalli.

Some of the most beautiful rock-cut caves are those at Ajanta, Ellora, Bhaja, Karle, Bagh, Nasik and Kanheri. Some of the chunar sand-stone rock-cut chaityas of Bhaja. Kondane. Karle and Ajanta, all in Maharashtra state are earlier excavations and belong to the first phase or Hinayana creed of Buddhism and are similar to the brick and wooden structures of Ashokan times. Some of the chaityas show that wood had been used in the roofing and entrance arches. The chaitya at Bhaja is a long hall 16.75 metres long and 8 metres broad with an apse at the end. The hall is divided into a central nave and an aisle on either side flanked by two rows of pillars. The roof is vaulted. The rock-cut stupa in the apse is crowned by a wooden harmika. The chaitya has a large arched torana or entrance with an arched portico.

Hinayana rock architecture reaches the peak of excellence in the splendid chaitya at Karle. An inscription in Karle mentions Bhutapala, a banker to be the founder of the chaitya hall but later scholars identify him with Devabhuti, the last of the Sunga rulers.

The chaitya has a double-storeyed facade and has three doorways in the lower part. It has an upper gallery over which there is the usual arch. The walls of the vestibule to the chaitya hall are decorated with sculptured figures of couples. The pillars separating the central nave from the aisles have a pot base, an octagonal shaft, inverted lotus capital with an abacus. The abacus has exquisitely carved pairs of elephants kneeling down, each with a couple in front and caparisoned horses with riders on them. The stupa at the apse end is tall and cylindrical with two tiers of railings around the drum. It is crowned by the original wooden chhatra. This is the most beautiful of the chaityas.

The second phase of Buddhist architecture is marked by the Mahayana creed of Buddhism seen in some of the excellent rock-cut chaityas at Ajanta in Aurangabad district of Maharashtra excavated between 5th AD and 9th century AD during the rule of the Vakatakas, the Guptas and the Rashtrakutas.

The caves were first discovered in the beginning of the 19th century. The caves are excavated from a semi-circular steep rock with a stream flowing below, and were meant for the use of the monks who spent the rainy season there in meditation.

The caves are at different levels and have stairs leading down to the stream. Five of the thirty caves arc chaityas or sanctuaries. The earlier group of two caved dated 2nd century BC belong to the style of Kondan and Nasik caves.

The chaityas have a vaulted ceiling with a huge horse-shoe shaped window or chaitya window over the doorway. They are large halls divided into three, parts-the central nave, apse and aisles on either side separated by a row of columns. The side aisles continue behind the apse for circumambulation. At the centre of the apse is a rock stupa with large figure of Buddha, sitting or standing. A remarkable feature of these Chaityas is the imitation of woodwork on rock. Beams and rafters were carved in the rock though they serve no purpose. From the unfinished caves, we get an idea of the method of excavation. Starting from the ceiling, they worked downwards. Solid blocks were left to be carved into pillars. After finishing the verandah, they excavated the interior. Tools used were the pick-axe, chisel and hammer.

The most perfect of this group of chaitya grihas is cave 19. Excavated at the end of the 5th century AD it is similar to the other chaityas in its plan and ribbed vaulted ceiling except for its single doorway and elaborate ornamentation. It has a pillared portico in front leading into a courtyard with the walls on either side heavily sculptured with figures. The interior pillars are well decorated with cushion shaped capitals. The corbel brackets are richly sculptured. The drum of the central stupa is elongated and carved. Projecting from the drum is an arched nasika or niche with the figure of a standing Buddha carved in it. The rounded dome of the stupa ~ is surmounted by a harmika and three tiers of chhatras, diminishing in size and supported by figures on four sides. On top of the chhatras and touching the ceiling is another small stupa with a miniature harmika. The facade of the cave is exquisitely carved. The chaitya-window has figures of yakshas and richly carved, friezes on either side. Two figures of standing Buddha flank the entrance. The walls of the hall and the ceiling of the aisles is richly painted with figures of Buddha, floral motifs, animals and birds.

PAINTINGS

Paintings which has been an accepted art since early times attained heights of excellence in Gupta period. These exquisite paintings or frescos are to be seen in the caves of Ajanta. The entire surface of the caves is exquisitely painted and shows the high standard reached in mural painting.

The theme of the painting on the walls is mostly the life of Buddha and Bodhisattvas and the Jataka stories. These topics cover a continuous narration of events on all aspects of human-life from birth to death. Every kind of human emotion is depicted. The paintings reflect the contemporary life of the times, dress, ornaments, culture, weapons used, even their beliefs are portrayed with life-like reality. The paintings include gods, yakshas, kinneras, gandharvas, apsaras and human beings.

The paintings show their intense feeling for nature and an understanding of the various aspects of all living beings. The ceilings are covered with intricate designs, flowers, plants, birds, animals, fruit and people. The ground for painting was prepared by paving it with a rough layer of earth and sand mixed with vegetable fibres, husk and grass. A second coat of mud mixed with fine sand and fibrous vegetable material was applied. A final finish was given with a thin coat of lime-wash, glue was used as a binder. On this prepared surface, the outlines were drawn and the spaces were filled with the required colours; with much attention given to shades and tones. Red, yellow, black, ochre, blue and gypsum were mostly used.

Some of the renowned paintings are that of the Bodhisattva holding a lily (cave 1), the painting of Padmapani, the Apsaras with a turban headgear (cave 17) the painting on the ceiling (cave 2) and the toilet scheme (cave 17) considered to be a masterpiece of the painter.

STHAMBAS

Sthambas or Pillars with religious emblems were put up by pious Buddhists in honour of Buddha or other great Buddhists. Fragments of sthambas belonging to Mauryan times and later were found at Sanchi, Sarnath, Amaravati and Nagarjunkonda.

A portion of the Ashoka Pillar, 15.25 metres high, surmounted by the famous lion-capital and a dharma chakra above the heads of the four lions stands embedded near the Dharmarajika stupa at Sarnath. The pillar bears the edict of Ashoka warning the monks and nuns against creating a schism in the monastic order. The broken fragments of the Pillar are now in the Museum at Sarnath. The lion-capital-the most magnificient piece of Mauryan sculpture is 2.31 metres high. It consists of four parts-(i) a bell-shaped vase covered with inverted lotus petals, (ii) a round abacus, (iii) four seated lions and (iv) a crowning dharmachakra with thirty two spokes. The four lions are beautifully sculptured. On the abacus are four running animals-an elephant, a bull, a horse and a. lion with a small dharmachakra between them. The dharmachakra symbolises the dharma or law; the four lions facing the four directions are the form of Buddha or Sakyasimha, the four galloping animals are the four quarters according to Buddhist books and the four smaller dharmachakras stand for the intermediate regions and the lotus is the symbol of creative activity. The surface of these pillars has a mirror like finish.

Another Ashokan Pillar of note is the one at Lauriya Nandangarh in Bihar. Erected in the 3rd century BC it is made of highly polished Chunar sand-stone. Standing 9.8 metres high it rises from the ground and has no base structure. It is surmounted by a bell-shaped inverted lotus. The abacus on it is decorated with flying geese and crowning it is a sitting lion. The pillar is an example of the engineering skill of the craftsmen of Mauryan times.

BUDDHIST ART

Buddhist art originated on the Indian subcontinent following the historical life of Gautama Buddha, 6th to 5th century BCE, and thereafter evolved by contact with other cultures as it spread throughout Asia and the world.

Early Buddhist art followed the Indian aniconic tradition, which avoids direct representation of the human figure. Around the 1st century CE an iconic period emerged lasting to this day which represents the Buddha in human form.

Buddhist art followed believers as the dharma spread, adapted, and evolved in each new host country. It developed to the north through Central Asia and into Eastern Asia to form the Northern branch of Buddhist art, and to the east as far as Southeast Asia to form the Southern branch of Buddhist art. In India, Buddhist art flourished and even influenced the development of Hindu art, until Buddhism nearly disappeared in India around the 10th century due in part to the vigorous expansion of Islam alongside Hinduism.

Aniconic Phase (5th century-1st century BCE)

During the 2nd to 1st century BCE, sculptures became more explicit, representing episodes of the Buddha's life and teachings. These took the form of votive tablets or friezes, usually in relation to the decoration of stupas. Although India had a long sculptural tradition and a mastery of rich iconography, the Buddha was never represented in human form, but only through some of his symbols. This reluctance towards anthropomorphic representations of the Buddha, and the sophisticated development of aniconic symbols to avoid it (even in narrative scene where other human figures would appear), seems to be connected to 70 of the Buddha's sayings, reported in the Dighanikaya, that disfavored representations of himself after the extinction of his body. This tendency remained as late as the 2nd century CE in the southern parts of India, in the art of the Amaravati school (see: Mara's assault on the Buddha). It has been argued that earlier anthropomorphic representations of the Buddha may have been made of wood and may have perished since then. However, no related archaeological evidence has been found.

Iconic Phase (1st century CE-present)

Anthropomorphic representations of the Buddha started to emerge from the 1st century CE in northern India. The two main centers of creation have been identified as Gandhara in today's Punjab, in Pakistan, and the region of Mathura, in central northern India.

The art of Gandhara benefited from centuries of interaction with Greek culture since the conquests of Alexander the Great in 332 BCE and the subsequent establishment of the Greco-Bactrian and Indo-Greek Kingdoms, leading to the development of Greco-Buddhist art. Gandharan Buddhist sculpture displays Greek artistic influence, and it has been suggested that the concept of the "man-god" was essentially inspired by Greek mythological culture. Artistically, the Gandharan school of sculpture is said to have contributed wavy hair, drapery covering both shoulders, shoes and sandals, acanthus leaf decorations, etc. The art of Mathura tends to be based on a strong Indian tradition, exemplified by the anthropomorphic representation of divinities such as the Yaksas, although in a style rather archaic compared to the later representations of the Buddha. The Mathuran school contributed clothes covering the left shoulder of thin muslin, the wheel on the palm, the lotus seat, etc.

Mathura and Gandhara also strongly influenced each other. During their artistic florescence, the two regions were even united politically under the Kushans, both being capitals of the empire. It is still a matter of debate whether the anthropomorphic representations of Buddha was essentially a result of a local evolution of Buddhist art at Mathura, or a consequence of Greek cultural influence in Gandhara through the Greco-Buddhist syncretism.

This iconic art was characterized from the start by a realistic idealism, combining realistic human features, proportions, attitudes and attributes, together with a sense of perfection and serenity reaching to the divine. This expression of the Buddha as a both a man and a god became the iconographic canon for subsequent Buddhist art.

Buddhist art continued to develop in India for a few more centuries. The pink sandstone sculptures of Mathura evolved during the Gupta period (4th to 6th century) to reach a very high fineness of execution and delicacy in the modeling. The art of the Gupta school was extremely influential almost everywhere in the rest of Asia. By the 10th century, Buddhist art creation was dying out in India, as Hinduism and Islam ultimately prevailed.

As Buddhism expanded outside of India from the 1st century CE, its original artistic package blended with other artistic influences, leading to a progressive differentiation among the countries adopting the faith.

- A Northern route was established from the 1st century CE through Central Asia, Tibet, Bhutan, China, Korea, and Japan, in which Mahayana Buddhism prevailed.
- A Southern route, where Theravada Buddhism dominated, went through Myanmar, Thailand, Cambodia, and Vietnam.

NORTHERN BUDDHIST ART

The Silk Road transmission of Buddhism to Central Asia, China and ultimately Korea and Japan started in the 1st century CE with a semi-legendary account of an embassy sent to the West by the Chinese Emperor Ming (58-75 CE). However, extensive contacts started in the 2nd century CE, probably as a consequence of the expansion of the Kushan Empire into the Chinese territory of the Tarim Basin, with the missionary efforts of a great number of Central Asian Buddhist monks to Chinese lands. The first missionaries and translators of Buddhists scriptures into Chinese, such as Lokaksema, were either Parthian, Kushan, Sogdian or Kuchean.

Central Asian missionary efforts along the Silk Road were accompanied by a flux of artistic influences, visible in the development of Serindian art from the 2nd through the 11th century CE in the Tarim Basin, modern Xinjiang. Serindian art often derives from the Greco-Buddhist art of the Gandhara district of what is now Pakistan, combining Indian, Greek and Roman influences. Silk Road Greco-Buddhist artistic influences can be found as far as Japan to this day, in architectural motifs, Buddhist imagery, and a select few representations of Japanese gods.

The art of the northern route was also highly influenced by the development of Mahayana Buddhism, an inclusive faith characterized by the adoption of new texts, in addition to the traditional Pali canon, and a shift in the understanding of Buddhism. Mahayana goes beyond the traditional Theravada ideal of the release from suffering (dukkha) and personal enlightenment of the arhats, to elevate the Buddha to a god-like status, and to create a pantheon of quasi-divine Bodhisattvas devoting themselves to personal excellence, ultimate knowledge and the salvation of humanity. Northern Buddhist art thus tends to be characterized by a very rich and syncretic Buddhist pantheon, with a multitude of images of the various Buddhas, Bodhisattvas and lesser deities.

Afghanistan

Buddhist art in Afghanistan (old Bactria) persisted for several centuries until the spread of Islam in the 7th century. It is exemplified by the Buddhas of Bamyan. Other sculptures, in stucco, schist or clay, display very strong blending of Indian post-Gupta mannerism and Classical influence, Hellenistic or possibly even Greco-Roman.

Although Islamic rule was rather tolerant of other religions "of the Book", it showed little tolerance for Buddhism, which was perceived as a religion depending on idolatry. Human figurative art forms also being prohibited under Islam, Buddhist art suffered numerous attacks, which culminated with the systematic destructions by the Taliban regime. The Buddhas of Bamyan, the sculptures of Hadda, and many of the remaining artifacts at the Afghanistan museum have been destroyed. The multiple conflicts since the 1980s also have led to a systematic pillage of archaeological sites apparently in the hope of reselling in the international market what artifacts could be found.

Central Asia

Central Asia long played the role of a meeting place between China, India and Persia. During the 2nd century BCE, the expansion of the Former Han to the West led to increased contact with the Hellenistic civilizations of Asia, especially the Greco-Bactrian Kingdom. Thereafter, the expansion of Buddhism to the North led to the formation of Buddhist communities and even Buddhist kingdoms in the oases of Central Asia. Some Silk Road cities consisted almost entirely of Buddhist stupas and monasteries, and it seems that one of their main objectives was to welcome and service travelers between East and West.

The eastern part of Central Asia (Chinese Turkestan (Tarim Basin, Xinjiang) in particular has revealed an extremely rich Serindian art (wall paintings and reliefs in numerous caves, portable paintings on canvas, sculpture, ritual objects), displaying multiple influences from Indian and Hellenistic cultures. Works of art reminiscent of the Gandharan style, as well as scriptures in the Gandhari script Kharoshti have been found. These influences were rapidly absorbed however by the vigorous Chinese culture, and a strongly Chinese particularism develops from that point.

China

Buddhism arrived in China around the 1st century CE, and introduced new types of art into China, particularly in the area of statuary. Receiving this distant religion, strong Chinese traits were incorporated into Buddhist art.

Northern Dynasties

In the 5th to 6th centuries, the Northern Dynasties, developed rather symbolic and abstract modes of representation, with schematic lines. Their style is also said to be solemn and majestic. The lack of corporeality of this art, and its distance from the original Buddhist objective of expressing the pure ideal of enlightenment in an accessible and realistic manner, progressively led to a change towards more naturalism and realism, leading to the expression of Tang Buddhist art.

Sites preserving Northern Wei Dynasty Buddhist sculpture:

- Longmen Grottoes, Henan
- Bingling Temple, Gansu

Tang Dynasty

Following a transition under the Sui Dynasty, Buddhist sculpture of the Tang evolved towards a markedly life-like expression. Because of the dynasty's openness to foreign influences, and renewed exchanges with Indian culture due to the numerous travels of Chinese Buddhist monks to India, Tang dynasty Buddhist sculpture assumed a rather classical form, inspired by the Indian art of the Gupta period. During that time, the Tang capital of Chang'an (today's Xi'an) became an important center for Buddhism. From there Buddhism spread to Korea, and Japanese embassies of Kentoshi helped it gain a foothold in Japan.

However, foreign influences came to be negatively perceived in China towards the end of the Tang dynasty. In the year 845, the Tang emperor Wuzong outlawed all "foreign" religions (including Christian Nestorianism, Zoroastrianism and Buddhism) in order to support the indigenous religion, Taoism. He confiscated Buddhist possessions, and forced the faith to go underground, therefore affecting the development of the religion and its arts in China.

Chán Buddhism however, at the origin of Japanese Zen, continued to prosper for some centuries, especially under the Song Dynasty (960-1279), when Chan monasteries were great centers of culture and learning.

The popularization of Buddhism in China has made the country home to one of the richest collections of Buddhist arts in the world. The Mogao Caves near Dunhuang and the Bingling Temple caves near Yongjing in Gansu province, the Longmen Grottoes near Luoyang in Henan province, the Yungang Grottoes near Datong in Shanxi province, and the Dazu Rock Carvings near Chongqing municipality are among the most important and renowned Buddhist sculptural sites. The Leshan Giant Buddha, carved out of a hillside in the 8th century during the Tang Dynasty and looking down on the confluence of three rivers, is still the largest stone Buddha statue in the world.

Korea

Korean Buddhist art generally reflects an interaction between Chinese Buddhist influence and a strongly original Korean culture. Additionally, the art of the steppes, particularly Siberian and Scythian influences, are evident in early Korean Buddhist art based on the excavation of artifacts and burial goods such as Silla royal crowns, belt buckles, daggers, and comma-shaped gogok. The style of this indigenous art was geometric, abstract and richly adorned with a characteristic "barbarian" luxury. Although Chinese influence was strong, Korean Buddhist art "bespeaks a sobriety, taste for the right tone, a sense of abstraction but also of colours that curiously enough are in line with contemporary taste" (Pierre Cambon, Arts asiatiques-Guimet').

Three Kingdoms of Korea

The first of the Three Kingdoms of Korea to officially receive Buddhism was Goguryeo in 372. However, Chinese records and the use of Buddhist motifs in Goguryeo murals indicate the introduction of Buddhism earlier than the official date. The Baekje Kingdom officially recognized Buddhism in 384. The Silla Kingdom, isolated and with no easy sea or land access to

China, officially adopted Buddhism in 535 although the foreign religion was known in the kingdom due to the work of Goguryeo monks since the early fifth century. The introduction of Buddhism stimulated the need for artisans to create images for veneration, architects for temples, and the literate for the Buddhist sutras and transformed Korean civilization. Particularly important in the transmission of sophisticated art styles to the Korean kingdoms was the art of the "barbarian" Tuoba, a clan of non-Han Chinese Xianbei people who established the Northern Wei Dynasty in China in 386. The Northern Wei style was particularly influential in the art of the Goguryeo and Baekje. Baekje artisans later transmitted this style along with Southern Dynasty elements and distinct Korean elements to Japan. Korean artisans were highly selective of the styles they incorporated and combined different regional styles together to create a specific Korean Buddhist art style.

While Goguryeo Buddhist art exhibited vitality and mobility akin with Northern Wei prototypes, the Baekje Kingdom was also in close contact with the Southern Dynasties of China and this close diplomatic contact is exemplified in the gentle and proportional sculpture of the Baekje, epitomized by Baekje sculpture exhibiting the fathomless smile known to art historians as the Baekje smile. The Silla Kingdom also developed a distinctive Buddhist art tradition epitomized by the Bangasayusang, a half-seated contemplative maitreya whose Korean-made twin, the Miroku Bosatsu, was sent to Japan as a proselytizing gift and now resides in the Koryu-ji Temple in Japan.

Buddhism in the Three Kingdoms period stimulated massive temple-building projects, such as the Mireuksa Temple in the Baekje Kingdom and the Hwangnyongsa Temple in Silla. Baekje architects were famed for their skill and were instrumental in building the massive nine-story pagoda at Hwangnyongsa and early Buddhist temples in Yamato Japan such as Hoko-ji (Asuka-dera). Sixth century Korean Buddhist art exhibited the cultural influences of China and India but began to show distinctive indigenous characteristics. These indigenous characteristics can be seen in early Buddhist art in Japan and some early Japanese

Buddhist sculpture is now believed to have originated in Korea, particularly from Baekje, or Korean artisans who immigrated to Yamato Japan. Particularly, the semi-seated Maitreya form was adapted into a highly developed Korean style which was transmitted to Japan as evidenced by the Koryu-ji Miroku Bosatsu and the Chugu-ji Siddhartha statues. Although many historians portray Korea as a mere transmitter of Buddhism, the Three Kingdoms, and particularly Baekje, were instrumental as active agents in the introduction and formation of a Buddhist tradition in Japan in 538 or 552.

Unified Silla

During the Unified Silla period, East Asia was particularly stable with China and Korea both enjoying unified governments. Early Unified Silla art combined Silla styles and Baekje styles. Korean Buddhist art was also influenced by new Tang Dynasty styles as evidenced by a new popular Buddhist motif with full-faced Buddha sculptures. Tang China was the cross roads of East, Central, and South Asia and so the Buddhist art of this time period exhibit the so-called international style. State-sponsored Buddhist art flourished during this period, the epitome of which is the Seokguram Grotto.

Goryeo Dynasty

The fall of the Unified Silla Dynasty and the establishment of the Goryeo Dynasty in 918 indicates a new period of Korean Buddhist art. The Goryeo kings also lavishly sponsored Buddhism and Buddhist art flourished, especially Buddhist paintings and illuminated sutras written in gold and silver ink. The crowning achievement of this period is the carving of approximately 80,000 woodblocks of the Tripitaka Koreana which was done twice.

Joseon Dynasty

The Joseon Dynasty actively suppressed Buddhism beginning in 1406 and Buddhist temples and art production subsequently decline in quality in quantity although beginning in 1549, Buddhist art does continue to be produced.

See also: Buddhism in Korea, Bangasayusang, Geumdong Mireuk Bosal Bangasang, Seokguram, Hwangnyongsa, Mireuksa, Gyeongcheonsa Pagoda, Tripitaka Koreana

Japan

Before the introduction of Buddhism, Japan had already been the seat of various cultural (and artistic) influences, from the abstract linear decorative art of the indigenous Neolithic Jamon from around 10500 BCE to 300 BCE, to the art during the Yayoi and Kofun periods, with developments such as Haniwa art.

Japan, the largest Buddhist country today, discovered Buddhism in the 6th century when missionary monks travelled to the islands together with numerous scriptures and works of art. The Buddhist religion was adopted by the state in the following century. Being geographically at the end of the Silk Road, Japan was able to preserve many aspects of Buddhism at the very time it was disappearing in India, and being suppressed in Central Asia and China.

From 711, numerous temples and monasteries were built in the capital city of Nara, including a five-story pagoda, the Golden Hall of the Horyuji, and the Kafuku-ji temple. Countless paintings and sculpture were made, often under governmental sponsorship. Indian, Hellenistic, Chinese and Korean artistic influences blended into an original style characterized by realism and gracefulness. The creation of Japanese Buddhist art was especially rich between the 8th and 13th centuries during the periods of Nara, Heian and Kamakura. Japan developed an extremely rich figurative art for the pantheon of Buddhist deities, sometimes combined with Hindu and Shinto influences. This art can be very varied, creative and bold.

From the 12th and 13th, a further development was Zen art, following the introduction of the faith by Dogen and Eisai upon their return from China. Zen art is mainly characterized by original paintings (such as sumi-e) and poetry (especially haikus), striving to express the true essence of the world through impressionistic and unadorned "non-dualistic" representations.

The search for enlightenment "in the moment" also led to the development of other important derivative arts such as the Chanoyu tea ceremony or the Ikebana art of flower arrangement. This evolution went as far as considering almost any human activity as an art with a strong spiritual and aesthetic content, first and foremost in those activities related to combat techniques (martial arts). Buddhism remains very active in Japan to this day. Still around 80,000 Buddhist temples are preserved. Many of them are in wood and are regularly restored.

Tibet and Bhutan

Tantric Buddhism started as a movement in eastern India around the 5th or the 6th century. Many of the practices of Tantric Buddhism are derived from Brahmanism (the usage of mantras, yoga, or the burning of sacrificial offerings). Tantrism became the dominant form of Buddhism in Tibet from the 8th century. Due to its geographical centrality in Asia, Tibetan Buddhist art received influence from Indian, Nepali, Greco-Buddhist and Chinese art.

One of the most characteristic creations of Tibetan Buddhist art are the mandalas, diagrams of a "divine temple" made of a circle enclosing a square, the purpose of which is to help Buddhist devotees focus their attention through meditation and follow the path to the central image of the Buddha. Artistically, Buddhist Gupta art and Hindu art tend to be the two strongest inspirations of Tibetan art.

Vietnam

Chinese influence was predominant in the north of Vietnam (Tonkin) between the 1st and 9th centuries, and Confucianism and Mahayana Buddhism were prevalent. Overall, the art of Vietnam has been strongly influenced by Chinese Buddhist art.

In the south, the kingdom of Champa has a strongly Indianized art, just as neighboring Cambodia. Many of its statues were characterized by rich body adornments. The capital of the kingdom of Champa was annexed by Vietnam in 1471, and it totally collapsed in the 1720s.

Southern Buddhist Art

During the 1st century CE, the trade on the overland Silk Road tended to be restricted by the rise of the Parthian empire in the Middle East, an unvanquished enemy of Rome, just as Romans were becoming extremely wealthy and their demand for Asian luxury was rising.

This demand revived the sea connections between the Mediterranean Sea and China, with India as the intermediary of choice. From that time, through trade connections, commercial settlements, and even political interventions, India started to strongly influence Southeast Asian countries.

Trade routes linked India with southern Burma, central and southern Siam, lower Cambodia and southern Vietnam, and numerous urbanized coastal settlements were established there.

For more than a thousand years, Indian influence was therefore the major factor that brought a certain level of cultural unity to the various countries of the region. The Pali and Sanskrit languages and the Indian script, together with Mahayana and Theravada Buddhism, Brahmanism and Hinduism, were transmitted from direct contact and through sacred texts and Indian literature such as the Ramayana and the Mahabharata.

This expansion provided the artistic context for the development of Buddhist art in these countries, which then developed characteristics of their own.

Between the 1st and 8th centuries, several kingdoms competed for influence in the region (particularly the Cambodian Funan then the Burmese Mon kingdoms) contributing various artistic characteristics, mainly derived from the Indian Gupta style. Combined with a pervading Hindu influence, Buddhist images, votive tablets and Sanskrit inscriptions are found throughout the area.

From the 9th to the 13th centuries, Southeast Asia had very powerful empires and became extremely active in Buddhist architectural and artistic creation. The Sri Vijaya Empire to the south and the Khmer Empire to the north competed for influence, but both were adherents of Mahayana Buddhism, and their art expressed the rich Mahayana pantheon of the Bodhisattvas.

The Theravada Buddhism of the Pali canon was introduced to the region around the 13th century from Sri Lanka, and was adopted by the newly founded ethnic Thai kingdom of Sukhothai. Since in Theravada Buddhism only monks can reach Nirvana, the construction of temple complexes plays a particularly important role in the artistic expression of Southeast Asia from that time.

From the 14th century, the main factor was the spread of Islam to the maritime areas of Southeast Asia, overrunning Malaysia, Indonesia, and most of the islands as far as the Philippines. In the continental areas, Theravada Buddhism continued to expand into Burma, Laos and Cambodia.

Myanmar

A neighbor of India, Myanmar was naturally strongly influenced by the eastern part of Indian territory. The Mon of southern Burma are said to have been converted to Buddhism around 200 BCE under the proselytizing of the Indian king Ashoka, before the schism between Mahayana and Hinayana Buddhism.

Early Buddhist temples are found, such as Beikthano in central Myanmar, with dates between the 1st and the 5th centuries. The Buddhist art of the Mons was especially influenced by the Indian art of the Gupta and post-Gupta periods, and their mannerist style spread widely in Southeast Asia following the expansion of the Mon Empire between the 5th and 8th centuries.

Later, thousands of Buddhist temples were built at Bagan, the capital, between the 11th and 13th centuries, and around 2,000 of them are still standing. Beautiful jeweled statues of the Buddha are remaining from that period. Creation managed to continue despite the seizure of the city by the Mongols in 1287.

Cambodia

Cambodia was the center of the Funan kingdom, which expanded into Burma and as far south as Malaysia between the 3rd and 6th centuries CE. Its influence seems to have been essentially political, most of the cultural influence coming directly from India.

Later, from the 9th to 13th centuries, the Mahayana Buddhist and Hindu Khmer Empire dominated vast parts of the Southeast Asian peninsula, and its influence was foremost in the development of Buddhist art in the region. Under the Khmer, more than 900 temples were built in Cambodia and in neighboring Thailand.

Angkor was at the center of this development, with a Buddhist temple complex and urban organization able to support around 1 million urban dwellers. A great deal of Cambodian Buddhist sculpture is preserved at Angkor; however, organized looting has had a heavy impact on many sites around the country.

Often, Khmer art manages to express intense spirituality through divinely beaming expressions, in spite of spare features and slender lines.

Thailand

From the 1st to the 7th centuries, Buddhist art in Thailand was first influenced by direct contact with Indian traders and the expansion of the Mon kingdom, leading to the creation of Hindu and Buddhist art inspired from the Gupta tradition, with numerous monumental statues of great virtuosity.

From the 9th century, the various schools of Thai art then became strongly influenced by Cambodian Khmer art in the north and Sri Vijaya art in the south, both of Mahayana faith. Up to the end of that period, Buddhist art is characterized by a clear fluidness in the expression, and the subject matter is characteristic of the Mahayana pantheon with multiple creations of Bodhisattvas.

From the 13th century, Theravada Buddhism was introduced from Sri Lanka around the same time as the ethnic Thai kingdom of Sukhothai was established. The new faith inspired highly stylized images in Thai Buddhism, with sometimes very geometrical and almost abstract figures.

During the Ayutthaya period (14th-18th centuries), the Buddha came to be represented in a more stylistic manner with sumptuous garments and jeweled ornamentations. Many Thai sculptures or temples tended to be gilded, and on occasion enriched with inlays.

Indonesia

Like the rest of Southeast Asia, Indonesia seems to have been most strongly influenced by India from the 1st century CE. The islands of Sumatra and Java in western Indonesia were the seat of the empire of Sri Vijaya (8th-13th century CE), which came to dominate most of the area around the Southeast Asian peninsula through maritime power.

The Sri Vijayan Empire had adopted Mahayana and Vajrayana Buddhism, under a line of rulers named the Sailendras. Sri Vijaya spread Mahayana Buddhist art during its expansion into the Southeast Asian peninsula. Numerous statues of Mahayana Bodhisattvas from this period are characterized by a very strong refinement and technical sophistication, and are found throughout the region.

Extremely rich and refined architectural remains are can be found in Java and Sumatra. The most magnificence is the temple of Borobudur (the largest Buddhist structure in the world, built from around 780-850 AD).

This temple modeled after Buddhist concept of universe, the Mandala which counts 505 images of the seated Buddha and unique bell-shaped stupa that contains the statue of Buddha. Borobudur is adorned with long series of bas-reliefs narrated the holy Buddhist scriptures. The oldest Buddhist structure in Indonesia probably is the Batu Jaya stupas at Karawang, West Java, dated from around 4th century AD.

This temple is some plastered brick stupas. However, Buddhist art in Indonesia reach the golden era during the Sailendra dynasty rule in Java. The bas-reliefs and statues of Boddhisatva, Tara, and Kinnara found in Kalasan, Sewu, Sari, and Plaosan temple is very graceful with serene expression, While Mendut temple near Borobudur, houses the giant statue of Buddha, Avalokitesvara, and Vajrapani.

In Sumatra Sri Vijaya probably built the temple of Muara Takus, and Muaro Jambi. The most beautiful classical Javanese art is the serene and delicate statue of Prajnaparamita (the collection of National Museum Jakarta) the goddess of transcendental wisdom from Singhasari. The Indonesian Buddhist Empire of Sri Vijaya declined due to conflicts with the Chola rulers of India, then followed by Majapahit empire, before being destabilized by the Islamic expansion from the 13th century.

3

Indian Buddhist Architecture

INDUS VALLEY CIVILIZATION

The Indus civilization or the Harappan civilization, which flourished during the Bronze Age i.e. 2500-2000 BC is ranked among the four widely known civilizations of the old world. Extensive excavation work that has been done since Independence has so far identified more than 100 sites belonging to this civilization. A few prominent among them are Dholavira (Gujarat), Kalibangan (Rajasthan), Lothal (Gujarat), Sarkotada (Gujarat), Diamabad (Maharashtra), Alamgirpur (U.P.), Bhagwanpura (Haryana), Banawali (Haryana), Kuntasi, Padri (Gujarat) and Mauda (Jammu).

Extensive town planning was the characteristic of this civilization, which is evident from the gridiron pattern for the layout of cities, some with fortifications and the elaborate drainage and water management systems. The houses were built of baked bricks, which is rare in contemporary civilizations at Mesopotamia and Egypt. Bricks of fixed sizes, as well as stone and wood were also used for building. Buildings in the lower area are rather monotonous, being mainly functional rather than decorative.

But many houses are two storeyed. The most imposing of the buildings is the Great Bath of Mohenjodaro. It is 54.86 metres long and 32.91 metres wide and with 2.43 metres thick outer walls. The Bath had galleries and rooms on all sides. Another important structure was the Granary complex comprising of blocks with an overall area of 55 x 43 metres.

The granaries were intelligently constructed, with strategic air ducts and platforms divided into units.

THE MAURYAN PERIOD

If the remnants of the Indus culture are excluded, the earliest surviving architectural heritage in India is that of the Mauryans. The Mauryan period was a great landmark in the history of Indian art. Some of the monuments and pillars belonging to this period are considered as the finest specimens of Indian art.

The Mauryan architecture was embalmed in timber, for rocks and stones were not as freely in use then. The art of polishing of wood reached so much perfection during the Mauryan period that master craftsmen used to make wood glisten like a mirror. Chandra Gupta Maurya had built many buildings, palaces and monuments with wood, most of which perished with time. In 300 B.C., Chandragupta Maurya constructed a wooden fort 14.48 km long and 2.41km wide, along the Ganges in Bihar. However, only a couple of teak beams have survived from this fort.

Ashoka was the first Mauryan Emperor who began to "think in stone". The stonework of the Ashokan Period (3rd century B.C.) was of a highly diversified order and comprised of lofty free-standing pillars, railings of the stupas, lion thrones and other colossal figures. The use of stone had reached such great perfection during this time that even small fragments of stone art was given a high lustrous polish resembling fine enamel. While most of the shapes and decorative forms employed were indigenous in origin, some exotic forms show the influence of Greek, Persian and Egyptian cultures.

The Ashokan period marked the beginning of the Buddhist School of architecture in India. It witnessed the construction of many rock-cut caves, pillars, stupas and palaces. A number of cave-shrines belonging to this period have been excavated in the Barabar and Nagarjuni hills and Sitamarhi in Bihar. These rock-cut sanctuaries, quarried from large masses of rocks called gneisses, are simple in plan and are devoid of all interior decorative carvings. The caves served as the residences of the monks. There are several inscriptions, which indicate that these rock-cut sanctuaries were constructed by Emperor Ashoka for the monks of the Ajivika sect, who are more closely related to the Jains than to the Buddhists.

The Ashokan rock-edict at Dhauli, near Bhubaneshwar, is considered to be the earliest rock-cut sculpture in India. It has a sculpted elephant on the top, which signifies the Emperor's conversion to Buddhism after his Kalinga victory. The monolithic Ashokan pillars are marvels of architecture and sculpture. These were lofty free standing monolithic columns erected on sacred sites. Originally there were about thirty pillars but now only ten are in existence, of which only two with lion capitals stand in situ in good condition at Kolhua and Laurya Nandangarh respectively. Each pillar was about 15.24 metres high and weighed about 50 tonnes and was made out of fine sandstone. The pillar consisted of three parts-the prop, the shaft and the capitol. The capitol consisted of fine polished stone containing one or more animal figures in the round. Made of bricks, they carried declarations from the king regarding Buddhism or any other topic. The pillars did not stand in isolation and were usually found near stupas in a spot either unknowingly marked by the Buddha himself or along the royal route to Magadha, the capital. The Sarnath pillar is one of the finest pieces of sculpture of the Ashokan period. The Ashokan pillars also throw light on the contacts India had with Persia and other countries. Two of the Ashkan edicts have also been found at Laghman, near Jalalabad in modern Afghanistan.

Ashoka was responsible for the construction of several stupas, which were large halls, capped with domes and bore symbols of the Buddha. The most important ones are located at Bharhut, Bodhgaya, Sanchi, Amravati and Nagarjunakonda. The Buddhist shrines or the monasteries were built in somewhat irregular designs following the Gandhara style of architecture. Built on the patterns of a fort and defended by a stone wall, the monastery evolved from the site of an ancient stupa. The principle buildings were housed within a rectangular courtyard with a stupa in the south and the monastery in the north.

Ashoka had also built a number of palaces, but most of them have perished. Ashoka's palace near Patna was a masterpiece. Enclosed by a high brick wall, the highlight of the palace was an immense 76.2 metres high pillared-hall having three storeys. The Chinese traveller Fahien was so impressed by this palace that he stated that "it was made by spirits" and that its carvings are so elegantly executed "which no human hands of this world could accomplish". Made mostly of wood, it seems to have been destroyed by fire. Its existence was pointed out during the excavations at Kumrahar, near Patna, where its ashes have been found preserved for several thousand years.

THE STUPAS

Sanchi Stupas

The early stupas were hemispherical in shape with a low base. The hemispherical shape symbolized the cosmic mountain. The later stupas assumed an increasingly cylindrical form. The early stupas were known for their simplicity.

Apart from the than ruins of stupa at Piprahwa (Nepal), the core of stupa No 1 at Sanchi can be considered as the oldest of the stupas. Originally built by Asoka, it was enlarged in subsequent centuries. An inscription by the ivory carvers of Vidisha on the southern gateway throws light on the transference of building material from perishable wood and ivory to the more durable stone.

Amaravati Stupa

Amaravati stupa, built in 2nd or 1st century BC was probably like the one at Sanchi, but in later centuries it was transformed from a Hinayana shrine to a Mahayana shrine. The diameter of the dome of the stupa at ground level was about 48.76 metres and its height was about 30 metres. Amaravati stupa is different from the Bharhut and Sanchi stupas. It had free-standing columns surmounted by lions near the gateways. The dome was covered with sculptured panels. The stupa had an upper circumambulatory path on the drum as at Sanchi. This path had two intricately carved railings. The stone is greenish-white limestone of the region.

Gandhara Stupa

The Gandhara stupa is a further development of stupas at Sanchi and Bharhut. In Gandhara stupas the base, dome and the hemisphere dome are sculpted. The stupa tapers upward to form a tower like structure. The stupas of Nagarjunakonda in Krishna valley were very large. At the base there were brick walls forming wheel and spokes, whish were filled with earth. The Maha Chaitya of Nagarjunakonda has a base in the form of Swastika, which is a sun symbol.

THE SUNGAS, KUSHANS AND SATAVAHANAS

The Mauryan dynasty crumbled after Asoka's death in 232 B.C. In its wake came the Sungas and Kushans in the north and the Satavahanas in the south. The period between 2nd century B.C. and 3rd century A.D. marked the beginning of the sculptural idiom in Indian sculpture where the elements of physical form were evolving into a more refined, realistic and expressive style. The sculptors strived at mastering their art, especially of the human body, which was carved in high relief and bore heaviness and vigour. These dynasties made advances in art and architecture in areas like stone construction, stone carving, symbolism and beginning of temple (or chaitya hall) and the monastery (or vihara) constructions.

Under these dynasties the Asokan stupas were enlarged and the earlier brick and wood works were replaced with stone-works. For instance, the Sanchi Stupa was enlarged to nearly twice its size in 150 B.C. and elaborate gateways were added later. The Sungas also reconstructed the railings around the Barhut Stupa.

The Sungas also built the toranas or the gateways to the stupas. An inscription at the Barhut Stupa indicates that the torana was built during the reign of Sungas i.e. 184-72 B.C. These toranas indicate the influence of Hellenistic and other foreign schools in the Sunga architecture.

The Satavahanas constructed a large number of stupas at Goli, Jaggiahpeta, Bhattiprolu, Gantasala, Nagarjunakonda and Amravati. During the Kushan period (1-3 A.D.), the Buddha was represented in human form instead of symbols. Buddha's image in endless forms and replicas became the principal element in Buddhist sculpture during the Kushan period. Another feature of this period was that the Emperor himself was shown as a divine person. The Kushans were the pioneers of the Gandhara School of Art and a large number of monasteries; stupas and statues were constructed during the reign of Kanishka.

THE SCHOOLS OF ART

Gandhara School of Art

The Gandhara School of Art (50 B.C. to 500 A.D.): The Gadhara region extending from Punjab to the borders of Afghanistan was an important centre of Mahayana Buddhism up to the 5th century A.D. The region became famous throughout the world since a new school of Indian sculpture known as the Gandhara School developed during that period. Owing to its strategic location the Gandhara School imbibed all kinds of foreign influences like Persian, Greek, Roman, Saka and Kushan. The origin of Gandhara art can be traced to the Greek rulers of Bactria and Northwest India. But it was during the reign of Kanishka that the art received great patronage.

The Gandhara School of Art is also known as the Graeco-Buddhist School of Art since Greek techniques of Art were applied to Buddhist subjects. The most important contribution of the Gandhara School of Art was the evolution of beautiful images of the Buddha and Bodhisattavas, which were executed in black stone and modelled on identical characters of Graeco-Roman pantheon.

Hence it is said, "the Gandhara artist had the hand of a Greek but the heart of an Indian." The most characteristic trait of Gandhara sculpture is the depiction of Lord Buddha in the standing or seated positions. The seated Buddha is always shown cross-legged in the traditional Indian way. Another typical feature of the Gandhara Art is the rich carving, elaborate ornamentation and complex symbolism. The best specimens of Gandhara art are from Jaulian and Dharmarajika stupa at Taxila and from Hadda near Jalalabad in modern Afghanistan. The tallest rock-cut statue of Lord Buddha is also located at Bamiyan in modern Afghanistan and dates back to 3-4 century AD.

The Mathura School of Art

The Mathura School of art flourished at the holy city of Mathura, especially between 1-3 A.D. It established the tradition of transforming Buddhist symbols into human form. Buddha's first image can be traced to Kanishka's reign (about 78 A.D.). The earliest sculptures of Buddha were made keeping the yaksha prototype in mind. They were depicted as strongly built with the right hand raised in protection and the left hand on the waist. The figures produced by this school of art do not have moustaches and beards as in the Gandhara Art. These figures can be seen in the museum of Mathura. The standing Buddha figures resembles the yaksha figures and indicates the Kushan influence. The seated figures are in the padmasana posture. The Mathura School not only produced beautiful images of the Buddha but also of the Jain Tirthankaras and gods and goddesses of the Hindu pantheon. Many scholars believe that the Mathura School of Art, although of indigenous origin, was greatly influenced by the Gandhara School of Art. The Guptas adopted the Mathura School of Art and further improvised and perfected it.

The Amravati School of Art

This school of art developed at Amravati, on the banks of the Krishna River in modern Andhra Pradesh. It is the site for the largest Buddhist stupa of South India. Its construction began in 200 B.C. and was completed in 200 A.D. The diameter of the stupa at the base was 51 metres. The height of the dome was 31 metres and its outer railing was 5 metres wide. The stupendous stupa could not withstand the ravages of time and its ruins are preserved in the London Museum.

TEMPLE ARCHITECTURE OF INDIA

As temples form the backbone of Indian medieval architectural heritage, it would be appropriate to discuss their basic architectural features before we move on to different styles of Indian architecture. Despite the vastness of the land, Indian temple architecture is remarkably uniform. It is, however, often distinguished into two chief styles, each having numerous sub-styles. The Northern or Indo-Aryan style is marked by a tower with rounded top and curvilinear outline while the Southern or Dravidian style has the tower usually in the shape of a rectangular truncated pyramid.

The standard type of the Hindu temple has remained fundamentally same from the 6th century AD to the present day. The construction of temples-whether in the north in the south-essentially followed a similar pattern. There is the sanctuary or the vimana of which the upper and outer pyramidal and tapering portion is called the shikhara, or pinnacle. The vimana is a rather dark place that houses the divine deity. This small area is called garbha griha, literally meaning 'womb house'. The entrance is through a doorway, normally from the eastern side. The doorway is reached through a mandapa or pillared hall, where devotees congregate for prayers. However, earlier temples may have had the mandapa at a little distance from the main temple (the Shore Temple in Mamallapuram near Chennai, circa 700 A.D.), although this practise was done away with in later constructions. Later it became necessary to unite both buildings, making way for the antarala or intermediate vestibule. A porch or a smaller room called ardha mandapa leads up to a hall (mandapa), which in turn goes into a maha mandapa. A tower generally surmounted the shrine-room while smaller towers rose from other parts of the building. The whole conception was set in a rectangular courtyard, which sometimes contained lesser shrines and was often placed on a raised platform. The most perfect examples of temples on this structure are the Khajuraho temples. Here, each chamber has its own separate pyramidal roof rising in gradual steps so that the final sanctum's roof towers up, surrounded by smaller spires, finally forming a graceful, rising stepped pyramid.

In some parts of India, the ascending pyramid roof format was not followed. The roof in such temples was still pyramidal, but was formed of layers that gradually became narrower as they rose. A courtyard was built around the temple, and sometimes a wall would be constructed to ensure seclusion. The outer walls were treated by carving in an orderly group of repetitive miniatures. The shikhara or tapering roof was specifically based on this design, which may have originated from the domed huts of central and eastern India.

THE PRATHIHARAS

The Pratiharas, who ruled over an extensive empire from Ujjain during the 8th and 9th centuries, were among the significant successors of the Guptas. The Pratihara temples of Central India have their own unique designs and decorative schemes. The important temples of Ujjain include the Mahakaleshwar temple, which has one of the twelve Jyotirlingas of India, Kal Bhairava temple, which finds a mention in the Skanda Purana, and Mangalnath temple, which is regarded as the birthplace of Mars, according to the Matsya Purana.

THE PALAS

The Pala School of Architecture (8-13th Centuries AD) flourished in Bengal and Bihar under the Pala and the Sena rulers. Nalanda was its most active centre, whose influence was spread to Nepal, Myanmar and even Indonesia. Stone sculptures of this period are found at Nalanda, Rajagriha, Bodh Gaya, Rajashahi and other places. The Pala School of art is seen at its best at Nalanda and several sculptures belonging to this period have been unearthed in excavations.

THE CHANDELAS

The Chandelas of Jijihoti or Bundelkhand were known as great builders during the 10th-11th centuries. It is they who built the temples at Khajuraho justly famous for their graceful contours and erotic sculptures. These 22 temples (out of the original 85) are regarded as one of world's greatest artistic wonders. The Khajuraho Temples do not illustrate a development over a long period of time but were built within a short period of hundred years from 950-1050 A.D. The Khajuraho Temples have highly individualistic architectural character and are generally small in size. Each temple is divided into three main compartments-the cella or garbha griha, an assembly hall or mandapa and an entrance portico or ardha mandapa. Some temples also contain the antarala or vestibule to the cella and the transepts or maha-mandapa. The Kendriya Mahadev temple is the largest and most beautiful of the Khajuraho Temples. The Shiva Temple at Visvanath and the Vishnu Temple at Chaturbhanj are other important temples at Khajuraho.

CAVE ARCHITECTURE OF INDIA

The earliest man-made caves date back to the 2nd century BC while the latest date to the 7th century AD. The splendid sculpture and lovely frescoes adorning these caves make them one of the glorious monuments of India's past.

Ajanta Caves

The cave temples of Ajanta, situated north of Aurangabad, were first mentioned in the writings of the Chinese pilgrim Huen Tsang who visited India between 629 AD and 645 AD. These caves were discovered by the British officers in 1819 AD. The thirty temples at Ajanta are set into the rocky sides of a crescent shaped gorge in the Inhyadri hills of the Sahyadri ranges. At the head of the gorge is a natural pool which is fed by a waterfall. The excavations spanned a period of about six centuries.

The earlier monuments include both chaitya halls and monasteries. These date from the 2nd to 1st centuries B.C. After a period of more than six centuries, excavations once again revived during the reign of the Vakataka ruler Harishena. The sculptures contain an impressive array of votive figures, accessory figures, narrative episodes and decorative motifs. The series of paintings is unparalleled in the history of Indian art, both for the wide range of subjects and the medium. The caves depict a large number of incidents from the life of the

Buddha (Jataka Tales). Overlapping figures suggest that the perspective and colors are harmoniously blended and that the line work is sinuous. However, the identities of the artists responsible for the execution of the Ajanta caves are unknown.

Bhimbetaka Caves

Bhimbetka is located in the Raisen District of Madhya Pradesh about 45 km to the southeast of Bhopal near a hill village called 'Bhiyanpur'. Bhimbetaka, discovered in 1958 by V.S. Wakanker, is the biggest prehistoric art depository in India. Atop the hill a large number of rock-shelters have been discovered, of which more than 130 contain paintings. Excavations in some of the rock-shelters revealed history of continuous habitation from early stone age (about 10000 years) to the end of stone age (c. 10,000 to 2,000 years) as seen from artificially made stone tools and implements like hand-axes, cleavers, scrappers and knives. Neolithic tools like points, trapezes and lunates made of chert and chalcedony, besides stone querns and grinders, decorated bone objects, pieces of ochre and human burials were also found here.

Elephanta Caves

The 6th century Shiva temple in the Elephanta caves is one of the most exquisitely carved temples in India. The central attraction here is a twenty-foot high bust of the deity in three-headed form. The Maheshamurti is built deep into a recess and looms up from the darkness to fill the full height of the cave. This image symbolizes the fierce, feminine and meditative aspects of the great ascetic and the three heads represent Lord Shiva as Aghori, Ardhanarishvara and Mahayogi. Aghori is the aggressive form of Shiva where he is intent on destruction. Ardhanarishvara depicts Lord Shiva as half-man/half-woman signifying the essential unity of the sexes.

The Mahayogi posture symbolises the meditative aspect of the God and here Lord Shiva is shown in his most quiet and serene form. Other sculptures in these caves depict Shiva's cosmic dance of primordial creation and destruction and his marriage to Parvati.

Mahakali Caves

These are rock-cut Buddhist caves situated in the Udayagiri hills, about 6.5km from Mumbai. These were excavated during 200 BC to 600 AD and are now in ruins. They comprise of 4 caves on the southeastern face and 15 caves on the northwestern face. Cave 9 is the chief cave and is the oldest and consists of a stupa and figures of Lord Buddha.

Jogeshwar and Kanheri Caves

Located in the western suburbs of Bombay, it is second largest known cave after the Kailasa cave in Ellora and houses a Brahmanical temple dating back to the 6th century AD.

Excavated between the 1st and 2nd centuries, the Kanheri is a 109-cave complex located near Borivili National Park in Bombay. The Kanheri caves contain illustrations from Hinayana and Mahayana Buddhism and show carvings dating back to 200 BC.

Karla and Bhaja Caves

About 50-60 kms away from Pune, these are rock-cut Buddhist caves dating back to the 1st and 2nd centuries BC. The caves consist of several viharas and chaityas.

RAJPUT ARCHITECTURE

The Rajputs were great patrons of art and architecture, the finest examples being their forts and palaces. The Rajput palaces are complex compositions built as inner citadels surrounded by the city and enclosed by a fortified wall as at Chittorgarh and Jaisalmer. Some forts, such as those at Bharatpur and Deeg, were protected by wide moats.

The oldest surviving palaces date from the mid-fifteenth century and are found at Chittor and Gwalior. The Man Mandir, the largest palace in Gwalior, was built by Raja Man Singh Tomar (1486-1516). The Man Mandir has two storeys above, and two below, ground level overhanging a sandstone cliff. This gigantic cliff is punctuated by five massive round towers, crowned by domed cupolas and linked by delicately carved parapets. The whole facade is enriched with brilliant blue tiles. The palaces of Jaisalmer, Bikaner, Jodhpur, Udaipur and Kota represent the maturity of the Rajput style. All of these palaces were built predominantly in the 17th and early 18th centuries. The huge fortified city of Jaisalmer is situated far out in the Thar Desert. The buildings are constructed with the local yellow brown stone and they have been remarkably preserved owing to their remote location.

The city of Bikaner is encircled by 5.63 km long stone wall in rich pink sandstone. There are five gates and three sally ports. The Jodhpur Fort dominates the city, which is surrounded by a huge wall with 101 bastions, nearly 9.5 km long. The Meherangarh fort stands on a cliff with a sheer drop of over 36 metres.

The foundation of Jaipur, the fabled "pink city", in 1727 AD represents the final phase of Rajput architecture. Built by Jai Singh, Jaipur represents a fusion of Eastern and Western ideas of town planning. The city is enclosed by a wall and has bastions and towers at regular intervals. The City Palace is at the center of the walled city and is a spectacular synthesis of Rajput and Mughal architectural styles. The famous building Hawa Mahal, or Palace of Winds, (1799) has a five-storeyed symmetrical facade composed of 953 small casements in a huge curve each with a projecting balcony and crowning arch. The Jantar Mantar, the largest of five observatories built by Jai Singh II in the early eighteenth century, is another interesting example of Rajput architecture.

JAIN ARCHITECTURE

The contribution of Jain art to the mainstream art in India has been considerable. Every phase of Indian art is represented by a Jain version and each one of them is worthy of meticulous study and understanding. Jain architecture cannot be accredited with a style of its own, for in the first place it was almost an offshoot of Hindu and Buddhist styles. In the initial years, many Jain temples were made adjoining the Buddhist temples following the Buddhist rock-cut style. Initially these temples were mainly carved out of rock faces and the use of bricks was almost negligible. However, in later years Jains started building temple-cities on hills based on the concept of 'mountains of immortality'.

Compared to the number of Hindu temples in India, Jain temples are few and spaced out. Surrounded by embattled walls, the temples are divided into wards, guarded by massive bastions at its ends, with fortified gateways as the main entrances. These temple-cities were not built on a specific plan; instead they were the results of sporadic construction. Natural levels of the hill on which the 'city' was being built accommodated various levels so that as one goes higher the architecture and grandeur increases. The only variation in these temples was in the form of frequent chamukhs or four-faced temples. In these the image of a Tirthankara faces the four sides, or four Tirthankars are be placed back to back to face four cardinal points. Entry into this temple is also from four doors. The Chamukh temple of Adinath (1618 AD) is a characteristic example of the four-door temple.

The great Jain temples and sculptured monuments of Karnataka, Maharashtra and Rajasthan are world-renowned. The most spectacular of all Jain temples are found at Ranakpur and Mount Abu in Rajasthan. Deogarh (Lalitpur, U.P.), Ellora, Badami and Aihole also have some of the important specimens of Jain Art.

THE INDO-ISLAMIC ARCHITECTURE

Indian architecture took new shape with the advent of Islamic rule in India towards the end of the 12th century AD. New elements were introduced into the Indian architecture that include: use of shapes (instead of natural forms); inscriptional art using decorative lettering or calligraphy; inlay decoration and use of coloured marble, painted plaster and brilliantly glazed tiles. In contrast to the indigenous Indian architecture which was of the trabeate order i.e. all spaces were spanned by means of horizontal beams, the Islamic architecture was arcuate i.e. an arch or dome was adopted as a method of bridging a space. The concept of arch or dome was not invented by the Muslims but was, in fact, borrowed and was further perfected by them from the architectural styles of the post-Roman period. The Muslims used the cementing agent in the form of mortar for the first time in the construction of buildings in India. They further put to use certain scientific and mechanical formulae, which were derived by experience of other civilizations, in their constructions in India. Such use of scientific principles helped not only in obtaining greater strength and stability of the construction materials but also provided greater flexibility to the architects and builders. This amalgamation of the Indian and the Islamic elements led to the emergence of a new style of architecture called the Indo-Islamic Architecture.

One fact that must be stressed here is that, the Islamic elements of architecture had already passed through different experimental phases in other countries like Egypt, Iran and Iraq before these were introduced in India. Unlike most Islamic monuments of these countries, which were largely constructed in brick, plaster and rubble, the Indo-Islamic monuments were typical mortar-masonry works formed of dressed stones. It must be emphasized that the development of the Indo-Islamic architecture was greatly facilitated by the knowledge and skill possessed by the Indian craftsmen, who had mastered the art of stonework for centuries and used their experience while constructing Islamic monuments in India.

In simple terms the Islamic architecture in India can be divided into religious and secular. Mosques and Tombs represent the religious architecture, while palaces and forts are examples of secular Islamic architecture. Forts were essentially functional, complete with a little township within and various fortifications to engage and repel the enemy.

Mosques: The mosque or masjid is a representation of Muslim art in its simplest form. The mosque is basically an open courtyard surrounded by a pillared verandah, crowned off with a dome. A mihrab indicates the direction of the qibla for prayer. Towards the right of the mihrab stands the mimbar or pulpit from where the Imam presides over the proceedings. An elevated platform, usually a minaret from where the Faithful are summoned to attend the prayers is an invariable part of a mosque. Large mosques where the faithful assemble for the Friday prayers are called the Jama Masjids.

Tombs: Although not actually religious in nature, the tomb or maqbara introduced an entirely new architectural concept. While the masjid was mainly known for its simplicity, a tomb could range from being a simple affair (Aurangazeb's grave) to an awesome structure enveloped in grandeur (Taj Mahal). The tomb usually consists of solitary compartment or tomb chamber known as the huzrah in whose centre is the cenotaph or zarih. This entire structure is covered with an elaborate dome. In the underground chamber lies the mortuary or the maqbara, in which the corpse is buried in a grave or qabr. Smaller tombs may have a mihrab, although larger mausoleums have a separate mosque located separately from the main tomb. Normally the whole tomb complex or rauza is surrounded by an enclosure. The tomb of a Muslim saint is called a dargah. Almost all Islamic monuments were subjected to free use of verses from the Holy Koran and a great amount of time was spent in carving out minute details on walls, ceilings, pillars and domes.

COLONIAL ARCHITECTURE

European colonists brought with them to India concepts of their "world view" and a whole baggage of the history of European architecture---Neo-Classical, Romanesque, Gothic and Renaissance. The initial structures were utilitarian warehouses and walled trading posts, giving way to fortified towns along the coastline. The Portuguese adapted to India the climatically appropriate Iberian galleried patio house and the Baroque churches of Goa. Se Cathedral and Arch of Conception of Goa were built in the typical Portuguese-Gothic style. The St. Francis Church at Cochin, built by the Portuguese in 1510, is believed to be the first church built by the Europeans in India. The Portuguese also built the fort of Castella de Aguanda near Mumbai and added fortifications to the Bassein fort built by Bahadur Shah, the Sultan of Gujarat, in 1532 AD. The Bassein fort is famous for the Matriz (Cathedral of St Joseph), the Corinthian pillared hall and the Porte da Mer (sea gate).

The Danish influence is evident in Nagapatnam, which was laid out in squares and canals and also in Tranquebar and Serampore. The French gave a distinct urban design to its settlement in Pondicherry by applying the Cartesian grid plans and classical architectural patterns. The Church of Sacred Heart of Jesus (Eglise De Sacre Coeur De Jesus), the Eglise de Notre Dame de Anges and the Eglise de Notre Dame de Lourdes at Pondicherry have a distinct French influence.

However, it was the British who left a lasting impact on the India architecture. They saw themselves as the successors to the Mughals and used architecture as a symbol of power. The British followed various architectural styles-Gothic, Imperial, Christian, English Renaissance and Victorian being the essentials.

The first buildings were factories but later courts, schools, municipal halls and dak bungalows came up, which were ordinary structures built by garrison engineers. A deeper concern with architecture was exhibited in churches and other public buildings. Most of the buildings were adaptations of the buildings designed by leading British architects of that time like Wren, Adam, Nash and others in London and other places. For instance, the Church of St. John at Calcutta was built in 1787 inspired by St. Stephens Church at Walbrooks, the Government House in Calcutta was built by Capt. Charles Wyatt modelled on the Kedleston Hall of Derbyshire, the Indian Government Mint in Calcutta is a half-scale replica of the Temple of Minerva at Athens and the Pachaiyappa's Hall in Chennai was modelled on the Athenium Temple of Theseus. Unlike Europe, however, these buildings were built mostly of brick and stuccoed with lime or chunam, sometimes "facades" incised to look like stones. Some later buildings were, however, built with stones. Churches, which were symbols of colonialism, were built in great style. Based on London prototypes, several churches evolved with variations as highly original works. The earliest example is the St. Mary's Church in Fort St. George in Chennai.

Neo-Gothic architecture flourished in different parts of India under the British, inspired by the Houses of Parliament in London. Colonel Thomas Cowper built the town hall in

Bombay during 1820 to 1835. Governor Sir Bartle Frere tried to give a truly imperial ambience to the city of Bombay. During his reign the old town walls were broken down and the Gateway of India was built in the Gothic style of architecture. The Secretariat, University Library, Rajabai Tower, Telegraph Office and the Victoria Terminus all followed the Victorian Gothic style, similar to buildings in London. Undoubtedly, the Victoria Terminus, designed by the architect Frederick Willaim Stevens modelled on the St.Pancras Station, is the finest example of Gothic architecture with a subtle hint of the Indo-Saracenic motifs, an extravaganza of polychromatic stone, decorated tile marble and stained glass. Stevens also designed other buildings like the Churchgate Terminus and the Municipal Building opposite the Victoria Terminus.

In Varanasi, one of the true Gothic monuments is Queen's College, built in a perpendicular style by Major Kitoe from 1847 to 1852. In Allahabad, the British built a series of edifices including the University, All Saints Cathedral, the High Court and the Mayo College. In Calcutta, a High Court was constructed following the Gothic style. The Howrah Bridge (1943), with its red brick facade surrounded by eight square towers represents a combination of the Oriental and Roman styles. Fort William, the stronghold of the British in mid 19th century that took 13 years to construct at a cost of more than $3.5 million and the Victoria Memorial in Calcutta (1921), designed by Sir William Emerson, are probably the most imposing of all British structures in India.

The passing of power from the East India Company to the British Crown, the rise of Indian nationalism and the introduction of Railways were the watersheds in the British Colonial Indian architectural history. New materials like concrete, glass, wrought and cast iron opened up new architectural possibilities. The British also started assimilating and adopting the native Indian styles in the architecture. All these factors led to the development of Indo-Saracenic architecture towards the end of the 19th century. Victorian in essence, it borrowed heavily from the Islamic style of Mughal and Afghan rulers. In fact it was a pot pouri of architectural styles; a hybrid style that combined in a wonderful manner diverse architectural elements of Hindu and Mughal with gothic cusped arches, domes, spires, tracery, minarets and stained glass. The Indo-Saracenic style was Indian on the outside and British inside since the facade was built with an Indian touch while the interior was solely Victorian. F.S.Growse, Sir Swinton Jacob, R.F.Chisholm and H.Irwin were the pioneers of this style of architecture. The Chepauk Palace in Chennai designed by Paul Benfield is said to be the first Indo-Saracenic building in India. Other outstanding examples of this style of architecture include the Law Courts, Victoria Memorial Hall, Presidency College and Senate House of Chennai, Muir College at Allahabad, Napier Museum at Thiruvanthapuram, the Post Office, Prince of Wales Museum and the Gateway of India in Mumbai, the Maharaja's Palace at Mysore and M.S.University and Lakshmi Villas Palace at Baroda.

The architecture of New Delhi was the crowning glory of the British Raj. Robert Byron described New Delhi as "The Rome of Hindostan". The British built New Delhi as a systematically planned city after it was made the capital in 1911. The British Viceroy made Sir Edward Lutyens responsible for the overall plan of Delhi. He was specifically directed to "harmonise externally with the traditions of Indian art". Thus, the Western architecture with Oriental motif was realised with chajjas, jalis and chhattris, as stylistic devices in the Viceroy's House (now Rashtrapati Bhawan). Herbert Baker added the imposing buildings of the South Block and the North Block, which flank the Rashtrapati Bhawan. Another Englishman called Robert Tor Tussell built the Connaught Place and the Eastern and Western Courts.

St Martin's Garrison Church marks the culmination of the British architectural ventures in India. The Church is a huge monolith with a high square tower and deeply sunken window ledges reminiscent of Dutch and German architecture.

MODERN ARCHITECTURE OF INDIA

After the British left India in 1947, Indian architecture dropped into an abyss. Indian architects, who were relegated to the role of being assistants to the British architects under the British Raj, took their own time to express their ingenuity. Perhaps, there was an identity crisis, a dilemma whether to bask in the glory of the past or move forward with times using new ideas, images and techniques. While in other fields like art, music and culture, the distinct Indian imprint was more enhanced in the post-Independence period; no such thing was discernible in the case of architecture. It is no doubt that the Indian architects were unable to achieve a transformative architecture despite the existence of great potential at the time of Indian Independence.

The post-Independence period saw the emergence of two schools of thought in architecture--the Revivalist and the Modernist. The Revivalists, who advocated "continuity with the past", could not break the shackles of the colonial legacy and left no significant impact on the neo-Indian architecture. The Modernists too depended heavily on the European and American models and tried to adopt them in India without taking into consideration the regional aspirations, diversities and requirements. The contemporary Indian architecture was also beset with problems like population explosion, lack of vision among the planners, lack of support from the government and a less than satisfactory standard of architecture education. The result was that during the initial years after the Independence, foreign architects continued to play a leading role in Indian architecture.

Jawaharlal Nehru, the first Prime Minister, had called for an open architectural competition for the design of the Ashoka Hotel in 1956, which was won by B.E.Doctor, an architect from Bombay. Using technology to create large pillar-less spaces, Doctor created a facade that borrowed from Islamic, Hindu, British and modern architecture.

Indian architecture witnessed a revolution when the Punjab government engaged Le Corbusier to design the new city of Chandigarh. Built in three stages, Corbusier divided the city into three sections. The 'head' consisted of political, bureaucratic and judicial buildings, the administrative parts of the city. The 'body' housed the university and residential complexes in the heart of the city. The 'feet' consisted of industrial sectors and the railway station. Apart from the initial layout of the city, Corbusier also designed several buildings in Chandigarh. The High Court building has a sloping roof, supported by concrete walls which allow air to pass through them. The Assembly is a squarish structure topped with a huge industrial chimney while the Secretariat is made up of hundreds of rooms with an airy exterior.

Taking inspiration from Le Corbusier's creativity, a young Indian architect D V Joshi designed the Institute of Indology in Ahmedabad. Charles Mark Correa, Doshi's contemporary, designed the Hindustan Lever pavilion for the India International Trade Fair in 1961. The pavilion was an exposed concrete structure resembling a crumpled packing case made of concrete with a zigzag ramp to walk along. Correa also designed the Gandhi Sanghralaya in Ahmedabad as a tribute to Mahatma Gandhi.

The Asiad Village in New Delhi, designed by Raj Rewell and built as a colossal complex with more than 800 residential units, landscaped courts, streets, restaurants and shops, all catering to sports persons who had assembled for the 1982 Asian Games, is one of the architectural landmarks of modern India. The lotus-shaped Bahai temple in New Delhi, designed by Fariburz Sabha in 1980 and completed in December 1986, is an awe-inspiring example of the ingenuity of the Indian architects.

However, the fact remains that the contemporary architecture in India has failed to inspire. Even after 50 years of Independence our cities are still symbolised by pre-independence buildings. For instance, Calcutta is symbolised by the Victoria Memorial, New Delhi by the Rashtrapati Bhawan, Mumbai by the Victoria Terminus and the Gateway of India and Chennai by the Victoria Memorial Hall. The post-independence buildings such as the New Secretariat building in Calcutta or the Vigyan Bhawan in New Delhi has nothing much to offer in terms of architectural style.

In contrast most major cities in the world have splendid modern buildings to boast off, like Sydney has its Sydney Opera House, Paris has new Grand Arch and the Georges Pompidos Centre, New York has its World Trade Centre, Chicago has the Sears Tower and Toronto has the C.N.Tower. Even cities in other Third World countries have several buildings to feel proud about, like Kuala Lumpur has its Petronas Tower, Shangai has the TV Tower, Hong Kong has its Hongkong and Shanghai Corporation building and the Bank of China Building and even Colombo has its new Parliament building.

In November 1998, the media reported that the foundation stone of World Centre of Vedic Learning, the world's tallest building would be laid at Karondi village, in Jabalpur in Madhya Pradesh. The building, which will be built by the Maharishi Mahesh Yogi Vedic University, is being designed according to the Maharishi Sthapatya Veda symbolising the victory of India's ancient knowledge of Vastu Vidya. The proposed centre for Vedic consciousness, which is modelled on Sao Paulo Tower of Brazil, would be 677 metres (2222 feet) high and 339 metres (1111 feet) wide at the square base. Once completed it will be more than 213 metres (700 feet) taller than the Petronas Tower in Kuala Lumpur and will achieve the distinction of being the world's tallest building. It was also reported that a consortium of architects and engineers who have designed several of the tallest structures in the world is undertaking the design of the building. Indeed, India will have something to cheer about if this building materializes!

Madhya Pradesh seems to be the only state in India which has several grand public buildings and international award winning projects. The New Assembly building in Bhopal and the Madhya Pradesh State Electricity Board office in Jabalpur, The Judicial Academy in Bhopal, the Rajiv Gandhi Jal Grahan Mission in Raipur and the proposed "White House" in Bhopal are some fascinating examples which show that global aesthetics is moving very fast into the smaller Indian cities. Paradoxically, it is the smaller cities and towns like Indore, Raipur, Rajkot, Baroda and Bhopal, with no greatly visible architectural traditions like that of Jaipur, Hyderabad or Lucknow, that are displaying unprecedented alacrity in adapting to 'international styles'. There is a growing brand of young and dynamic architects, which include Charles Correa, Prashant Diwakriti, Ajay Kataria, Anjum Gupta, Vineet Chadha, Nikhil Sompura and others, who do not shy away from experimentation. Most often these architects employ a hybrid style that is a free mix of Roman, English, Gothic, Rajasthani and Mughal styles. This new-age architectural aesthetics has redefined the idea of space. The emphasis now seems to be on having more open spaces, green spaces and natural lighting. It is, however, not possible to term this new trend as a 'representative' architecture of our times as it is highly restricted in geographic terms and also confined to the affluent lot.

SCULPTURE IN INDIA

As far as the origin of sculpture is concerned, it goes back to the Stone Age. The Megalithic people buried their dead and constructed monumental stones over them and worshipped them. The change over from worshipping the ancestral spirits to a personal God is reflected in making icons of the God with his specific attributes. Tiny terra-cotta seals discovered from the Indus Valley reveal carvings of peepal leaves, deities and animals. The famous figurine of the dancing girl of Mohenjodaro bears witness to the fact that the tradition of sculpture and bronze casting goes back to the Indus Valley Civilisation and shows tremendous sophistication and artistry.

The sculpture in India started appearing from 3rd century BC with the stone pillars of Ashoka, the stupas and Toranas of Sanchi, Bharhut, Amravati and the rock-cut viharas of Barabar, Bhaja, Pitalkhoda, Karle, Bedsa, Ajanta and others and continued till the12th century AD. During the reign of the Mauryan emperor Ashoka, nearly 85,000 stupas were constructed. Many awe-inspiring statues exhibiting a serene Buddha, with a glowing face were crafted in large numbers. Though, Buddhism deplored idol worship, human forms of Lord Buddha began to be depicted with features like a halo around the head, the dharmachakra engraved upon his palms and soles of his feet, and the lion throne representing his royal ancestry. The earliest archaeological evidence of sculpture work in metal, terracotta, wood and stone in the Indian sub-continent is provided by the remains found at the pre-Harappan sites of Baluchistan, the Makran areas of Pakistan and Kalibangan in Rajasthan, dating back to 3000 BC. Literary evidence from the Rigveda states that copper and bronze-smithy was a specialized science and that craftsmen were held in high esteem. Whether it is in wood, stone or ivory, the Indian carver-craftsman has been extremely versatile in applying his techniques and designs to various media. Carved wooden facades and fixtures of dwellings, domestic shrines, temples, churches and palaces of Rajasthan, Gujarat, Kashmir and Kulu in Himachal Pradesh are marked by intricate designs. In Punjab and Haryana, there exists a tradition of clay wall relief in appliqué. India is also famous for producing a startling range of terracotta figures, ritual and secular utility objects and toys for children.

Modern Sculptors: Modern sculpture, like other mediums of art, has experienced a revival. While the traditionalists continue to follow the rhythmic, decorative tradition of the Gupta and Chola periods, there is a growing breed of modern sculptors who are endeavouring to simplify the art form and to bring in contemporary elements and social awareness into their art. Sculptors of this group freely assimilate art forms of Europe and other places to evolve their own individualistic styles. Some of the modern sculptors are Amarnath Sehgal (Conquest of Moon, Collection in White House, Rising Spirit), P. Ramachandra Kamat, Panchal Rajnikant, Dhanraju Bhagat, Jairam, D.P.Choudhury, Sankha Choudhury, Raghav Kaneria, S.Dhanapal, P.V.Janakiram, C.Dakshinamoorthy, P.S.Nandhan, S.Parmavisam, Vidyashankar Sthapathy, S.Nandagopal, Chintamoni, Nandgopal Shankar, Niranjan Pradhan, Pradosh Kusum Das Gupta, Meera Mukherjee and Jashu Shilpi.

WORLD HERITAGE SITES

In 1972, the General Conference of UNESCO adopted a resolution with overwhelming enthusiasm creating thereby a 'Convention concerning the protection of the World Cultural and Natural Heritage'. The main objectives were to: (a) Define the World Heritage in both cultural and natural aspects, (b) Enlist sites and monuments from member countries which are of exceptional interest and universal value the protection of which is the concern of all mankind and (c) Promote co-operation among all Nations and people to contribute for the protection of these universal treasures intact for future generations.

India is an active member State on the World Heritage from 1977. It has been working in close co-operation with other International agencies like International Council of Monuments and Sites (ICOMOS), International Union for the Conservation of Nature and Natural Resources (IUCN) and International Centre for the study of Preservation and Restoration of Cultural Property (ICCROM).

The Department of Culture and Archaeological Survey of India, apart from observing this World Heritage Day on April 18 and the World Heritage Week from 19th November every year. It is specially aimed to involve the youth of the country through NSS/NCC units in such works as protection, preservation and propagation of the great heritage for which our India is world famous.

The various Indian monuments and sites included in the World Heritage List are the Ajanta Caves, Ellora Caves, Agra Fort, Taj Mahal, Sun Temple at Konarak, the Group of Monuments at Mahabalipuram, Kaziranga National Park, Manas Wildlife Sanctuary, Keoladeo National Park, Churches and Convents of Goa, Group of Monuments at Khajuraho, Group of Monuments at Hampi, Fatehpur Sikri, Group of Monuments at Pattadakal, Elephanta Caves, Brihadeeshwara Temple at Thanjavur, Sundarbans National Park, Nanda Devi National Park, Buddhist Monastery at Sanchi, Humayun's Tomb at Delhi and Qutab Minar and associated monuments at Delhi. The UNESCO World Heritage Committee has bestowed world heritage status on the Darjeeling Himalayan Railway in December 1999.

4

Buddhistic Ethics and Social Criticism

Buddhism arose in India during a period of intense intellectual and social ferment. It was a period during which the authority of the Vedas had been placed in doubt, the concept of god as a supreme being and creator was in question, the hereditary restrictions on caste mobility were under attack, and the efficacy of Brahminical rituals was being challenged. The authors of the Upanishads had opened the door for various heterodox currents to emerge in society, and amongst the most significant of these were the Lokayatas who polemicized against religious charlatans, and the Nyayavadis whose rational epistemology created the foundation for intense philosophical debate and encouraged the investigation of the real world based on reason and logic, freed from the burden of superstition and irrational adherence to burdensome rituals. Various ideological sects competed for the attention and acceptance of the ruling elites and the public. The most important amongst these were the Jains and the Buddhists. Although each of the various sects made original and interesting contributions to philosophy, it was the early Buddhists who attempted to provide a unified philosophical system where ethical conduct and social criticism lay at the very core of their ideological system.

Although today, Buddhism is viewed as a religion by many of its followers, the early Buddhists sects were either strongly atheistic or agnostic. The atheists believed that rather than "God having created man in his own image" it was man who had created "God" in his image. In their view, the liberation of humanity was contingent upon humanity shedding the delusion that "God" existed.

Other parables from surviving Buddhist texts indicate agnosticism. For instance, there is a suggestion that Buddhist followers ought not to waste their time on unsolvable metaphysical questions such as "does god exist". The search to identify the "one true god" or to speculate on the nature of god was seen as an exercise in futility.

But the most frequently cited argument against god by the Buddhists was that if an omnipotent and omniscient being such as "God" truly existed, and who was also all good, there could not be the kind of dukkha (suffering) that was so widespread in the real world.

These shlokas (verses) from the Bhûridatta Jataka illustrates this point:

If the creator of the entire world they call "God" be the lord of every being, why does he order such misfortune, and not create concord?

If the creator of the entire world they call "God" be the lord of every being, why let prevail deceit, lies and ignorance, why create such inequity and injustice?

If the creator of the entire world they call "God" be the lord of every being, then an evil master is he, knowing what's right did let wrong prevail!

Unlike religions that ascribed earthly miseries to human sinfulness that brought upon the wrath of a vengeful god who needed to be feared, Buddhism saw the root of human suffering in ignorance that could only be ended through the acquisition of wisdom. Rather than expect some supernatural entity to end human suffering, the Buddhists argued that it was in human hands to end their sorrows through conduct and action driven by knowledge and correct understanding of human nature and the physical world. Hence, the aspiration for knowledge (jigyasa) was seen as the answer to blind faith. Although the Buddhists were not alone in developing this view, the elaboration of this point of view became pivotal to early Buddhist philosophy.

Central to Buddhist philosophy was an understanding of human nature and what caused dukkha-i.e. human suffering. They saw human personality as constituting five attributes, i.e. body, feeling, perception, disposition and consciousness, and used this framework to develop their understanding of human suffering. Citing examples of conditions that led to human suffering, such as aging, sickness and death, or association with the unpleasant, (or separation from the pleasant), or the inability to get what one wished-they concluded that suffering was a condition of stress and conflict inherent within human existence and interaction with the world.

They also connected suffering to the very impermanence of things. They observed how people lamented over the loss of a loved one, or experienced sorrow when something or someone that had once given them happiness became separated from them. They noted that even human pleasures were not immune from suffering because they didn't last forever, and the loss of pleasure inevitably left people feeling deprived. Seeing as how clinging to things (that were necessarily impermanent) was one of the primary causes of dukkha, they cautioned against excessive attachment.

At the same time, they recognized a recurring and more general type of existential unease and anxiety (aniccha) that arises from the very transience of life, and our inability to control or comprehend all worldly phenomenon, which they characterized as viparinama-dukkha.

But the Buddhists did not see dukkha only emanating from the difficulties of an individual. They also saw suffering emerge on a much larger scale from hostile social conditions such as poverty, war, and social oppression which they described as dukkha-dukkha.

As a formula (char-mulya) for addressing these different types of suffering, the Buddhists advocated a four-fold scheme of a) recognizing the problem i.e. suffering (dukkha); b) identifying the cause of the suffering-such as craving stemming from ignorance (samudaya); c) establishing the goal of ending the problem (nirodha)-i.e. the cessation of suffering (nirvana);

d) conducting life in a manner that was consistent with the cessation of suffering-following the right path or engaging in the right practice (marga).

Followers were thus goaded into developing both a sense of personal ethics and a social conscience:

> *"He who has understanding and great wisdom does not think of harming himself or another, nor of harming both alike. He rather thinks of his own welfare, of that of others, of that of both, and of the welfare of the whole world. In that way one shows understanding and great wisdom." Anguttara Nikaya-(Gradual Sayings)*
>
> *"By protecting oneself (e.g., morally), one protects others; by protecting others, one protects oneself." Samyukta Nikaya (Kindred Sayings)*

Human actions (kamma, kaama, or karma) in the Buddhist framework were to be judged based on both the intention or motive (chetanaa) and the consequences (vipaaka) of the action. Altruistic actions which helped in the establishment and promotion of a just society were encouraged in the dharmaniyama (moral duty code).

{The discourses, or suttas in the Digha Nikaya, illustrate how there was deep concern with the creation of social conditions favorable to the cultivation of Buddhist values and the expansion of social equity and justice. These views undoubtedly influenced the creation of a "welfare state" during the reign of emperor, Ashoka (B.C. 274-236)}

In their theories of causality Buddhists challenged the view that human destiny was unaffected by the ethics or morality of human actions. They countered the doctrine of amoral causation (akriyavaada) whose adherents argued that there was no merit in doing good and no demerit for doing evil. (An extreme expression of such thinking was seen in philosophers who denied all morality and saw no crime in the killing of any person.)

Realizing that such a world-view could lead to the rejection of moral distinctions and personal responsibility for ones actions, they argued strenuously against such beliefs. They also argued against the theory of Makkali Ghosha (or Ghoshala) who believed that human fate was predetermined, and therefore denied that human actions had any bearing on the results of things (ahetuvaada) and maintained that human intention and effort were essentially powerless in changing human destiny, and therefore advocated fatalism (niyati).

They also countered philosophers from the school of "absolute skepticism" who doubted everything and never committed themselves to any specific position in doctrinal debates. Philosophers from this school such as Sanjaya Belarthaputra (who was known as a theorist of endless equivocation or an equivocationist (amraavikkhepavaadin)) were criticized in the Brahmajaala Sutta (or Sutra) as "eel-wrigglers" who were incapable of taking a definitive stance on the vital philosophical questions of the day. Such skepticism was seen as emanating from both the fear of being in error and the lack of knowledge (or inability) to provide reasonable answers to question put forward for discussion. Such all-pervading doubt coupled with a cynical skepticism (vichikicchaa) was viewed as a serious mental hindrance, a fetter in the path to wisdom.

Other theories that contradicted the notion that human actions mattered were theories of accidentalism (ahetu-apachayavaada), theistic determinism (ishvaranimmaanavaada) and past-action determinism (purvaketavaada or purvekatahetu). All of these were opposed by the Buddhists. Accidentalism was an indeterminist theory which held that whatever was experienced was uncaused and unconditioned by human intervention. Theistic determinism was a determinist theory, which held that whatever was experienced was due to God's will or by plan of a "Supreme-Being". Past-action determinism was also a determinist theory, but it held the belief that whatever was experienced, whether pleasurable or painful or indifferent was entirely due to ones past actions (from a previous life), and ones present actions had no relevance.

The danger in each of these theories was highlighted in these words: "Thus for those who fall back on these three erroneous views as essential dogma, there is neither the will to do what is ought to be done, or not to do what is ought not to be done, nor necessity to do this deed or abstain from that deed. No moral improvement or intellectual culture can be expected from them."

Some of the theories in circulation at that time built on a germ of truth but generalized to the point of absurdity. For instance the accidentalists were correct only to the extent that certain things did indeed appear to happen by random chance or accident. But they failed to recognize that sometimes what may have seemed to be accidental was more due to inadequate understanding or improper or incomplete perception, and that other activities had a clearly discernible cause. To deal with the extreme generalizations of such theorists, they introduced a middle standpoint for their epistemology and ethics.

They thus rejected the theory admitting that everything exists (sabba atthii ti) and in permanence-i.e. the extreme of eternalism (sassatavaada), and its opposite which advocated that nothing actually exists (sabba natthii ti) i.e. nihilism (the denial of all reality in real-world phenomenon) or the extreme of annihilationalism (ucchedavaada). Related to their critique of the eternalist and nihilist philosophies was their rejection of both hedonism and self-mortification (attakilamathaanuyoga) which they viewed as painful, fruitless, unprofitable and ignoble.

Buddhist texts also expressed suspicion about claims by heretical teachers of being constantly "all-knowing" and "all-seeing" and in possession of "all-embracing knowledge-and-vision." Such claims were countered with arguments relating to the actual behaviour of such charlatans in different situations. For instance, they wondered why such "all-knowing" and "all-seeing" spiritual teachers lost their way in an unfamiliar place or why they were unable to escape from trouble while countering a fierce animal such as dog, elephant, horse or bull. Moreover, if they were really omniscient, they wouldn't need to ask for people's names, clans, or the name of a village or market town or make enquiries about anything. That they did such things indicated that their knowledge was evidently limited just like that of any average worldly person (puthujjana).

Unlike religions that were based on revealed truth or the sanctity of every word in a holy textbook, the Buddhist belief system prescribed reasoning based on investigation as the means of determining ones dhamma, (or dharma as in Hindu practise). In a parable in the Kaalaama Sutta, followers of Budhism are advised not to accept any moral codes on the following ten grounds: (1) Vedic authority (anussava), (2) tradition (paramparaa), (3) hearsay or report (itikiraa), (4) textual authority (pittakasampadaa), (5) apparent agreebility of the view (sama o no garu), (6) authority of the holder of the view (takkahetu), (7) apparent logicality of the view (nayahetu), (8) the fact that the view is an accepted standpoint (aakaaraparivitakka), (9) inadequate reflection on reasons (bhabbaruupataa), or (10) the fact that the view agrees with one's own (ditthinijjhaanakkhanti).

In this manner, the Buddhism developed a very sophisticated philosophical system in which social ethics were integrated with rational investigation of human nature, social organization and the physical world. Buddhist ideas and concepts left a powerful impression on other Indian philosophical and religious belief systems, and over time, many commonalities developed amongst the competing ideologies.

However, there were also certain problems with the Buddhist world view which prevented its complete acceptance by intellectuals committed to the scientific method. For instance, although the Buddhists rejected the theory of past action determinism, they did posit the existence of a soul which survived a person's death and carried with it the merits and demerits of a person's past lives. Presumably this concept was essential to the Buddhist goal of encouraging right conduct but it was rejected by those who considered the soul as inseparable from the body and did not believe that the soul survived death. Those who rejected the concept of transmigration of the soul naturally couldn't accept the idea that human destiny had anything to do with merits and demerits accumulated in previous incarnations of the "soul". In their view, morality and ethics were entirely social constructs and had to be dealt with accordingly. The realists (such as the Nyayavadis) who shared the Buddhist concern for morals and ethics in society argued that while morals and ethics ought to be encouraged, they could only be enforced through societal laws and judicial codes.

Another problem facing the Buddhists was that in many ways, their views were too advanced for their times. Society had not yet developed to the point where education was universal, and knowledge of the real world sufficient to prevent superstitions and irrational beliefs from being completely abandoned by the masses. In an era where society had only limited control over nature, it was inevitable that sections of society would continue with beliefs in deities and supernatural phenomenon in the hope that they may be spared from natural disasters or that their crops might withstand attacks from pests and disease. Thus although the Buddhists had a very important and salutatory effect on Indian society, the most advanced Buddhist concepts could be understood and practised by only a minority in society.

Over time, the spirit of inquiry and rational investigation that had spurred the early Buddhist scholars towards dialectical thinking and critical social analysis became more and more replaced by narrow and literalist interpretations of the earlier texts. For instance, advice against accepting something that appeared "logical" without personal verification was taken to mean that logic could be rejected. Advice against wasting ones time on unsolvable metaphysical questions was also taken too literally and many Buddhist scholars remained aloof from the metaphysical debates pursued by other philosophical schools such as those of the Jains and the Nyaya Vaisheshikas. What they didn't anticipate was that some of these debates might lead to useful advances in mathematics or deeper understanding of human thought processes and new insights on human memory and psychology. These led to valuable advances in the interpretation of moods and emotions-thus benefiting Indian art, literature and music.

In addition, later Buddhist monks lapsed into some of the very things that had been attacked by the early Buddhists such as indulgence in unnecessary and elaborate rituals, belief in supra-natural phenomenon, and alienation of the priests from the masses. Activities such as meditation which were encouraged as a means to gaining wisdom became ends in themselves, and were turned into idealistic fetishes. Although Buddhist monks dutifully delivered sermons on right conduct and right action, they often failed to engage in relevant and timely social criticism- and did not always connect the textual suggestions to concrete practice. Intra-Buddhist disputes developed around less significant details, even as some of the most important ideas that had initially shaped the philosophy were pushed into the background. As a result Buddhism as it was practised came to be associated with idealism and inaction. Whereas the early Buddhists saw no merit in worshipping god or its images, later Buddhism developed a pantheon of deities not very different from other Indian religions.

Thus even as Buddhism had spread almost throughout Asia by the 5th-6th C AD, it gradually began to lose its distinct edge and liberating influence on much of Indian society. Within the Indian subcontinent, strains of Buddhism survived in Sri Lanka, Bengal, Bhutan, Sikkim, parts of Bihar and Nepal, and parts of Sindh, Punjab, Kashmir and Afghanistan. In parts of Orissa and adjoining regions (such as Chhattisgarh and Telengana), Tantric (and other) influences reshaped the practice of Buddhism. Yet, Buddhism continued to have an impact outside India and developed pockets of influence as far West as Syria, as well as in much of Central Asia (including what is now Uzbekistan, Tajikistan, Kyrgyzia, Kazakhstan) and Tibet. In the East, its influence was felt on virtually every nation including Burma, Thailand, Malaya and Indonesia, Laos, Cambodia, Vietnam, China, Korea and Japan.

As noted earlier, the vast literature of Buddhism (like much of Hindu or Jain literature) was not a literature of revelation and authority. Its essays on social ethics and moral responsibilities, its treatises on philosophy and science, its art and poetry were but pointers to a path to wisdom. This gave Buddhism both flexibility and adaptability. Owing to its non-hegemonic character and humanist appeal, Buddhism was adopted without coercion or force. It was also successfully fused with Hinduism in many parts of South East Asia just as elements of it had been integrated into Hindu practices in India. In China, it was integrated with Taoism and Confucian principles; in Japan with Shinto beliefs. For several centuries, within India and outside, several people followed multiple faiths and identified as both Buddhists and Hindus, or as both Buddhists and Tantrics, (or Buddhists and Taoists) and so on. During the Gupta period (and in other reigns), philosophers from various schools of thought received royal patronage and temple grants were conferred for the construction of Buddhist and Hindu monuments alike.

It is also important to recognize that the form of Buddhism that was embraced in each nation was often quite different. For instance, in Western and Central Asia, it was not the philosophical or intellectual aspects of Buddhism that were popularized, but rather, its personal moral codes. Buddhist prosletysers imbued their stories of the Buddha with examples of miraculous healing and super-natural compassion so as to win more followers.

While such tendencies were also to be seen as Buddhism travelled within India or outwards, in Burma, Sri Lanka and Thailand, Buddhism developed organizational structures that appear to have been much more resilient. It was perhaps realized that the development of Buddhist virtue would require leadership and constant interaction with the community. In these nations, Buddhism did not degenerate into the extremes of mysticism or retreatism that became commonplace in certain parts of India (such as in the foothills of the Western Himalayas). Burmese and Thai monks maintained a practical and benevolent connection with the community, and thus retained a measure of respect within the community. This also appears to be the case in Japan. In Korea, the emphasis on gaining wisdom was taken very seriously, and Buddhist monks took the lead in promoting mass literacy. This propelled the growth of technologies associated with the production of paper, writing instruments, inks, and furniture. And unlike in India, (where due to Upanishadic influences, "inner" wisdom came to be favored over outer wisdom), Buddhist concern for disseminating the writings of the Buddha had significant positive secular impact. In Korean (and other Eastern) Buddhism, there was the correct realization that a Buddhist mindset, or that a Buddhist society could not be constructed overnight. There was thus the emphasis on the (helical) upgradation of individuals and society towards greater "Buddhahood". This philosophical element was perhaps signficant in that it prevented the sort of philosophical stagnation that occurred in India, where followers too often sought immediate succuor, and thus not only became divorced from reality, but also lost sight of the strategic potential of the philosophy.

In addition, it ought to be noted that Buddhism in India also had to contend with strongly anarchic and ultra-democratic tendencies. Precisely because its philosophical structure emphasized the relative and changing nature of truth, different tendencies under the Buddhist mantle competed for leadership through argument and debate. Initially, this led to important advances in democratic practices within the Sanghas. But over time, it also led to clashes of egoes, hair-splitting and deadlock. While some Buddhist sects compromised and fused with other tendencies (even alien tendencies), others remained fiercely autonomous. To survive, Buddhism had to confront both the tendency to be co-opted, as well as the tendency to atomize.

However, the catastrophic demise of Buddhism in India was triggered by the onslaught of Islam which first obliterated the remnants of Buddhism in Central Asia, and then later in Afghanistan and India. By and large, Buddhism survived only in those countries that escaped invasions by Islamic conquerors. As a gentle faith that encouraged its followers to abjure violence, it was perhaps unable to protect itself from iconoclasts and proselytizers who intended to enforce a new religio-political order. Accustomed to centuries of peaceful co-existence, India's Buddhists had not anticipated the need to develop viable strategies for self-defence that could have combated the violence of India's Islamic conquerors who virtually obliterated Buddhism from the land of its birth.

Yet, it also appears that (in large part) later Buddhism had deviated considerably from the rational principles outlined in the early texts. Monasteries often became isolated from mainstream society, and monks who focused exclusively on meditative practices and idealistic or esoteric philosophical speculation contributed little to social progress. Some have even argued that the monastic orders had degenerated into sheer parasitism and were becoming a heavy social drain. Consequently, value judgements on the demise of Buddhism and the rise of Islam in India need to be made with a measure of caution.

Nevertheless, it must be acknowledged that the ascent of Islam was concomitant with the eclipse of Buddhism, and since the influence of Buddhism was greatly dependant on the existence of the monastic orders, the destruction of monasteries and their conversion to mosques and institutions of Quranic learning simply lead to mass conversions to Islam.

In the long term, this could have had the effect of stunting India's future intellectual development, since the destruction of important institutions of Buddhist learning also led to a notable decline in the opportunity (and social sanction) to study secular subjects such as logic and epistemology (which were also taught at Buddhist universities-such as Bhagalpur).

It might also be observed that the destruction of Buddhist centers of learning coincided with the destruction of extremely valuable textual materials-which could have been potentially rediscovered, and revived or reinterpreted by future generations of Indians so as to achieve a society that was more thoughtful and learned. Islamic texts did not offer anything comparable in terms of causality or epistemology. Nor did they offer the psychological, sociological, or moral insights that had been developed under the ambit of Buddhism. Nor was there any comparable stress on seeking knowledge or constantly updating ones understanding of nature and human society.

One can, therefore, only speculate as to the full consequences of this profound sociolgical and cultural loss (and discontinuity).

But East of India, Buddhism did survive, and in countries such Korea, Thailand and Burma, it continued to enjoy a loyal popular following. Philosophical innovations also took place, and as noted earlier, Buddhist scholars in China, Korea and

Japan offered their own commentaries and somewhat individual interpretations of Buddhist concepts and formulations outlined in later (5-7th C.) Indian texts. And although the sacking of monasteries and centers of learning (such as Nalanda and Vikramshila in Bihar) led to records of the original Buddhist texts being permanently destroyed, it has been possible to reconstruct some of them from translations that survived outside India such as in Thailand and Tibet. Notwithstanding the virtual erasure of Buddhism in India, it is possible to infer from these reconstructed texts and other archaeological records (and surviving monuments and artifacts) that Buddhism had a very powerful impact in shaping the destiny of India, and in triggering a social and cultural renaissance that would take Indian and other Asian civilizations to a higher level of social, cultural and material development.

5

Buddhist Philosophy

It has been pointed out above that Buddhism is a religion which does not center around a perception of a god, but in practise can tolerate the belief in any god or gods. Of all major religions of the world, Buddhism is probably the most philosophical one. And there has been in Buddhism a tendency to define Buddha's teachings rather as a philosophy than a religion, at least in the more narrow sense of the term.

As was pointed out by A.B. Griswold in his essay "What is a Buddha Image", published 1962 by the Fine Arts Department of the Thai government, many relevant works representing a tendency to emphasize the philosophical side of Buddhism over the pietistic side were published in the 19th century.

Among them are Henry Alabaster's Wheel of the Law (London, 1871), and the following works by T.W. Rhys Davics: Buddhism (London, 1878), Buddhism, its History and Literature (New York and London, 1896), Buddhist India (London, 1903), Dialogues of the Buddha (translations from the Pali Canon, with explanations, 3 volumes, London, 1899, 1910, 1921), and the article Buddhism in the Encyclopaedia Britannica, 11th edition.

A.B. Griswold states in his essay that the works of Rhys Davics are particularly interesting, as his views are similar to those of many learned Buddhists in Thailand today. Both, Davics and Alabaster, consider that the Theravada is essentially a doctrine of rationalism, paralleling modern scientific and humanistic thought, an ethical and psychological system in which no deity has a significant part. Following Rhys Davics, A.B. Griswold claims that Buddhism has one aim and one only: to abolish suffering. It proposes to do so, not by the aid of divine intervention but by purely human means: that is, by examining the law of cause and effect, and acting accordingly.

Considered the causes of suffering are craving, malice and delusion; if they can be eradicated, Buddhism teaches, suffering will disappear. The remedy sounds simple, but no one supposes it is easy to apply. All Buddhists are expected to play their part in the struggle against craving and malice, by exercising self-restraint and kindness toward all living creatures; but only relatively few are able to participate directly in the struggle against delusion. That task is assigned more to the monkshood (not priesthood, as it is often called), which is expected to lead the struggle against ignorance, bigotry and mental torpor, and to promote good conduct by precept and example.

A.B. Griswold explains that the Buddha lived at a time and place in which nearly everyone believed in the transmigration of souls, taking it for granted that each individual would be re-born again in various conditions on earth, or in heaven or hell for periods of various length. The condition of each re-birth was a reward or punishment for actions committed in previous ones, in accordance with the will of the god in whom one put one's faith; and the gods sometimes tested this faith by requiring the devotee to commit the most outrageous actions.

In contrast to such beliefs, the Buddha taught that retribution does not depend on the will of any god, but on a natural law whose workings can be discovered by the use of human intelligence. There is nothing capricious about it; every man or woman can discriminate between good actions and evil ones, without fear that some god will unexpectedly change the rules; the gods, if such there be, are incapable of setting aside the laws of nature. Favoritism cannot operate; and no act of faith can erase the consequences of an evil deed.

In the interpretation given by A.B. Griswold the Buddha did not deny transmigration, but as he flatly denied the soul it is clear that he interpreted it very differently from most of his contemporaries. The law of impermanence, he taught, applies to all living beings: men, animals, and any other conceivable category. Life is inevitably accompanied by growth, and growth cannot occur without decay. What is commonly called the individual is in constant disintegration, a process which in man and the higher animals begins even before emerging from the womb.

No being, not even a god, is an enduring entity. Each is a compound of elements such as form, matter, perception, and so on; and in each the relationship of the component parts is constantly changing, never remaining the same for any two consecutive moments. It follows that individuality and personality are mere figures of speech and the soul an illusion. Yet that does not mean in the least that good and evil are indifferent; somehow or other, though it is not always easily perceptible, every action brings its retribution; and though there is no soul to be reincarnated, the energy of past action, good or evil continues forever.

This energy, under the impact of craving and delusion, is what is re-born. When simple people, who could not grasp this argument, asked the Buddha whether or not they should believe in transmigration, he advised them to be on the safe side: by acting as if it were true, and doing their best to lead a virtuous life, they would gain the rewards of a tranquil conscience and lose nothing even if they guessed wrong; but if they thoughtlessly rejected it and followed their own evil desires, they would lead a tormented life and finally, if it turned out after all that they were mistaken, they would be "like travellers without provisions".

A.D. Griswold admits that many Indian and European scholars today say that Rhys Davics, Henry Alabaster, and the others who believed the Theravada to be a doctrine of rationalism were all wrong. They say that the rationalist view is a 19th century invention, largely due to King Mongkut (Rama IV, 1851-1868), and that there is no justification whatever to be found for it in the Canon. They assert that the Buddha took transmigration quite literally, just like everyone else; that he was no less superstitious than the generality of educated persons of his time; that he believed firmly in the gods; that he thought himself able to perform miracles; and that he taught his disciples spells to drive away troublesome sprites.

It is true that these scholars can point to a great many passages in the Buddhist Canon that would seem to prove their argument; but A.B. Griswold defends the rationalistic line, saying that the rationalists can point to others, less numerous but somehow more convincing, in which Buddha is seen as a skeptic, gentle but thoroughgoing: he counsels his disciples not to put their faith in tradition or in any honored teacher, even himself, but to rely on their own powers of reason; he limits the meaning of re-birth to an impersonal abstraction; and he not only condemns magic and superstition but even rejects the whole supernatural basis of religion, placing its moral values firmly in human psychology instead.

In fact two contradictory currents of thought, one rational and the other pietistic, run side by side through the Canon, where anyone can see them for him-or herself. The Buddhism that prevailed before King Mongkut's time emphasized the pietistic and the marvelous, just as popular Buddhism still does today. But King Mongkut did not need to invent the current of rationalism: it was already there, though less noticed; he called attention to its importance and shifted the emphasis at the highest level.

In the opinion of A.B. Griswold the two currents of thought are not really as irreconcilable as they at first appear. The contradiction vanishes if passages of the one sort are taken to be factual, and the other as metaphorical. The Buddha knew that teaching is useless unless it is adapted to the capacity of the listener. In addressing sophisticated people he used the technical terms of Indian philosophy, but gave them a new meaning; whereas in talking to simple people he used familiar concepts as allegories and homely anecdotes to point a moral.

Sometimes the simple people remembered the anecdote more distinctly than the moral, or mistook the allegory for the recital of a real event. One does not have to follow their example;

and usually there is a clear hint to stop people from doing so. For instance the three daughters of Mara try to tempt the Buddha from the path of virtue, and of course they fail miserably, but not before putting on a seduction scene worthy of Hollywood, the account of which reads as if it were intended to be a real event; but what are the ladies' names? Craving, Discontent and Lust. There could be no clearer warning to the reader who might be disposed to take the story literally.

In the interpretation of A.B. Griswold, most people in the Buddha's time believed-as a great many people in India and Southeast Asia still believe today-that a huge population of unseen but powerful creatures haunt the sky and earth, from the great Vedic and Brahmanical gods to the humbler village divinities, from the gods of planets, sun and rain, to the sprites of mountains and rocks, trees and ponds, fields, building-foundations, parasols, and almost any sort of object.

The Buddha did not try to erase these creatures from the general belief-that would have been impossible-but he drastically reduced their importance and at the same time put them to use as figures of speech. So it comes about that Buddhist literature depicts fierce dragons and earth-sprites as being converted to the Doctrine, and Indra, the formerly ferocious Vedic god of thunder and lightning, as little more than a nimble servitor of the Sage.

As A.B. Griswold explains, a person who has extinguished all craving, malice and delusion in himself is exempt from re-birth no matter how it may be defined. In the technical terminology, when such a person dies he "passes into parinibbana", which is the ultimate goal of all Buddhists. It may sound strange to a Westerner who has been nourished on the hope of eternal felicity in heaven; but in Buddhist logic the law of impermanence is inexorable, and a sojourn in any conceivable heaven can be no more than temporary. Since a god is no less subject to craving, malice and delusion than a man, he is just as liable to act in such a way that punishment will follow; and so, if a sojourn in heaven is admitted as a possibility, it will inevitably be followed by more lives of abject misery in other conditions throughout countless millions of aeons.

The only escape is parinibbana, which some people equate with total extinction, and others with a disembodied state of changeless bliss. The Buddha himself refused to define it; but he said that anyone who achieves it "will be no more seen by men or gods." In other words, such a person becomes totally and irrevocably inaccessible to all, and to their prayers.

It is generally agreed that when the Buddha knew his own death was approaching, he told his disciples they must take the initiative and carry on his work without him. The rationalists among them could think for themselves; but it would be harder for the others, less strong-minded but no less devoted, who had relied on him to do their thinking for them. A.B. Griswold states that it can easily be seen how desperate their plight was.

Among people who believed in transmigration, the death of someone whom they trusted and loved would ordinarily leave them some hope that they might meet him again in a future life. But in this case their beloved master, in achieving the goal they were all to strive for, deprived them of any such hope. Only a few of them had advanced so far that they could feel confident of achieving parinibbana themselves when it came their turn to die; the rest including all those to whom transmigration was the most literal reality found themselves facing a hideous eternity of re-births without any possible access to their beloved master.

REMINDERS, REVERED IMAGES

A.B. Griswold, in his essay "What is a Buddha Image", presented an interesting and convincing theory on how a philosophy marked by a considerable disrespect for deities became a religion in which images of the founder of the philosophical school, the Buddha, became subjects of animistic worship, in the sense that the images are considered animated and worshiped as powers in their own right.

A.B. Griswold starts with a rather hypothetical reconstructions of what might have happened at the time of the Buddha's death:

"Memory is a frail thing; and unless some means of preserving it could be found, the recollection of the Sage's person, and hence of his priceless guidance, would gradually fade. As the Buddha lay dying, all this was tragically evident to his disciple Ananda, who had served him with affectionate care for more than half a lifetime, making up in devotion what he lacked in intellectual power. Could not the disciples, he asked sadly, be allowed to perform some regular act of homage to the memory of the Master in whom they had put their faith? Could they not have some sort of substitute, a reminder of his Person no less than of his Doctrine, to keep them from falling back into the superstitions from which he had rescued them?"

"As a concession to such needs the Buddha replied that the faithful might make pilgrimages to the scenes of the Great Events of his career. When they visited these places they would visualize the Events connected with them, remember his victories over evil and ignorance, and so be inspired to imitate him. If that was not sufficient, they could gather his bodily relics (sariradhatu), such as bones and teeth, after his cremation; they could build stupas, mounds of earth or masonry, to contain them; and the stupas, by reminding people of the Doctrine, would make their hearts glad and happy."

A.D. Griswold explains that according to the orthodox classification, there are four categories of reminder: sariradhatu or dhatucetiya, bodily relics; paribhogacetiya, reminders by association; dhammacetiya, doctrinal reminders; and uddesikacetiya, indicative reminders.

The meaning of the first, sariradhatu or dhatucetiya, is self-evident.

The second, paribhogacetiya, reminders by association, include anything associated with the Buddha himself by physical contact, such as his alms bowl and robes, the footprints he left on river-bank and mountain-top, the benches he sat on, the

Bodhi tree at Bodhgaya which sheltered him at the moment of enlightenment, and in a more general way the sites of all the great events. Stupas containing his bodily relics are sometimes placed in this category, some-times in the first category.

The third, dhammacetiya, was originally the whole body of the Doctrine, remembered by word of mouth, but later was extended to include written extracts from the Canon, and stupas built to contain such extracts.

The fourth, uddesikacetiya, indicative reminders, are what might be called "reminders by convention". They are objects, neutral in themselves, which the general opinion might recognize as substitutes for paribhogacetiya, and indeed are usually man-made replicas of them. Trees grown from seeds or cuttings taken from the original Bodhi tree may be put in this category, in the sense that they have come into existence as a result of human intervention; but sometimes, in view of their genetic connection with the original, they are considered to be paribhogacetiya. Replicas of stupas containing bodily relics, when they themselves contain none, are indicative reminders; so are replicas of the footprints; and so are replicas of the scenes of the Great Events, or any essential part of them, in painting or bas-relief or any other suitable medium.

This last category of reminders assumed increasing importance with the spread of Buddhism to distant lands, as they enabled people who lived far away to make pilgrimages, by the power of mental projection, to the holy sites without actually leaving home.

According to A.B. Griswold, educated opinion in India long held the notion of image-making in contempt: images were needed only by the ignorant, who could not grapple with sublime abstractions. In the earliest Indian bas-reliefs depicting scenes from the Buddha's life, the Buddha himself is invisible. He is represented by an aniconic symbol only, such as a stone altar slab or bench, a tree, a serpent, a pair of footprints, or a stupa.

The symbols are depictions of the chief features at the scenes of the Great Events and other incidents: the Bodhi tree at Bodhgaya, and the stone slab under it; the nearby statue of the Serpent King (Naga) who had protected the Buddha from the storm while he meditated; the disk or wheel commemorating the preaching of the First Sermon, the event which "set the Wheel of the Doctrine in motion"; the footprints the Buddha had stamped in rock or clay as souvenirs for the faithful, and the stupas commemorating his parinibbana.

In the bas-reliefs are seen people worshipping these symbols as if they were worshipping the Buddha in person. Some of the worshippers, it may be suspected, had only recently been converted to the Doctrine, and had previously been in the habit of worshipping very similar objects in an entirely different context. In the older cults the solar disk and the serpent had long been worshipped, and so had stones and trees, either in their own right or as the abode of powerful sprites who conferred all sorts of favors when properly approached, but who took terrible vengeance when displeased.

Buddha images, it seems, were first invented about the beginning of the Christian Era, either in Gandhara or at Mathura. A.B. Griswold says that in a curious way they grew directly out of the old symbols, almost as a seedling grows out of a coconut: and just as it takes some time for the coconut shell to rot away, so vestiges of the symbols long clung to the images: the slab as pedestal, the footprints as feet, the serpent or the tree as shelter, the wheel as halo, and various other combinations. And since in the popular mind these symbols were still animated by the sprites inherent in them, people felt that certain images, though representing the Sage of Rationalism (as A.B. Griswold calls the Buddha), possessed the powers and personalities of sprites.

In due course Buddhism was brought from India to Southeast Asia, and the art of image-making as well. One of the most reliable chronicles that have remained, the Jinakalamali, makes it clear what an important role the images had in spreading the Doctrine. Some of them were reputed to possess great magical power, and the timely miracles they performed were a great help in converting the people.

A.B. Griswold recommends that such stories should not be dismissed as fanciful. The power of the images was real enough, he says, though it exerted itself differently at different levels. The staunchest rationalist would admit that Reminders of the Doctrine can start a mental process that will end by dispelling the fear of demons.

In the traditional belief, moreover, every Buddha image inherits some fraction of the teja, "fiery energy", which the Buddha himself possessed in incalculable abundance, and which is conventionally represented by a fiery halo, a flame springing from the top of the head, the gilded surfaces of bronze or stone, and so on.

It is not difficult to guess why some images were thought to possess much more magical power than others. One that was believed to be very old would seem to have demonstrated its unusual potency by its unusual power of survival; and if it was thought to be directly copied from one of the original authentic images it would naturally hold more teja than those whose resemblance to the Buddha's person, transmitted through copying at many removes, was less perfect.

Old local beliefs played their part in a variety of ways. If statues of the Buddha sheltered by the Serpent King were particularly popular in Cambodia, and in Thailand during the Khmer period, it was surely because converts from the old serpent cults saw them as inheritors of the serpent's power. Images carved from certain stones, or the wood of certain trees, which had previously been worshipped as the abode of sprites, were still instinctively felt to be animated by those terrifying creatures. And if a particular image happened to be present when a very striking and unusual event occurred, people might easily think it responsible for the "miracle".

Such beliefs now and than produced incongruous results. Siamese chronicles make no attempt to veil the fact that ambitious rulers resorted to unscrupulous tricks and even the threat of open warfare to get hold of the most powerful images, or to cause political rivals to loose the images which were thought to protect them. Each city needed at least one powerful image for its protection, and if the enemy got hold of it he would very likely be able to take the city, too. Thus certain images became deeply involved in political affairs.

As A.B. Griswold pointed out, the chronicles dealing with events from the 13th to the 16th century record that allegedly some images themselves did not always behave very well. Some of the most famous ones were very unpredictable, and often downright cranky, acting in a way the Buddha himself would have condemned in the strongest terms. Like powerful sprites, they gave material rewards when flattered, but in moments of annoyance inflicted disease, set buildings on fire, and caused earthquakes.

The feeling that certain images behave in so un-Buddhist a way lasted right down to modern times. Two of them, the Emerald Buddha and the Phra Bang, were said to have detested each other; and towards the end of the 18th century, when they were brought to Thonburi together, it is believed that they caused all sorts of trouble, including a brief revolution, so they had to be separated. As late as 1867, when they were both in Bangkok (occupying separate buildings, but still not far enough away from each other), their alleged jealousy was said to have caused two disastrous crop-failures within three years.

One still hears of Buddha images that bring bad luck to their owners. The only remedy in that case is to present them to a monastery, where their mischievous tendencies will be kept in check.

A.B. Griswold relates that not many years ago he experienced an amusing example of misplaced piety. In the gallery of a monastery at Ayutthaya there was a long row of apparently identical images, one of which had been singled out for particular favors by an admirer. He had presented it with a silk scarf, and he spent a good deal of time in front of it in a reverential attitude, with palms pressed together as if in prayer. Why had he singled out this particular image, which differed in no way from the dozens of others in the same row?

A.B. Griswold relates that upon inquiry he found that a week earlier it had inspired the man to place a bet on a certain horse, which won the race handily and paid off well; so now he wanted to express his gratitude and at the same time seek further inspiration. A.B. Griswold judged that the supposed personality of the image reminds one more of a Neapolitan saint than of the Buddha; it is hard to believe that the Founder of the Doctrine himself would have given such encouragement to gambling.

Tradition explains such eccentricities by saying that they are not caused by the Buddha image as such, but by the sprite inhabiting it. The old belief that almost any noteworthy object is animated by its particular sprite has already been cited, and Buddha images are no exception. When they are made of certain sorts of wood or stone, those worshipping them may believe that the sprites were already in them before they were carved into Buddha images, and the process of carving did not wholly change their original nature.

States A.B. Griswold nonchalantly: "In any case the trouble-makers are rare. Most images behave with perfect decorum."

A.B. Griswold points out that not only old animistic believes are responsible for the widespread opinion that Buddha images are actually alive. The Brahmanical rite of "opening the eyes" of inert, inanimate objects that have to be brought to life by a particular ceremony also plays its part.

Siamese chronicles contain a large number of records which indicate the extend to which Buddha images have long been believed to be animated. One of the most famous and beautiful images in Thailand is the Jinaraja Victorious King at Phitsanulok, cast when that city was part of the Kingdom of Sukhothai. Not long afterwards Sukhothai, including Phitsanulok, was conquered by the rival Kingdom of Ayutthaya. The annals record a curious event: in 1438, when the Crown Prince of Ayutthaya proceeded to Phitsanulok, to become Viceroy of the conquered provinces, tears of blood were seen to flow from the eyes of the statue.

Until today, images are often presented with cloth robes to wear, and some are presented with gem-studded golden crowns and costly garments. The Emerald Buddha has three changes of costume: a princely attire for the hot season, a monastic robe for the rainy season, and a mantle of gold mesh for the cool season.

The old laws of Ayutthaya provided severe punishments for anyone mutilating a Buddha image. To cut off its head was to commit murder, to scrape the gold leaf from its surface was to skin it alive; and anyone who would commit so evil an act was a criminal of the worst sort.

During the long years of warfare that ravaged northern Siam in the late 18th century, many images were broken and others fell into ruin from neglect. As soon as peace was restored, the ruler of Chiang Mai set about restoring the damage; an inscription tells "he thought of the old images, lying broken in field and forest, neglected and exposed to sun and rain; and he took pity on them in his heart".

A mission with a similar purpose was performed by Prince Wang Na at the command of his brother, King Rama I (1782-1806). He proceeded to Ayutthaya, Sukhothai, Phitsanulok and other cities to rescue the images that had been neglected during the Burmese wars, and brought many hundreds of them, of life-size or larger, to Bangkok by raft. The colossal image called Sri Sarbejna ("the Omniscient One"), which had been the object of the deepest veneration at Ayutthaya, proved to be too badly damaged to repair; so it was reverently entombed in a large stupa built for the purpose at Wat Pho. The others were distributed among various monasteries in Bangkok and Thonburi; more than half of them were deposited at Wat Pho, where they may still be seen.

They were given a curious restoration treatment: they were covered with a thick coating of plaster and gilt lacquer, which completely obscured their beauty but did not prevent their teja from functioning. In recent years the plaster has been removed from many of them, revealing the beauty of the patinated bronze; but they were then almost immediately given a new coating of gilt lacquer, though not thick enough to disguise them as completely as before. Those at Wat Benchamabophit, also known as Marble Temple, can be seen to better advantage:

at the suggestion of Prince Damrong, they were left ungilded so as to serve as examples of style to students and archaeologists.

At Phitsanulok there was a companion image of the Jinaraja, named Jinasiha, Victorious Lion. Both images were objects of particular veneration to King Rama I; before ascending the throne he used to go to Phitsanulok as often as he could spare the time from his campaigns against the Burmese and in the civil war, and there he would offer homage to the statues. The monastery where they were located had fallen into ruins, but when peace was restored a new Vihara was built for the Jinaraja, and in 1829 the Jinasiha was brought to Bangkok.

The raft which bore it, towed by hundreds of gilded and gaily decorated barges, stopped at the landing-stage of the Prince Wang Na's Palace; and after three days of rejoicing it was conveyed by land to the Excellent Abode Monastery (Pavaranivesa), a vast throng of people pulling the many ropes that were required for so heavy a burden.

In his essay "What is a Buddha Image", published by the Fine Arts Department of the Thai government, A.B. Griswold presented some more curious stories connected with the belief that images have a life of their own. In a monastery in Ang Thong Province there is a colossal reclining Buddha image of masonry, which, according to historical records, on one occasion during the reign of King Rama V (1867-1911) manifested the power of speech. One afternoon, in the presence of the abbot and a large group of monks and novices, deep muffled sounds were heard to issue from its bosom. "Are you not well, Sir?" the abbot asked politely. The image replied: "Thank you, I am quite well; and you?" "Sir, I am well." "But trouble is on its way," said the image; "within two months, there will be a bad outbreak of cholera." Upon being asked what counter measures could be taken, the image provided a recipe to be compounded from certain herbs; and when the cholera came, exactly as predicted, the medicine proved to be an effective cure.

A.B. Griswold outlines that the belief that miniatures worn around the neck confer invulnerability can be explained in more than one way. Some people would say that the teja inherent in the image transmits itself to the wearer and makes him immune from harm; others might argue that by reminding the wearer of the Doctrine, and particularly that part of it that counsels constant alertness, it enables him to keep out of harm's way.

Critics of such an opinion may point out that in the manner of this explanation, any irrationalism could be rationalized. The may be reminded that irrationalism, rationally explained, does not turn irrationalism into rationalism. Furthermore, those wearing images in the belief they are amulets protecting them from harm do not understand them simply as reminders to keep them alert. And by rationalizing amulets as reminders, the question remains unanswered whether or not the images worn as amulets protect the wearer on account of their own power.

In spite of such arguments, A.B. Griswold sees the rationalizing of images as reminders as sufficient to defend the opinion that Buddha images are somehow animated. He states in his essay cited above: "We can now begin to see why such miniatures were made in huge quantities to be buried away inside stupas and colossal images. They were a sort of electric charge, suffusing the stupa or the statue with teja: even if most of them proved to be inert, or nearly so, on the basis of probability at least a few of them would turn out to be particularly effective. Looked at in another way, they were intended to assure the durability, the invulnerability, of the Reminder that contained them: and even if they failed in that, and the Reminder was ever broken open, they would pour forth in an explosion of fiery energy, teja, conferring their benefits as reminders and protectors far and wide upon future generations."

> *"We can now see, too, why images inspire such fervent devotion. They fill the function for which the various sort of reminder, cetiya, were designed, but they also do rather more. They act as substitutes for the Buddha himself in a sort of mystical worship that reminds us of the bhakti of Hindu religions; and some people have a feeling that although the Buddha himself is inaccessible, he can be worshipped through his substitutes and*

somehow answer prayers through them too. At a less sublime level they are magical protectors, jealous gods who must be kept in a good humor, since they are equally capable of bestowing enormous favors and of bringing on a general disaster."

MAKING MERIT

According to A.B. Griswold, the most obvious reason why Buddha images have been created in Thailand in such stupendous quantity is simply the intent to make merit (tam boon). And he explains that by doing good deeds, those who believe in transmigration lay up a store of merit for the future, like prudent people making deposits in a savings bank. To enter the monkhood for several days or months; to help in the construction or maintenance of a monastery; to contribute to education; to make gifts to the needy; to give alms to monks; to perform any act of kindness, great or small: all such things, and many others, are recognized as acts of merit. And of course it is an act of merit to create any sort of reminder, uddesikacetiya, from a great monument to a little heap of sand in the form of a stupa, from a colossal image to a tiny votive tablet.

The amount of merit acquired, it is felt, is a function of the effort expended by the donor in proportion to his means. That explains why the rich like to commission images of gold or precious stone, and why King Rama III (1824-1851) founded the vast reclining Buddha, over 40 meters long, at Wat Pho. Great efforts are expected of the possessors of great sources; but a poor man may earn as much merit by creating a simple reminder of clay.

It has been explained that in spite of the fact that Buddhism doesn't consider the Buddha a god, Buddha images seem to rank higher in Buddhism than crucifixes in Catholicism. Buddha images are considered animated in their own right, while crucifixes are symbols and symbols only. As A.B. Griswold pointed out, Buddhist may believe that a Buddha image can miraculously talk, and in this case, the spirit of the Buddha image is considered the talking force.

Catholicism also knows images that miraculously talk but Catholicism interprets such occurrences as the Holy Spirit talking through the medium of the image, and not the image talking on its own. A.B. Griswold in his essay "What is a Buddha Image" named the Buddha "Sage of Rationalism". His essay also indicates that he sees himself on the side of those who attempt a rationalist interpretation of Buddhism. In spite of this, he defends what appears to be image worship even by Buddhist rationalist, and he does so with a seemingly rationalist explanation. The more this appears to be contradictory, the more interested one may be in his chain of arguments.

A.B. Griswold:

"But what of the rationalists? Would they not view all such notions, if not with contempt, at least with a mildly amused skepticism? Yet we often see modern-minded Buddhists, including the leaders of the rationalist movement, prostrating themselves before an image and making offerings of flowers and incense."

"The usual answer is that they are expressing their gratitude to the memory of the Teacher who conferred the priceless gift of the Doctrine on mankind. While this answer may seem strange to a Westerner, I am sure it is right. In all countries that take their forms of politeness from India, the manifestations of respect accorded to a teacher looks very much like worship."

"Still, we might think it an exaggerated way to express gratitude to a Master who long ago passed into Total Extinction, or at least far beyond the range of human behavior, and who can consequently derive no possible satisfaction from such homage. But the rationalist knows that the expression of gratitude is really for the benefit of the living, reinforcing the power of the Reminder in his own feelings and in the feelings of others; and even in the West it sometimes occurs that the most skeptical writers, who have no belief in any sort of future life whatever, will dedicate a book to the memory of some deceased friend."

"There is still another reason for such outward acts of piety on the part of Buddhist rationalists. Though they are indeed atheists, in the sense that they allow no significant place for a god or gods, they are not at all bigoted; and unlike the atheists of Communist countries they have no thought of undertaking a crusade against religion. Though for their own part they consider faith to be rather a hindrance than a help to clear thinking, they freely admit that many people need faith as a support for good morals. Tolerance is a cardinal principle of Buddhism; they recognize the good features of all religions, and in particular they respect the traditional forms of Buddhist worship."

"And they believe that good manners are the counterpart, in small things, of good morals in large ones. This is a good thing for Westerners to bear in mind, even those Westerners who have no particular sympathy for Buddhism."

"Among the souvenirs a tourist takes home with him from Bangkok there will very likely be a few Buddha images. [The export of Buddha images has been prohibited only after A.B. Griswold's essay was first published.] They should not be used as door-stops or decorations for a bar, placed on the floor, made into lamps or coffee-tables, dressed up in humorous costumes, given nicknames, turned over to the children to play with, or treated in any other manner that does not befit objects of religious significance. To put them in unsuitable places is not only bad manners, which would hurt the feelings of any Buddhist who happened to visit the house; it is also a singularly unsatisfactory way to bring out the beauty of a work of art. No one in his right mind, no matter how little he might care about Christianity, would hang a crucifix on his wall upside down. Buddha images were made with the expectation that they would be placed in a position of honor-generally speaking, at such a height that their legs are at the level of the spectator's eye-and that is the way they can be seen to best advantage."

"Buddha images, however, are not 'works of art' in the ordinary sense. The purpose in making them was not to delight a connoisseur or to win praise from a critic; nor was it, except in a secondary way, to please the eye at all. As we have seen, they are religious mechanisms of a very peculiar kind. Nevertheless a great many of them are also objects of beauty by any standards; and there is certainly no harm in a non-Buddhist seeing them as such, provided he remembers that that is not the whole story. Unfortunately Western taste often seems to prefer a severed head or hand, rather than the complete image, and instances have been recorded of thieves mutilating images in monasteries to obtain such fragments for sale. I would not go so far as to say that we should refuse to display a detached head or hand that has been dug up, if the body has been lost-though in the eyes of an old-fashioned Buddhist such a display is rather gruesome and indeed likely to bring bad luck-but we should always remember that the whole image is much more valuable, and more worthy of display, than a mere fragment; and we should do everything we can to discourage the mutilation of images."

"Apart from that, we can only sense the inner beauty of a Buddha image by discovering what it means to Buddhists on different levels of understanding."

"Its surfaces and silhouette may please the eye, or even cause a gasp of surprise by their beauty. But they exist only as the capsule that contains the fiery energy; without that, whether we define it as magic or as psychological power, the image would not even have come into existence."

EPISTEMOLOGY

Siddhartha Gautama the Buddha is portrayed in Buddhist literature as ridiculing the sacrificial rituals of the Brahmans and accusing the priests of fabricating them for no better reason than to make money from the wealthy and to manipulate the powerful. Attacking the sacrificial practices of the Brahman priests in this way eventually led to challenging the authority of the Vedic literature that the priests considered sacred. An early Buddhist philosopher who challenged the authority of sacred texts was Nagarjuna, whose arguments called into question the very possibility of justified belief. In a text called Vigrahavyavartana (Averting Disputes), Nagarjuna argued that all opinions are warranted by an appeal to experience, or to various forms of reasoning, or to the authority of tradition. Now among the opinions that one may hold, said Nagarjuna, is the opinion that all opinions are warranted in one of those ways. Nothing, however, seems to warrant that opinion. If one should claim that that opinion is self-warranting, then why not grant that all other opinions are also self-warranting? On the other hand, if that opinion requires substantiation, the result will be an infinite regress. Therefore, concluded Nagarjuna, no opinion can be grounded. Realizing that one can never arrive at certainty thus becomes for Nagarjuna the most reliable way of freeing oneself from the various delusions that cause unhappiness in the world. Dispelling delusions is therefore not a matter of discovering truth, but a matter of realizing that all opinions that pass as knowledge are not really knowledge at all.

Although Nagarjuna's scepticism managed to capture the spirit of some passages of Buddhist literature that depict the Buddha as questioning the authoritarianism of other teachers, it did not leave adequate room for distinguishing truth from error. Most Buddhist philosophers who came after Nagarjuna, therefore, placed an emphasis on both eliminating error and securing positive knowledge. Dignaga, modifying theories of knowledge that Brahmanical thinkers had developed, argued that there are just two types of knowledge, each having a distinct subject matter unavailable to the other: through the senses one gains knowledge of particulars that are physically present, while the intellect enables one to form concepts that take past and future experiences into consideration.

In an important work called Klambanaparakra (Examining the Support of Awareness) Dignaga developed an argument that his predecessor Vasubandhu had made. Here Dignaga argued that a cognition is accurate only if the subject matter of the cognition is identical to that which causes the awareness to arise. So, for example, if one sees a dead tree in the dark and takes it to be a man, then the subject matter of the cognition is a man, which is not identical to the dead tree that is causing the cognition; the cognition is therefore inaccurate. Given this principle, said Dignaga, it follows that none of our sensory cognitions is accurate, because each of them is really caused by atoms massed together; nevertheless, we are never aware of anything as a mass of atoms. Instead, what we are aware of is such things as human beings, elephants and trees. These notions of things as human beings or elephants, however, are purely conceptual in nature and are not in accord with the realities that exist in the external world. Therefore, he concluded, the only objects of our awareness are concepts; we are never directly aware of realities as they occur outside the mind.

Dignaga's essays rekindled an interest in epistemological questions among Buddhist philosophers that lasted for several centuries. As influential as his theories in logic and the sources of knowledge were, there was little in them that explicitly referred to previous Buddhist doctrine. It was left to the systematic philosopher Dharmakarti to draw out the implications that questions of logic and epistemology had for people interested in the traditional Buddhist preoccupation with eliminating delusions concerning the nature of the self in order to win freedom from discontent.

Dharmakarti's system of epistemology was centred around his criticism of the Brahmanical doctrine of the special authority of the Veda, which the Brahmans supposed had been revealed to humanity by God. He combined this criticism with a defence of the doctrine that the Buddha was a source of knowledge. The Brahmanical claim of authority for their scriptures is based upon the notion that God is omniscient and compassionate; this idea, said Dharmakarti, is extravagant and laughable. The Buddhist claim for the authority of the Buddha, on the other hand, is based on the modest claim that the Buddha was an ordinary man who could see the root cause of discontent, knew how to eliminate the cause, and took time to teach other human beings what he had discovered. Moreover, argued Dharmakarti, the Buddha taught nothing but principles that every human being could confirm. Full confirmation of the Buddha's teachings was said to be impossible for a person whose vision was still clouded by delusions. On the other hand, to a person who had learned to listen to wise counsel, reflect on it and then put it into practice, all the teachings of the Buddha on the question of winning nirvana would be confirmed.

The form of reflection that Dharmakarti recommended was based upon a systematic study of the principles of legitimate inference; most delusions, he contended, stem from forming hasty generalizations from limited experience. Most doctrinal matters about which philosophers dispute, he said, cannot be decided with certainty. In this respect, Dharmakarti adopted the cautious attitude of the Buddha and Nagarjuna towards unwarranted opinions and assumptions. At the same time, he tried to show that the extreme scepticism that had characterized the work of such thinkers as Nagarjuna was also unwarranted. This epistemological 'middle path', consisting of modest claims about the extent of the Buddha's knowledge and yet insisting that the Buddha's doctrines were true and distinguishable from falsehoods, set the tone for most of the Buddhist philosophy that evolved in India until the time that Buddhism stopped being an important factor in the philosophical milieu of the Indian subcontinent. The focus on epistemological issues enabled Buddhists to set aside the sometimes bitter disputes over the question of which Buddhist scriptures were authentic.

METAPHYSICS

Given the emphasis in Buddhist teachings on the role of erroneous belief as a cause of unhappiness, it was natural that Buddhist philosophers should focus on questions of ontology and the theory of causation. Ontology was important, since a kind of intellectual error that was supposed to lead to unhappiness was being mistaken about what exists. The theory of causation was important, since the eradication of the cause of unhappiness was supposed to result in the removal of unhappiness itself.

The earliest attempts to systematize the teachings of Buddhism were in the genre of literature known as 'Abhidharma', in which all the factors of human experience were classified according to a variety of schemata. The study of the relationships among these classes of factors eventually evolved into a detailed theory of causality, in which several types of causal relationship were enumerated. There were many schools of Abhidharma, and each had its own set of schemata for the classification and enumeration of the factors of experience. Indeed, each had its own interpretation of what the very word 'Abhidharma' means; among the possible interpretations of the word, a common one is that it means a higher or more advanced doctrine, or a doctrine that leads to a higher form of wisdom. The variety of approaches taken in Abhidharma literature makes it difficult to discuss this literature in any but the most general way. Among most schools of Abhidharma, there was a commitment to the idea that the best strategy for coming to an understanding of any complex being is to analyse that being into its ultimate parts. An ultimate part is that which cannot be analysed into anything more simple. Most Buddhist systematists held to the principle that the ultimately simple building blocks out of which things are made are ultimately real, while complex things that are made up of more simple parts are not ultimately real; they are held to be real only through the consensus of a community. As was seen above in the section on human nature (§1), for example, there was a strong tendency for Buddhists to accept that a person's character is the product of many components; these components were held to be real, but the person was held to be ultimately unreal. The idea of a person may be a fiction, but it is one that makes the running of society more manageable, and therefore it can be regarded as a consensual reality, in contrast to an ultimate reality.

The philosopher Nagarjuna questioned the whole attempt to make a distinction between consensual and ultimate truths. One interpretation of his philosophical writings is that he was trying to show that every attempt to understand the world can only be an approximation on which there may be some degree of consensus; there is, however, no understanding that can claim to have arrived at an adequate description of things as they really are. Along with this radical criticism of the very enterprise of trying to discern ultimate from consensual realities, Nagarjuna criticized the doctrine that the simple constituents that serve as causes of more complex beings are more real than the complex beings themselves. This principle had rested on the assumption that the more simple a being is, the closer it is to being independent. In fact, he argued, the apparently simple constituents are no less dependent than their apparently complex effects. To this fact of being dependent upon other things, Nagarjuna gave the name emptiness; since all beings are dependent for their existence on other beings, he said, all beings are empty.

Later Buddhist philosophers, beginning especially with Dharmakarti, devoted their energy increasingly to refuting the claims, advanced by some Brahmanical thinkers, that the whole universe can be traced back to a single cause. Dharmakarti argued that if all things in the history of the world had a single cause, such as God or some type of primordial matter, then there would be no way to account for all the formal variety in the world at any given time, nor would it be possible to account for the fact that events unfold in sequences. If all the formal and temporal diversity are already inherent in the cause, he argued, then the cause is not a single thing after all. One might argue that the diversity exists in the single cause only as a potential of some kind; this, however, only raises the problem of explaining how that potential is actualized. If the potential is activated by something outside the cause that possesses it, then the outside agency must be counted among the causal factors along with the primary cause, in which case there is no longer a single cause. Besides general arguments directed against the view that all things could have any single cause, Dharmakarti also gave arguments against the existence of a creator God in particular. The universe, he observed, shows no signs of having been designed by anyone intelligent. Even if it were conceded for the sake of argument that the world might have been made by some intelligent being, there is still no sign that this being had any concern for any living beings. Later generations of Buddhist philosophers expanded upon Dharmakarti's arguments against the existence of a single intelligent creator, but most of these expansions took the form of replying to the objections of opponents rather than formulating new arguments (see Causation, Indian theories of §6).

During the last five hundred years that Buddhism was an important factor in Indian philosophy (600-1100), criticism of Buddhist doctrines by Brahmanical and Jaina religious philosophers, as well as from anti-religious materialists, forced Buddhist thinkers to refine some of their arguments and even to abandon some of their doctrinal positions. Arguments among Buddhists became much less a feature of Buddhist philosophy than arguments against non-Buddhist opponents. Within Buddhism itself, there was a tendency to try to reconcile differences that in earlier centuries had divided Buddhists against each other, at least doctrinally. This new spirit of overcoming sectarianism resulted in several ingenious attempts to fuse the old Abhidharma schools, the Madhyamika schools, the Yogachara schools and the Buddhist epistemologists. Few new issues were raised in this last five-hundred-year period, and not many new arguments were discovered to defend old positions. Careful scholarship tended to replace philosophical innovation as the principal preoccupation of later Buddhist intellectuals, such as antarakaita, Kamalala, Jñanaramitra and Ratnakarti. It was during this period of the decline of Buddhism in India that Buddhist philosophy was introduced into Tibet. Once established there, it received a new impetus from a range of Tibetan intellectuals who were able to study many of these doctrines with a fresh perspective.

BUDDHIST PHILOSOPHY OF JAPAN

Buddhism transformed Japanese culture and in turn was transformed in Japan. Mahayana Buddhist thought entered Japan from the East Asian continent as part of a cultural complex that included written language, political institutions, formal iconography and Confucian literature. From its introduction in the sixth century through to the sixteenth century, Japanese Buddhism developed largely by incorporating Chinese Buddhism, accommodating indigenous beliefs and reconciling intersectarian disputes. During the isolationist Tokugawa Period (1600-1868), neo-Confucian philosophy and Dutch science challenged the virtual hegemony of Buddhist ways of thinking, but served more often as alternative and sometimes complementary models than as incompatible paradigms. Only since the reopening of Japan in 1868 has Japanese Buddhist thought seriously attempted to come to terms with early Indian Buddhism, Western thought and Christianity.

Through the centuries, Buddhism gave the Japanese people a way to make sense of life and death, to explain the world and to seek liberation from suffering. When it engaged in theorizing, it did so in pursuit of religious fulfilment rather than of knowledge for its own sake. As an extension of its practical bent, Japanese Buddhist thought often tended to collapse differences between Buddhism and other forms of Japanese religiosity, between this phenomenal world and any absolute realm, and between the means and end of enlightenment. These tendencies are not Japanese in origin, but they extended further in Japan than in other Buddhist countries and partially define the character of Japanese Buddhist philosophy.

In fact, the identity of 'Japanese Buddhist philosophy' blends with almost everything with which we would contrast it. As a development and modification of Chinese traditions, there is no one thing that is uniquely Japanese about it; as a Buddhist tradition, it is characteristically syncretistic, often assimilating Shinta and Confucian philosophy in both its doctrines and practices. Rituals, social practices, political institutions and artistic or literary expressions are as essential as philosophical ideas to Japanese Buddhism.

Disputes about ideas often arose but were seldom settled by force of logical argument. One reason for this is that language was used not predominately in the service of logic but for the direct expression and actualization of reality. Disputants appealed to the authority of Buddhist sutras because these scriptures were thought to manifest a direct understanding of reality. Further, as reality was thought to be all-inclusive, the better position in the dispute would be that which was more comprehensive rather than that which was more consistent but exclusive. Politics and practical consequences did play a role in the settling of disputes, but the ideal of harmony or conformity often prevailed.

The development of Japanese Buddhist philosophy can thus be seen as the unfolding of major themes rather than a series of philosophical positions in dispute. These themes include the role of language in expressing truth; the non-dual nature of absolute and relative, universal and particular; the actualization of liberation in this world, life or body; the equality of beings; and the transcendent non-duality of good and evil.

LANGUAGE

The practical, soteriological nature of Buddhism makes it wary of what Wittgenstein called the bewitchment of the mind by language. Yet the view that Buddhism disregards language is an oversimplification, especially in Japan. Japanese Buddhism has a positive appreciation of language, particularly of its non-referential usage. Buddhist thought first came to Japan in the form of sutras and commentaries written in Chinese characters. Written language was still so novel, and categories of thought so limited, that the content of these texts could be read as manifestations of new realities rather than as ideas referring to Buddhism. Some of the earliest literature composed in Japan, such as the poetry collection Man'yasha, mentions kotodama, the spiritual power of words that makes things present. Although scholars articulated this theory of language only much later and aligned it with Shinta (see Motoori Norinaga), it may apply to the early understanding of Chinese Buddhist as well as indigenous words. Words had the power not only to manifest things in the world but also to change them; before Buddhist texts represented a doctrinal and ethical system, they provided incantations to heal illness and bring prosperity to the land.

The ritualistic use of language continued through the centuries and was often central to the expression of doctrine.

Practitioners often used single words or phrases as the condensed form of a doctrine or lengthy sutra. Kakai, for example, recited the Sanskrit formulas for the Womb and Diamond Mandalas to better envision these pictorial representations of the cosmic order. He proposed that intoning mantras could make the basic sounds of the cosmos audible. He used dharma or magical formulae not only as a means of purifying body and mind and allowing him to understand the point of every Buddhist scripture, but also as the means by which his patron bodhisattva could fulfill all wishes. Even when later Pure Land School teachers such as Shinran suspected discursive language and discouraged belief in worldly benefit through magical transformation, they taught that the sincere invocation of Amida Buddha's name has the power to actualize the salvation of all sentient beings. Buddhists of the Nichiren schools chanted the name of the Wondrous Lotus Sutra, namu myaharenge kya, as a condensation and realization of all doctrines contained in it. Rinzai Zen teachers advocated the practice of kanna or 'contemplating the [crucial] phrase' of a dialogue, or of compressing the already condensed Heart Sutra into a single word. As long as the words are 'live' and not dead repetitions, Zen teachers conceived such practices as shortcuts to enlightenment that immediately put the practitioner in a frame of mind to realize the point of Buddhist doctrines.

The transformative as well as expressive nature of language is evident in perhaps the most important collection of premodern Japanese philosophical literature, the Shabgenz (Treasury of the True Dharma Eye), by the thirteenth-century Zen master Dugen. One chapter begins: 'As for the Buddha Way, not to voice it is impossible.' This statement does not command one to proclaim the teachings of Buddhism, but rather connects one's attainment of truth with its expression in the world. Such expression includes but is not limited to language. Another chapter of the Shabgenz states, 'All buddhas and patriarchs are able to voice the Way', that is, to express truth in all their words and actions. By virtue of their realization of non-duality or no ultimate opposition, they can directly express the Way and not merely refer to it. They can also experience as the words of the

Buddha 'the preaching of non-sentient beings', the 'sounds of the valley streams and the forms of the mountains'. This idea, explained further below, seems to collapse any ultimate distinction between sign and signified. Words express themselves, as do valley streams and the forms of mountains. This 'expressing' or 'voicing of the Way' does not stand for or represent something other than itself, and language used representationally is not privileged to express reality. The limitation placed on the power of representational language here is accompanied by an expanded meaning of 'expression' or 'voicing of the Way' that includes both linguistic and nonlinguistic forms.

DOCTRINE AND TRUTH

When early readers began to understand Buddhist texts as expressions of doctrines, and implicitly to grasp written language as signs signifying ideas, they came to understand the world in terms of formerly unseen relations. The Buddhist categories they applied were Chinese translations of Sanskrit terms, and this usage remained predominant even after modern Japanese scholars turned to Indian sources. The categories included names for the basic factors or elements of existence and the relations of cause and effect, conditioned and unconditioned, part and whole, relative and absolute.

The first systematic study of these categories and relations occurred in the so-called six schools of Nara, during the historical period of the same name (710-81). These 'schools' were more bodies of doctrine than independent sects with their own adherents. Often the doctrines were studied together in the same locale, such as the great temple Tadaiji. The Japanese version of the Indian Abhidharmakona school stressed the analysis of some seventy five conditioned and unconditioned constituents (dharmas) of existence and some ten types of direct and indirect causes that give rise to the conditioned factors.

As abstract as it appears, this analysis was intended as a kind of psychological examination to remove obstacles on the path to liberation. The Jajitsu (Establishment of Truth) school proceeded to show the emptiness, or lack of substantial reality, of all constituents. The Ritsu (Precept) school conveyed very specific ethical and administrative rules to regulate the ordination and life of monks and nuns, and taught that the observance of precepts was one purification necessary for enlightenment. As discussed below, however, it did not provide an ethical theory or general principles for determining good and evil.

The Sanron (Three Treatises) school derived from Indian Madhyamika philosophy (see Buddhism, Madhyamika: India and Tibet). It practiced the refutation of all claims of the existence or non-existence, truth or falsity, of separate elements and doctrines. The discursive language used to refute all views ultimately pointed to its own limit, beyond which lay absolute truth. The Hosse school formed the scholastic counterpart to Indian Yogachara or 'consciousness-only' philosophy. It criticized the Madhyamika tendency to absolutize emptiness, explained the role of consciousness in the appearance of self and world, and taught that enlightenment requires a conversion of the deep unconsciousness, called the 'storehouse' consciousness. It rejected the teaching that enlightenment is equally attainable by all. The sixth school, the Kegon (Flower Garland), was historically no more influential than these last two, but introduced a principle crucial to an understanding of the treatment of doctrines and truth in subsequent Japanese Buddhism.

The Nara schools took over doctrines and analyses from their Chinese counterparts virtually without change. These doctrines were partially incompatible with each other, but the discrepancies seemed little cause for dispute. Various doctrines and categories show up in later Japanese Buddhist philosophy, often as a foil for more innovative ideas. An example is the way the Abhidharma breakdown of reality and time forms the springboard of one chapter of Dugen's Shabgenz, 'Ocean Reflecting Samadhi'. This work first accepts the Abhidharma analysis of the causal arising of all elements but then disrupts it to proclaim the totality and sufficiency of each moment. In general, the failure of scholastic doctrines to challenge later generations of Japanese Buddhist thinkers is a sign that the latter have been more at home with practical reasoning and reconciliation than with formal argumentation and adjudication of claims. Indeed, until its introduction from the West there was in Japan no formal logic, where the rules of validity are separable from the content of the argument. This lack does not necessarily point to a deficiency in the ability to reason, however, but may have to do with a way of relating absolute and relative, universal and particular. The philosophy of the Kegon school best epitomizes that way.

The Kegon school accounted for the variety of doctrines by placing them in a scheme of increasing difficulty and comprehensiveness. The level of the teachings matches the hearer's capacity to understand. Partial teachings, in other words, are 'skillful means' designed to lead one to more difficult and comprehensive teachings. The Kegon school typifies the inclusion characteristic of much of Japanese and Chinese Buddhist thought. One Buddhist school would incorporate rather than exclude the doctrines of rival schools, but would regard them as incomplete and place them on a lower level. To be sure, the hermeneutic of inclusion was often politically motivated, intended to increase a power base by incorporating and not alienating other groups; but it also followed the dialectical principle that rival or alternative beliefs were partial truths that fit into a larger scheme.

The Kegon scriptural hermeneutic privileged its own source sutras and was rivalled by a similar scheme offered in the tremendously influential Lotus Sutra, but it developed a philosophy of totality and interrelation crucial for understanding most Japanese Buddhist thinking. According to this philosophy, each part or constituent of reality perfectly reflects the whole, and the whole depends upon each and every constituent part. All individual parts are therefore equivalent as conditions of the whole, and at the same time they are distinct and interdependent. The implications of this philosophy of nature for a theory of truth are the key to approaching Japanese Buddhist thought. There is no whole, universal or absolute, without its manifestation in concrete, distinct and relative particulars. In the twentieth century, Nishida Kitara reformulated this principle paradoxically: the more relative a truth is-that is, the more deeply embedded or embodied in particulars-the more absolute it is. The absolute must encompass the relative, not stand in opposition to it. In general, Japanese Buddhist philosophy developed through a kind of synecdochic argumentation that appealed not to a priori reasons or empirical evidence, nor simply to scriptural sources of authority, but to this mutual accommodation of relative and absolute.

UNIVERSAL AND PARTICULAR

Three interrelated themes display the mutual accommodation of relative and absolute, universal and particular: the locus of liberation, its actuality and the equality of beings.

Indian Mahayana sutras introduced the idea that liberation does not lead to a transcendent realm different from this world, but they often spoke of the 'three immeasurable eons' required for its attainment. In contrast, many seminal Buddhist thinkers in Japan developed one Chinese view of the locus of liberation: the idea of becoming a buddha in this very body (sokushin jubutsu). For Saichu (767-822), the founder of the Tendai school, it meant only a partial realization of buddhahood; but by the time of Tendai scholar Annen (841-89?) it referred to buddhahood attained in this very life. Kukai (774-835), founder of the rival Shingon school, taught that yogic practices involving body (mudras or symbolic hand gestures), speech (mantras) and mind (mental concentration and visualizations) could unify the practitioner with the Buddha Mahavairocana. Such practices made it possible to attain buddhahood in this very body. This doctrine, popularized by Kukai, provided a theoretical basis for the bodily aspects of practice and the enactment of rituals that were important especially in the esoteric traditions of Tendai and Shingon Buddhism.

In summary, the idea of becoming a buddha in this very body or life involved a temporal and a metaphysical reduction. First, it collapsed the various stages of the path to enlightenment that were so important in various Buddhist traditions, and reduced the 'three immeasurable eons' to one lifetime. Second, it collapsed any remnant of a difference between the physical reality of life on earth and a transcendent realm, between the transient human body and the transcendent dharma-body. The body we are born with is the site of realization and symbolically embodies the entire universe, the 'truth-body' of the Buddha. Dugen modified the idea further and proclaimed that 'this very mind is buddha' (sokushin zebutsu) when the discursive mind was disengaged. Although Dugen speaks of 'mind' and not body, no psychophysical dualism is implied here.

Other Buddhist reformers of the Kamakura period (1192-1333) qualified the idea that liberation was possible in this world or life. Hunen and Shinran placed this possibility in the Pure Land, which they usually considered as immediately accessible if intermediate between this world and the realm of final enlightenment. Even where it was imagined as a different world, this Pure Land was not nearly so remote a goal as Indian views of nirvana, and was sometimes in effect made immanent in this world. Ippen explicitly stated that the Pure Land was indeed identical with this world. Nichiren too emphasized this world as the locus of salvation.

The affirmation of this world in Japanese thought is often called phenomenalism (see Phenomenalism), but this description neglects the principle or absolute said to interpenetrate all phenomena. One tenet of Kegon philosophy was that 'principles are not impeded by things' (rijimuge). Tendai Buddhism stressed the Mahayana doctrine of the 'identity of the phenomenal and the real' (genshazoku jissa), and proposed that the phenomena of the world are aspects of Buddha. Dugen wrote that the 'true reality' (jiss) is in fact all things, and that birth and death (impermanence) (see Muju) is Buddha or nirvana. To understand these developments in Japanese Buddhism, however, one needs to consider the question of the actuality of liberation.

Many Indian Mahayana sutras teach that all sentient beings possess the nature of Buddha. The Lotus Sutra proclaims further that the historical Buddha is not a man who attained awakening but rather is a manifestation of the universal buddhahood that is available to all. It rejected schemes that differentiated levels of potential in beings and that excluded the lowest level from eventual enlightenment. Saichu advocated universal buddhahood, based on the language of the Lotus Sutra. Universal buddhahood and 'becoming Buddha in this very body' are ideas based on the notion of hongaku, the Chinese doctrine that all beings are 'originally or inherently awakened'. Inherent enlightenment, in contrast to 'acquired enlightenment', is timeless and independent of spiritual development. For some contemporary scholars such as Tamura Yoshira, the hongaku idea is definitive not only of Buddhism in medieval Japan but of Japanese culture in general, since it underlies the ideals of equality, harmony and conformity (Tamura 1987).

The ideas of inherent and acquired enlightenment do not form logical contraries, since both depend upon the buddha-nature in all beings, but rather pose a practical question: how is this innate enlightenment related to practice? Legend has it that Dugen encountered this question in his boyhood Tendai training and made it an existential problem: why undergo rigorous practice when we are endowed with 'dharma nature' by birth? Dugen's answer is thought to be a criticism of the hongaku idea, but can also be seen as its limit. He proposed 'the unity of practice and realization': 'The dharma [truth] is not manifested unless one practices; it is not attained unless there is realization'. The practice of concentrated mind-body, epitomized in zazen or seated meditation, is a way to actualize our inherent nature. In §1 above, Dugen's words were quoted: 'As for the Buddha Way, not to voice it is impossible... ' and this sentence concludes: 'not to study [practice] it is remote.' Dugen thus collapses the distinction between practice as means and enlightenment as end. Instead, zazen, the practice of awakening, becomes the manifestation of enlightenment.

Like Dugen, other Kamakura Period Buddhist reformers reacted against the complacency encouraged by the idea of original enlightenment, but modified rather than rejected it. For Hunen and Shinran the only 'practice' that counts is the nembutsu or invocation of the Buddha Amida. In his form as the Bodhisattva Dharmakara, Amida enunciated a primal vow that made his enlightenment contingent on that of all sentient beings. Those with sincere faith in Amida's vow were assured of rebirth in the Pure Land, where final enlightenment will be possible. In the original story, countless lifetimes elapse before Dharmakara becomes Amida Buddha, but the logic of the conditions may suggest a non-dual, timeless relation: since Amida Buddha is indeed here to save us, our liberation need only be actualized in this moment. Some writings of Shinran explicitly suggest that to recollect Amida Buddha with a believing mind (shinjin) is already to actualize buddhahood, without waiting to be reborn in the Pure Land. Moreover, this entrusting invocation is strictly speaking not a practice at all; that is, it is not accomplished through one own efforts or 'self-power' but rather is a gift of Amida, a result of Amida's 'other-power'. Ippen stated that 'the nembutsu is what recites the nembutsu'. Although faith in personal effort is considered futile, as in some interpretations of inherent enlightenment, true reality must be activated by personal faith. This again is a variation on the theme of the actualization of reality.

The idea of universal buddhahood supported both syncretistic tendencies in Japanese Buddhism and the equality of all beings. The first undermined any ultimate difference between Buddhist and Shint? objects of veneration, and the second any difference between the human and natural worlds, or what we today call culture and nature.

Syncretistic tendencies were formalized in the theory of honji suijaku. This theory regarded indigenous Shintu deities (kami) as trace manifestations (suijaku) of buddhas and bodhisattvas, who were their original ground or true nature (honji). The theory appears to establish a hierarchical relationship, with the bodhisattvas as more basic and important than the kami, and thus Buddhism as more fundamental than Shintu. This interpretation implies that the Shintu gods cannot exist without the Buddhist ideal beings. It not only reverses the historical order of their appearance in Japan; it misplaces the emphasis. In fact, the honj-suijaku theory often worked to set the two realms and their objects of veneration on a par with one another. If a kami functioned as a trace or attribute of a bodhisattva, the particular bodhisattva was best manifested in the kami. The reality of the one depended upon that of the other. This interdependence was explicit in a Tendai version of honji suijaku theory according to which the true nature could only be perceived in its manifestations. A fourteenth-century Shintu school simply reversed the order of bodhisattva and kami. Moreover, specific Buddhist and Shinta ideal beings are sometimes identified with one another and then contrasted with other pairs. In the twentieth century, a 'new religion' called Gedatsukai in effect identifies the Buddha Mahavairocana and the Shinta deity Tenjinchigi as honji, and gives other Buddhist-Shinta deities the status of suijaku. These examples illustrate that the accessibility of ideal beings was more important than any rank order, which was historically variable.

The theory of original ground and trace manifestation was developed in the late Heian Period (794-1185), contemporaneous with the idea of inherent enlightenment. Yet the underlying association of Shintu and Buddhism is evident much earlier and lasted until much later. At the very beginning of Japanese Buddhism, the Nihon shoki (Chronicles of Japan) report that the Emperor Yamei (d. 587) 'believed in the Law of the Buddha and reverenced the Way of the Gods'. Yet the name 'Way of the Gods' (Shintu) was a Chinese, quasi-Buddhist concept. In effect, Buddhism prevailed and was established as the state religion, at least temporarily, through the efforts of Yamei's sister, Empress Suiko, and especially of his son, Prince Shutoku, who wrote commentaries on sutras and built temples. In the Nara Period (710-81), Shintu shrines were incorporated into Buddhist temples in order to protect land interests, and Buddhist altars built near shrines ensured the protection of Shintu.

At one locale the god of war, Hachiman, was named the Bodhisattva Daijizaiten in 783; at others he was associated with different bodhisattvas. In the ninth century, Kakai proposed a 'dual aspect' theory that, for example, identified the sun goddess Amaterasu with Mahavairocana, the Buddha of Great Illumination, whom Kakai further identified with the dharmakaya or truth-body of Buddha. Although Tokugawa Period (1600-1868) nativists such as Motoori Norinaga reasserted the superiority of indigenous Shintu, the Buddhist inclusion of Shinta was not effectively challenged on a national scale until the early Meiji government's policies (in the 1870s) of 'separating gods and buddhas', persecuting Buddhism and establishing State Shintu. Religion and state have had separate legal status since the Second World War, but Buddhist and Shintu teachings and customs still coexist in Japanese family life. Japanese Buddhist thought extended the idea of universal buddhahood to the equality of all beings. In particular, the idea of inherent enlightenment lent support to the doctrine of the Buddha-nature of non-sentient beings that is often alluded to in medieval Japanese literature. It was both Tendai and Nichiren doctrine that the grass and trees-in other words, beings not possessed of a sensitive mind-can become buddhas: 'Grasses, trees, mountains and rivers all attain buddhahood' became a frequent saying in medieval Buddhist texts. A chapter of Dugen's Shabgenz quotes the enlightenment verse of Chinese poet Su Dongpo:

> *The sounds of the valley streams are His long, broad tongue;*
>
> *The forms of the mountains are His pure body.*
>
> *At night I heard the myriad sutra-verses uttered*
>
> *How can I relate to others what they say?*
>
> *(Cook 1989: vii)*

For Dugen, this verse provides one answer to the questions, 'where is buddha?', 'what is buddha?' and 'how does he preach?' The preaching of nonsentient beings, a frequent theme in Dugen, is echoed earlier in the poetry of Saigy?. It expands Dugen's view of 'expression' to the world of nature. Whether the traditional Japanese love of nature preceded or succeeded the absolute significance accorded to the phenomenal world cannot be determined.

THEODICY AND ETHICS

Japanese Buddhist treatments of theodicy and ethics also reveal ways in which Buddhism was transformed in Japan.

Theodicy is meant here in Max Weber's general sense of an explanation that make the injustices of life intelligible and accounts for evil in the world. In classical Indian thought, the notion of karma answers the problem of both moral and natural evil. Karmic retribution means that every deed or action has consequences and evil deeds bring about suffering. Suffering is not punishment by a God who is free to punish or not, but rather is an inevitable consequence of evil actions. There are accordingly practical reasons to avoid evil and do good. In early Indian thought the notion of karma entailed that of transmigration. Karma is, as it were, the momentum of our actions that propels us through samsara, the continuous cycles of birth and death. This transmigration occurs through various lifetimes and life forms, mythologized as the six realms of hell, hungry ghosts, animals, fighting demons, humans and gods. The Buddha taught a way of liberation that is a release from transmigration and its cause, karma, whether good or evil. In later Japanese Buddhist philosophy, attachment to self and the concomitant ignorance of the reality of no-self were stressed as the root cause of samsara.

After Buddhism was introduced to Japan, people easily accepted the notion of karmic retribution but not the literal belief of rebirth as animals or lower life forms. Transmigration through the six realms of samsara played a larger role in Japanese literature and theatre than in philosophical discussions, which focused more on the practical path to liberation. Good deeds were not the means to liberation; they did not, for example, ensure rebirth in the Pure Land, whether taken as the physical abode or spiritual state wherein final liberation is possible. Hunen, and later Shinran in his Tannish? (Lamenting the Deviations) went so far as to state that: 'If a good person attains birth in the Pure Land, how much more so the evil person'.

The apparent incompatibility between any notion of rebirth and the Indian Buddhist doctrine of no-self or no-soul was not an issue in traditional Japanese Buddhist thought. Moreover, even after the Japanese understood this doctrine they, like the Chinese, continued to believe in the spirits of ancestors who remain somehow present among the living. That folk belief has played a stronger role in everyday life and religious practices than has Buddhist doctrine.

Logically, the disassociation of good deeds and liberation would seem to compromise the theodicy offered by the notion of karmic retribution, and ancestor veneration to compromise the doctrine of no substantial self which is the basis of compassion with all living beings. In effect, however, the compromises have meant little more than finding a middle course, or superimposing the two metaphysically incompatible beliefs. Belief in karmic retribution has encouraged the avoidance of deeds conventionally deemed evil, and thus supported conventional ethics; but karmic retribution does not entail any final resolution to misery.

Only religious practice, whether conceived as self-power or other-power, holds out the prospect of final liberation, or at least the actualization of one's inherent enlightenment. In the meantime, one is to do good and avoid evil; more specifically, one is to adhere to conventional Buddhist precepts such as not killing, stealing, lying and so on. Similarly, veneration of ancestral spirits, including Buddhist patriarchs, has encouraged a respect for tradition and social order, while non-ego has been extolled as the basis of right action in both Japanese Buddhism and Confucianism. If we seek in Japanese Buddhist philosophy a coherent theory of ethics as a separate branch of philosophy, we find instead a variety of practical reasons; for a moral theory, we would have to refer to Confucianism.

This general description receives closer definition in the views of Shinran and Dugen. Dugen's ethical views reflect both the penchant to practical reasoning and the transcendence of ethics in the realization of enlightenment. Dugen's sermons to monks training under him admonish them to keep the precepts while recognizing that their content is relative to the situation. Ultimately, the practice of keeping precepts is subsumed into zazen or the practice of realization. Dugen's more philosophical writings transform practical admonitions such as 'do good' and 'do no evil' into proclamations of the realized state: 'the non-production of evil, the performance of good'.

Ultimately, both Dugen and Shinran would have us transcend the duality of good and evil to manifest, through uncontrived actions, absolute non-dual reality or 'suchness', which is perfect as it is. There is no cause-effect relation between morality and enlightenment, and so the issue is not the situational relativity of morality but, once again, the problem that the absolute is not complete without its manifestation in the phenomenal. Here ethical issues would give way to the problem of inherent enlightenment. The contemporary interpreter D.T. Suzuki advocated Zen enlightenment as the solution and simply proclaimed it to be 'beyond good and evil' (Suzuki 1964). On the other hand, the idea of inherent enlightenment has come under attack in the 1990s as perpetuating the status quo of society and blinding Japanese Buddhism to the need for reform guided by a social ethics.

6

Buddhist Philosophy of Korea

Buddhism was transmitted to the Korean peninsula from China in the middle of the fourth century ad. Korea at this time was divided into three kingdoms: Kokuryô, Paekche and Silla. Both Kokuryô and Paekche accepted Buddhism as a state religion immediately after it was introduced, to Kokuryô in 372 ad and to Paekche in 384 ad. However, it was not until two centuries later that Silla accepted Buddhism as a state religion. This was because Silla was the last of the three kingdoms to become established as a centralized power under the authority of one king.

It is not coincidental that Buddhism was accepted by these three states at the very same time that a strong kingship, independent of the aristocracy, was created. These newly established kingships needed a new ideology with which to rule, separate from the age-old shamanistic tradition which had been honored among the previous loose confederations of tribes. Buddhism fulfilled this need. It became a highly valued tool which kings used shrewdly, not only to provide their societies with a political ideology but to give them a foundation from which to build a viable system of ethics and philosophical thinking. Given this historical legacy, Korean Buddhism came to possess a feature which set it apart from the other East Asian traditions: it became 'state-protection' Buddhism.

Although this was not a particularly sophisticated phenomenon on a philosophical level, this feature had a lasting influence on all aspects of Buddhist thought in Korea. In general, Korean Buddhism has followed a course of development more or less parallel to that of the greater East Asian context, although with notably closer ties to China than to Japan. There is no historical evidence which indicates any direct intellectual transmission from India, Buddhism's birthplace; rather, most of the philosophical development of Buddhism in Korea occurred as Korean monks travelled to China to study and obtain Buddhist texts which had either been written in or translated into Chinese. Despite such close ties to China, however, Korean Buddhism has developed its own identity, distinct from that of its progenitor.

Compared to Indian and Central Asian Buddhism, which developed along clear historical lines, the development of Buddhism in China was largely dependent on the personalities of individual monks, and was thus affected by such factors as their region of origination and the particular texts which they emphasized. Thus, in the process of assimilating Indian Buddhism, the Chinese created and developed a number of widely varying schools of Buddhist thought. In Korea, however, such a diverse number of philosophical traditions was never established. Rather, one of the distinct features of Korean Buddhism has been its preference for incorporating many different perspectives into a single, cohesive body of thought.

THREE KINGDOMS PERIOD (372-668 AD)

When Buddhism arrived on the Korean peninsula, Korea was in a period of transition, changing from loose tribal societies to states ruled by centralized kingships. Buddhism was strongly patronized by the kings, as it provided them with a valuable political ideology, but nevertheless it had to face the challenge of countering the indigenous belief system based firmly on shamanistic ritualism. In response to this challenge, certain Buddhist doctrines which tended to undermine animistic beliefs received special emphasis in Korea. An example of these is the doctrine of karma, which asserts the importance of ethical action by humans and denies the power of gods and spirits in shaping human destiny. However, Buddhism also resorted to the tactic of assimilation. The heavenly being Hanunim, a shamanistic deity, was absorbed into the Buddhist conception of heaven. Similarly, the indigenous shamanistic worship of mountains, earth deities and dragons all became integrated into the Buddhist religious system.

Only fragmentary bits of information are available concerning Buddhist philosophy during its early existence in Korea. As previously discussed, the development of Buddhist studies in Korea ran almost parallel to that in China. Both Mahayana schools, such as Tientai, Huayan and Dilun, as well as Hinayana schools, including Abhidharma and the Sarvastivada and Vinaya traditions, were introduced. However, it seems that Madhyamika philosophy formed the mainstream of Buddhist doctrinal thought during this period. Names of Korean monks from the Kokuryô and Paekche kingdoms are often mentioned, particularly in Japanese records, as masters of Madhyamika theory or as founders of the Sanron (in Chinese, Sanlun) school in Japan (the Sanlun school was based on the sinicized interpretation of the Indian Madhyamika).

We can learn much about the Korean interpretation of Madhyamika theory by investigating the contributions of Sûngnang, an eminent Korean monk. Although we have no exact record of his date of birth, according to the Biography of Fadu in the Liang Gaosengzhuan (The Liang Biographies of the Eminent Monks), Sûngnang succeeded to the lineage after the Master Fadu passed away in 500 ad. Sûngnang's unique interpretations represented a turning point not only for Sanlun studies but for Chinese Buddhist studies as a whole. Through the decisive contributions of Sûngnang, Sanlun was established by Jizang (549-623 ad) as one of the major schools in Chinese Buddhist history. Sûngnang's own works have not been transmitted, but his philosophical ideas are cited throughout Jizang's writings.

During Sûngnang's time, Chinese Buddhist studies were divided into Northern/Abhidharma and Southern/Satyasiddhi. Sanlun was considered part of the Satyasiddhi school, whose doctrine was based on Abhidharma theory and centered around the Hanayana concept of the Four Noble Truths. Sûngnang, however, made a distinction between Satyasiddhi and Sanlun, and he demarcated a boundary between the Old and New

Sanlun. He is best known for his two-truth theory, in which he distinguished between conventional and ultimate truth. In his view, these are not ontological truths, but represent rather a convenient pedagogical device for teachers. In discussions concerning truth, some say that it is existence, some say that it is nonexistence, others say that it is either existence or nonexistence, while still others say that it is neither existence nor nonexistence. Sûngnang claimed, however, that none of these statements represent the complete truth, but merely indicate one aspect of it. Thus, in his view, the two truths represent different expressions of the excellent teaching of the Middle Path.

For Sûngnang, the Middle Path was not a state situated between existence and nonexistence, or duality and non-duality. Rather, he saw it as consisting of three levels: on the first level, the existence of all beings is considered as conventional truth, and the emptiness of all things is regarded as ultimate truth. Here, emptiness is called ultimate truth in response to the followers of Abhidharma who advocated the existence of dharmas. On the second level, the existence and emptiness of the first level are both viewed as conventional truth while the denial of both is seen as ultimate truth. This is Sûngnang's rebuttal to the Satyasiddhi school, which admits the dualism of existence and emptiness, positing emptiness as ultimate truth. Finally, on the third and last level, it is recognized that both truths as well as all three levels, are merely teaching devices. Thus, the three gates or three levels are expounded only in order to realize the truth of not three. This non-acquisition of, and non-abiding in, one level or one truth is initially named the ultimate.

The structure of Sûngnang's theory indicates a process of continuing dialectics to a level of infinity. As such, it negates any fixed concepts which regard the ultimate as a state arrived at through progression. For Sûngnang and his followers, a highest level does not exist; rather, this dialectic method of denial continues endlessly. The ultimate truth, then, cannot be the ultimate; it is not an absolute reality. This is why Sûngnang asserted that the two-truth theory was not a principle but only a pedagogical tool. He showed clearly that it is not possible to verbalize or conceptualize about ultimate truth. Any attempt to do so will only bring one back to the level of conventional truth. This unique philosophy marked the beginning of the New Sanlun school and was elaborated on first by Zhouyong and then by Jizang, who finalized its ideas in the latter half of the sixth century.

UNIFIED SILLA PERIOD (668-935 AD)

This period was one of religious maturity and innovation; as such, it represented the culmination of Buddhist influence in Korea, both culturally and doctrinally. Buddhism fully blossomed and flourished at this time, reaching heights that it would never see again. On the one hand, influences from China were still felt, as new schools of thought were introduced by Silla monks returning from the Tang dynasty. On the other hand, Korean Buddhist scholarship by such eminent monks as Wônhyo (617-86) played an important role in the development of Chinese Buddhist thought as well. However, unlike the Tang tendency towards sectarianism, Unified Silla leaned towards a synthesis of various aspects of Buddhist thought into a type of interdenominational philosophy, the so-called t'ong pulgyo, or Buddhism of total interpenetration. The syncretic approach of Korean Buddhist philosophy can be best understood under the following headings: the reconciliation of doctrinal disputes, the Silla Hwaom School, the Silla Vijñnavada School, and the introduction of Sôn (Chan) Buddhism from China.

RECONCILIATION OF DOCTRINAL DISPUTES

One of the most important proponents of this syncretic approach was the noted monk and scholar Wônhyo. In his view, the various disputes which arose among Buddhist scholars were similar to the story of the blind men's description of an elephant: each man was only defining one aspect of the animal. In one sense, they were all wrong, because each failed to fully describe the elephant. In another sense, however, they were not entirely wrong, as what they were describing was not something other than the elephant.

Wônhyo was not interested in merely partial or incomplete understandings, however; rather, he focused on integrating a variety of doctrines into one complete view, as seen from a higher perspective. This view has been termed hwajaeng, or the 'reconciliation of doctrinal controversy'. The hermeneutical device used in this doctrinal reconciliation is well represented in his unique genre of Buddhist commentarial work, chong-yo, as well as in his concepts of kae (unfolding or opening) and hap (folding or sealing) the truth. Wônhyo is believed to have composed approximately seventeen of these chong-yo, of which only five are extant. Chong translates as doctrine or theme, and yo means essence. Thus, for example, one of his works, the Yolban'gyong chongyo, translates as the 'Doctrinal Essentials of the Nirvana Sutra'. Here, 'doctrine' refers to the various ideas which are discussed, and 'essentials' integrates them into one primary framework of thought. Similarly, by his usage of the word 'unfolding' (kae), Wônhyo indicates a variety of ideas and analyses, while through 'folding' (hap) he denotes how these themes may be synthesized into one cohesive unit of understanding. Doctrine, then, reflects the unfolding of the one into the many, whereas essence refers to the folding of the many back into the one.

Another device which Wônhyo used in order to reconcile opposites and thus denote their non-duality was his theory of essence-function (Korean: ch'e-yong) (see Ti and yong). In his Taesung kisillon so (Treatise on Awakening Mahayana Faith) he asserts that Mahayana is a synonym for One-Mind. This One-Mind represents essence, or ch'e, while the variety of mental and physical states, or the arising of dharmas, represents function, or yong. In terms of its internal logic, essence-function is no different from the kae-hap (folding and unfolding) formulation. According to Wônhyo, when the essence of Mahayana, or One-Mind, is unfolded, immeasurable and limitless meaning can be found in its doctrine. Conversely, when the doctrine is folded, it returns to its essence, which consists of two aspects: the absolute and the phenomenal. The limitless meanings of One-Mind are identical to this essence and are completely amalgamated within it. Therefore, One-

Mind unfolds and folds freely, and establishes and refutes without restrictions.

In this way, the myriads of sensory impressions are brought to a permanent end and return to the source of One-Mind. Thus, there is nothing that is not advocated and nothing that is not refuted. Wônhyo calls the advocacy concession or acceptance (hwanho), and he labels the refutation variously as deprivation (t'al), negation (kyon), return (wang) or prohibition (purho).

Wônhyo was particularly concerned with using his hermeneutic tools to reconcile the Madhyamika and Yogachara doctrines. In his view, Nagarjuna's Malamadhyamakasutra and Dvadaanikayasutra offer a thorough dialectic critique of all views which a person might advocate, to the extent that they abolish both the views refuted and the act of refutation. However, because Madhyamika dialectics do not affirmatively acknowledge both the subject and object of this refutation, the approach is purely negative, and thus nothing is established. On the other hand, the Yogachara school accomplishes a thorough analysis of all mental states and accordingly establishes both the shallow and profound teachings. However, because the Yogacharins do not continue on to refute what they have established, theirs is a purely positive approach, and thus, nothing is refuted. Doctrinal controversy arose between the two schools due to the fact that the Madhyamikas attached to refutation and deprivation, whereas the Yogacharins attached to establishment and acceptance. Each recognized only a part of the truth; although neither was entirely wrong, at the same time neither was altogether correct.

Wônhyo was able, based on his unique usage of unfolding and folding, to reconcile these differences by including them into a single Buddhist teaching, that of One-Mind, which allows for both affirmation and negation. According to Wônhyo, the Taesung kisillon, a noted Mahayana text upon which he based his well-known commentary, is a syncretic work which embraces the positions of both Madhyamika and Yogachara. He asserts that while it refutes all relative views, it also embraces them comprehensively within the all-encompassing One-Mind.

SILLA HWAÔM SCHOOL

Another vital contribution to Korean Buddhist thought was made by Ûisang (625-702), who was a contemporary of Wônhyo and is known as the founder of the Korean Hwaôm school (Huayan in Chinese) based on the Avatamsaka Sutra. Unlike Wônhyo, who had never been to China, Ûisang spent almost ten years there and studied under Zhiyan (602-68), the second patriarch of the Chinese Huayan school. The Hwaôm ilsung popke to (Diagram of the Dharmadhitu of the One Vehicle of Hwaôm) is Ûisang's only major extant work, and is comprised of his Haein sammae to (Diagram of Ocean Seal Samadhi) and an autocommentary.

The Ocean Seal, as it is commonly known, written while Ûisang was in China, is a poem consisting of 210 characters. It opens with the word pop (dharma) and closes with pul (Buddha), thus signifying the cause-and-effect relationship between the two. By placing both of these characters in the centre of a diagram in the form of a maze, Ûisang articulated the basic theme of Hwaom philosophy which asserts that beginning and end, or cause and effect, occupy the same position while still retaining their own distinctive characteristics. In this way, he depicted Hwaôm philosophy as a mystery of simultaneous mutual penetration. In addition, he pointed to the Hwaôm soteriological position that within the fifty-two stages of a bodhisattva's career, the first stage of initial faith itself embodies all fifty-two stages, including the final stage of marvellous enlightenment. Of this position, a well-known Hwaôm aphorism states, 'The moment one arouses an enlightenment thought (bodhicitta), instantly perfect enlightenment is attained.'

Although Ûisang's expression of Hwaôm theory in the Ocean Seal was not his own creation, it succeeded in ably representing the main ideas of the school, both symbolically and graphically. The Ocean Seal is traditionally presented to monks upon completion of their course of study, a mark of how highly esteemed it is in the Korean Buddhist tradition. It is also chanted in Korean Buddhist ceremonies as a dharana, having been endowed with a special mantric power. Along with

Wônhyo's philosophy of the reconciliation of opposites, Ûisang's contributions to Hwaôm theory helped to create the Korean tradition of t'ong pulgyo and provided the foundation for the synthesis of the doctrinal or scriptural schools (Kyo) and the meditational schools (Sôn) by Chinul in the following Koryô dynasty.

SILLA VIJÑANAVADA SCHOOL

There were actually three different systems of Yogachara (or Mind-Only) philosophy which were transmitted into Korea from China during the Unified Silla period. The first can actually be traced back to the Three Kingdoms period, when Won'gwang (d. 630) returned to Korea after studying the Mahayanasanùgraha (in Chinese, Shelun) in China. However, it was not until Wônch'uk (612-96) arrived on the scene that any significant study of Yogachara was undertaken in Korea. Wônch'uk is considered the major figure among Silla monks studying Yogachara doctrine. His system is classified as the Old Yogachara, founded by the Indian monk Paramartha (499-569). This is in order to distinguish it from the New Yogachara, which was founded by the Chinese monk Xuanzang (602-64). Xuanzang translated Dharmapala's Vijñaptimatrat siddhi into Chinese and his new school, which was established on the basis of this text, became known as the Faxiang (Dharma Characteristics) school.

The two Yogachara schools, Old and New, differed in their theoretical approaches and there were conflicts between them. Wônch'uk and his disciples eventually established their own school, called the Ximing school. This was followed by the Silla Vijñanavada school, which included such noted monks as Tojung and T'aehyon. Vijñanavada theory in Silla developed its own unique characteristics quite distinct from those of Xuanzang's school in China. The Silla school not only effected a synthesis of the various Vijñanavada schools in China, but it also adopted theories from other Chinese schools, such as Tientai and Huayan. It achieved this synthesis through its understanding of the term 'One Vehicle', an approach made possible by the work of Wônhyo. Like Wônhyo, the Silla Vijñanavada school attempted to reconcile the teaching of Madhyamika with that of Yogachara; but by using the concept of one sound as its reference point. Here, Wônch'uk was referring to the Buddha's teaching, which has one meaning but is given different explanations depending on one's level of understanding. Wônch'uk's concept of 'one sound' is, of course, comparable to the concept of the One Vehicle, as both are nothing but teaching devices used to comprehend various understandings from a higher vantage point.

INTRODUCTION OF SÔN

A new epoch occurred in Korean Buddhism upon the transmission of Sôn (Chan) Buddhism from China. This new movement, with its strong emphasis on meditational practice, entered Korea not long after it was introduced into China. According to traditional accounts, it was Pômnang (fl. 632-46) who first introduced Chan Buddhism to Korea, following his study under Daoxin (580-651), the fourth patriarch of the Chinese Chan school. His lineage was passed down through Sinhaeng, Chunbôm and Hyeûn until it reached Chisôn Tohon (824-82), who founded the Mount Huiyang school, the oldest Sôn lineage in Korea, in 879. Within a hundred-year period, from the eighth to the ninth centuries, eight other mountain schools were founded. From this time onwards, the term Nine Mountains has come to represent Korean Sôn schools in general, and this number remained unchanged during the early Koryô period.

In contrast to the Chinese Chan schools, which were categorized as the Five Schools and Seven Orders and which maintained sharp sectarian distinctions, the Korean Nine Mountain schools were classified according to the identities of their founders. Only a monk who had originally studied in China was entitled to be the founder of a new school. Furthermore, in the Korean tradition, the relation between teacher and disciple was considered more important than the philosophical doctrine espoused. This differed sharply from the Chinese Chan tradition, in which lineage affiliation was based directly on doctrine. The Korean approach was to regard what they called the Five Schools and Seven Orders not as different schools, but rather as different families of the same school. For this reason, the Nine Mountain schools, regardless of their founders, were all considered to belong to the Chogye order. The name Chogye (in Chinese, Zaoxi) was taken from the mountain associated with Huineng, who was regard as the progenitor of Chan before its division into five schools and seven orders.

Eight of Korea's nine mountain schools (the exception was the Mount Sumi school) were derived from or related to the Chinese Hongzhou school. As noted by Zongmi (780-841), the noted Chinese Buddhist commentator and philosopher, the Hongzhou school had a close doctrinal affiliation with Huayan. Most of the Korean monks who came to China to study Buddhism were already familiar with Hwaôm philosophy, as it was the predominant school in Korea at that time.

Therefore it is not surprising that they were attracted to the Hongzhou school. However, the fundamental difference between Huayan and Chan must not be overlooked: while the former emphasizes scriptural study, the latter rejects it, choosing rather to espouse 'a separate transmission outside the scriptures'. This crucial difference may also have attracted the Silla monks, who were perhaps frustrated with the philosophically elaborate and priest-centred Hwaôm school.

Immediately upon Sôn's introduction to Unified Silla, an antagonistic tension was created between the new Sôn and the old doctrinal schools, particularly Hwaôm. Sôn masters perceived the scripture-based Hwaôm school as antithetical to their practice-oriented mission. Later, however, they altered their approach in an effort to synthesize the messages of the two schools.

KORYÔ PERIOD (918-1392)

Upon the collapse of the Silla dynasty, the Korean peninsula reverted back to three kingdoms, until King T'aejo unified the country and subsequently founded the Koryô dynasty. Under the Koryô, Buddhism was fully supported not only by the royal family but by the entire apparatus of the Korean government. The price, however, was tight government control.

Despite these controls, discord between the radical Sôn schools and the more conservative doctrinal proponents continued, and it was not till Ûich'ôn (1055-1101) that a serious attempt was made to reconcile these conflicts. Although his background was in Hwaôm, Ûich'ôn studied various schools of Buddhist thought throughout his career. Most notably, he travelled to China in 1085 and studied with renowned teachers of the Huayan, Tientai, Pure Land, Vinaya and Chan sects there. Upon returning to Korea, he attempted to incorporate Sôn into the system of Tientai (in Korean, Ch'ônt'ae). He felt that meditation was essential not only for followers of Sôn but for members of all Buddhist schools, and he criticized the polarization of the two approaches, doctrinal and meditational. From his perspective, which favoured scriptural study yet also emphasized meditational practice, although dharma is devoid of words and appearances, it is not separate from them. Similarly, doctrinal study and meditation do not oppose each other but should be seen as complements; each is a requisite tool for the attainment of awakening.

Yet Ûich'ôn was unable to accept the radical doctrine of the Sôn of his time. He acknowledged the validity of Sôn only on the condition that it remained based on scriptural teachings. For him, the Sôn dictum of 'transmission outside the scriptures' was not acceptable as a valid Buddhist teaching. He believed that the practitioners of his time, by abandoning the scriptures, were veering dangerously towards heresy. He felt that his own kyogwan kyomsu, or 'parallel cultivation of doctrinal study and contemplation', was the correct approach. Viewing the system of Ch'ônt'ae as one which harmonized Sôn and scriptural study, Ûich'ôn attempted to consolidate the Sôn school into the Ch'ônt'ae order. However, he was unable to accomplish this, thanks not only to his early death, but also to of his narrow understanding of Sôn.

It was Chinul (1158-1210) who effectively assimilated Sôn into the mainstream Korean Buddhist tradition, if not in its entirety, at least in the area of doctrine. Chinul lived during one of the most difficult times in the history of Koryô Buddhism. Having become dependent on the support of the government, Koryô Buddhism had lost most, if not all, of its earlier spiritual vitality; corruption was at its peak and discipline in the monasteries was increasingly lax. Chinul perceived the Buddhism of his day as subject to 'ten kinds of disease', and his endeavours to effect a rapprochement between the Sôn and doctrinal schools were founded on his deep concern about this decline.

If Wônhyo's philosophy of harmonization was aimed at ending the doctrinal disputes among the various schools, Chinul's intent was to provide a theoretical scheme for harmonizing Sôn with the scriptural schools, and to offer a radical approach to the issue of final enlightenment based on the doctrinal teachings of Mahayana. He attempted ultimately to provide a systematic, theoretical framework which would incorporate both theory and experience. Being a Sôn monk, he was deeply aware that only through one's own experience can one attain final, ultimate liberation. The primary value of his theory, then, was that it clearly displayed an understanding of the necessity of practice.

Unlike Ûich'ôn, whose viewpoint was rooted in the doctrinal teachings, Chinul's foundation was in Sôn. His syncretic vision was therefore to establish a new Sôn school which would incorporate not only various teachings of the traditional Chan schools in China, but various doctrinal teachings as well. His primary intent was to systematize a comprehensive soteriological scheme for Sôn which would be pertinent to practitioners of various levels of capacity. He was inspired in this task by the great Chinese Buddhist thinker Zongmi, a patriarch of both the Huayan and the Heze school of Chan. Chinul, deeply frustrated with the deterioration of Sôn in his time, was especially attracted by the balanced approach of the Heze school, which encompassed both the intellectual understanding of the scriptural teachings and the radical, anti-intellectual spirit of Chan. Chinul's soteriological scheme of sudden enlightenment followed by gradual self-cultivation reflects the Heze approach.

In an inscription written by Kunsu Kim (fl. 1216-20), it is said that Chinul established three main approaches to Sôn practice, directly reflecting his own enlightenment experiences: the balanced practice of meditation and wisdom, inspired by the Platform Sutra (see Platform Sutra); faith and understanding according to the complete and sudden teachings, inspired by the Li Tongxuan's Exposition of the Huayanjing (Avatamsaka Sutra); and finally, the shortcut approach of hwadu (in Chinese, huatou) investigation. We can elucidate Chinul's philosophical system by examining these three approaches.

BALANCED CULTIVATION OF MEDITATION AND WISDOM

In his Susim kyol (Secrets on Cultivating the Mind), Chinul elucidates a method for cultivating the mind after a sudden, initial enlightenment experience. According to him, sudden enlightenment represents a realization of the nature of true mind as having two aspects: voidness and calmness in its essence, and numinous awareness in its function. These in turn correspond to the two aspects of dharma, immutability and adaptability. Mind is in its essence originally void and calm, and yet at the same time it adapts freely in infinite ways, depending on one's level of consciousness. Thus if one's consciousness is deluded, Mind appears ignorant, while if it is awakened, Mind manifests a numinous awareness.

In Chinul's system, gradual practice should follow after the sudden, initial awakening to the nature of True Mind. Chinul correlates the essence and function of Mind with meditation (samadhi) and wisdom (prajñ), respectively: in the task of cultivation, meditation is the essence and wisdom is the function of Mind; they are inseparable, nondual aspects of the same thing. This dynamic concept of the interrelationship of meditation and wisdom further entails that in cultivating Mind one should be alert in the void and calm mental state, and calm in the state of numinous awareness: calm and alertness represent meditation and wisdom, which are inseparable and nondual, and thus must be practiced simultaneously in cultivation.

Even if one attains a sudden awakening to the nature of Mind and thus realizes the identity of meditation and wisdom, the balanced cultivation of meditation and wisdom is still important: due to the residue of defilements and the karmic force deriving from long-standing habits, one's mind-nature does not always have its original harmony. The two nondual, inseparable aspects of mind, essence and function, can become bifurcated, as if they were two different, separate entities. An excess of essence can produce too much calmness, which in turn leads to dullness, while an excess of function can produce over-alertness, thereby easily causing distraction.

Since Chinul follows the sudden approach to enlightenment, in which enlightenment precedes cultivation, his interpretation of meditation and samadhi as essence and function differs from that of the gradual school of Sôn. In the latter, where practices are centred on the gradual removal of defilements in order to achieve perfect Buddhahood, meditation is used to counter the defilements in the conditioned realm, and wisdom is used thereafter to counter discriminative thinking. These two different methods are intended to ultimately achieve a penetrating insight into the nature of reality. However, although Chinul does not exclude the possibility that the gradual approach to meditation and wisdom may be used as an expedient means for counteracting defilements, he felt it should be allowed only after the experience of sudden awakening. In fact, Chinul urges that at all levels of practice, as well as at all stages of a practitioner's development, both meditation and wisdom should be combined, just as the principle of balance, that is, of calmness and alertness, must be maintained in order to access the enlightenment experience.

FAITH AND UNDERSTANDING ACCORDING TO THE COMPLETE AND SUDDEN TEACHING

More often than not, the doctrinal teachings based on scriptures were considered by Sôn masters as a grave fallacy, an impediment to attaining final enlightenment. From their perspective, this is especially true because the conceptual or discriminatory nature of doctrinal teachings cannot invoke the

Absolute, which is ineffable. On the other hand, Hwaôm, as one of the doctrinal schools, considered Sôn as merely representing the sudden teaching,-which they considered a lesser teaching than the final, complete doctrine of Hwaôm. These two main branches of Mahayana Buddhism thus seemed to contradict each other, not only in terms of doctrinal framework, but also in their soteriological schemes.

Chinul believed that Sôn and Hwaôm were not necessarily contradictory, but could serve to complement each other. He felt that the conceptual framework of Hwaôm could help to enhance practitioners' understanding, especially those with a lesser capacity, of the mind-to-mind transmission of the esoteric teachings of Sôn. He was especially concerned about the Sôn practitioners of his time, whom he felt had strayed from correct practice due to their lack of a proper understanding of scriptural teachings. He feared that they were meditating in a state of ignorance and thus in vain. Chinul felt that proper guidance in the scriptural teachings was necessary for them to achieve final enlightenment

However, it was not an easy task to synthesize the two, thanks to their different orientations. Hwaôm philosophy systemized the path to enlightenment into fifty-two stages, beginning with the ten levels of faith and ending with the stage of Buddhahood. Often a temporal scheme was assumed, such as a period of three incalculable aeons, or more than several lives, from the initial stage of faith to the final attainment of Buddhahood. Within this progressive scheme, Hwaôm soteriology postulated a process of learning, practice and realization, in which each stage proceeds sequentially in a causal relationship. Chinul thus incorporated the soteriology of Hwaôm, which assumes a progressive development within a temporal scheme, into the sudden teaching approach of Sôn. It was in Li Tongxuan's Exposition of the Avatamsaka Sutra that he found a means of incorporating the two systems into a viable soteriological scheme.

Inspired by Li Tongxuan's unique interpretation of the Huayan soteriological structure, and recapitulating the latter's essential message, Chinul was able to propose, as another possible approach to Sôn practice, the method of faith and understanding as detailed in his Wondon Songbullon (Complete and Sudden Attainment of Buddhahood). Chinul noted that unmoving wisdom, or the wisdom of universal brightness, is essentially identical with the deluded mind. Through a sudden awakening to this essential identity, one can enter directly the initial abiding stage, the stage of the arising of bodhicitta, in which one may directly experience the fact that one is a Buddha. From this stage onward, the subsequent stages of the bodhisattva path can be instantly achieved because of the functioning of inherent Buddhahood. Such a soteriological structure is possible due to the fact that unmoving wisdom is not merely a fruit to be attained at the final stage, but also a cause for the final attainment of buddhahood. Moreover, from the initial stage of faith to the final attainment of buddhahood, it is the unmoving wisdom of Buddha which operates unceasingly.

SHORTCUT APPROACH OF HWADU INVESTIGATION

Although Chinul incorporated the theoretical framework of Hwaôm into Sôn practice, he did not forget to indicate that theories and conceptual frameworks need to be abandoned at a certain stage. In their place, Chinul proposed his method of hwadu investigation, which is like a finger pointing to the moon. Chinul never lost sight of the fact that the goal of Sôn practice is to transcend conceptual understanding, thus leaving behind all discriminatory thoughts. As a means of achieving this goal Chinul found the investigation of hwadu most effective, a method, which in his words, cuts through iron and split nails.

Hwadu is often considered a synonym for kongan (in Chinese, gongan). More precisely, however, the hwadu is the essential point of the kongan, which is used as a topic of meditation in the Sôn school. The purpose of hwadu investigation is to help practitioners break through views based on their conceptual understanding of the dharma and to ultimately return them to the source of all discriminative thought. Thus, Chinul referred to the function of the hwadu as one of cleansing knowledge and understanding.

The hwadu method is also called the shortcut approach, as it involves no conceptual descriptions but rather points one directly to the truth right from the inception of practice. In his Kanhwa Kyorui Ron (Resolving Doubts About Observing the Hwadu), Chinul discusses the three mystery gates, or three different methods, differentiated according to one's capacity for attaining the ultimate teaching of the Sôn school: (1) the mystery of essence, which involves the conceptual understanding of the Buddha-dharma, such as the doctrine of the unimpeded interpenetration of all phenomena of the Hwaôm school; (2) the mystery of the word, which helps one eliminate the defects of conceptual understanding and ultimately destroy it; and (3) the mystery of mystery, in which practitioners abandon the interpretive analytical approach altogether and investigate the word itself. This method transcends any trace of a sign which a word may signify and finally results in the awareness of the noumenal state, that is, the void and calm state of mind.

In making hwadu the cardinal approach of Sôn practice, Chinul was influenced by Dahui Zonggao (1089-1163), a disciple of Yuanwu Gejin of the Linji school in China. Inspired by the Dahui yulu (The Records of Dahui), Chinul was the first Korean Sôn master to introduce the hwadu into Korean Sôn practice. Hwadu became a hallmark of Korean Sôn and, combined with the concurrent cultivation of meditation and wisdom, and the doctrine of sudden awakening and gradual practice, represents the essence of Korean Sôn.

In summary, Chinul systematized a Korean approach to Sôn practice which stood apart from all other schemes. Its uniqueness lay in the fact that it synthesized the doctrinal teachings into Sôn practice, provided a theoretical framework for Sôn practice, and maintained the fundamental spirit of Sôn teaching by postulating hwadu investigation as a shortcut to the final attainment of enlightenment. With only slight variations through the ages, this structure has been maintained by Korean Sôn practitioners ever since.

After Chinul's time, Koryô Buddhism began to gradually decline. This was primarily due to the political instability of the

Koryô court after the Mongol invasion, but it was caused in part by the corruption of the Buddhist monasteries and monks. However, there were still contributions made by such monks as Kyônghan Paegun (1290-1374), T'aego Pou (1301-82) and Naong Hyegûn (1320-76), who tried to restore the strength of Buddhism in the latter Koryô. All three had returned from Yuan China after studying under the Linji (in Korean, Imje) school, which places a strong emphasis on hwadu practice. The most radical and confrontational methods of the Linji school became very popular in Korea and had a great impact on Korean Sôn practice. However, due to the general social instability of the times, there was insufficient support for a sustained reinvigoration of Buddhism.

In this period of decline the Korean literati, whose official education was grounded in neo-Confucian philosophy, succeeded in supplanting Buddhism as a state-sponsored ideology (see Confucian philosophy, Korean). Chinese philosophies, such as Daoism and neo-Confucianism, became increasingly influential, and monks like Kyônghan and Naong began to study these schools of thought. This represents the beginning of another unique trend in Korean Buddhism, as monks began to emphasize the study of non-Buddhist philosophies. Korea became more and more Confucianized, first in a political sense and later throughout society as a whole. This move toward Confucianism began gradually in the latter period of Koryô and accelerated with the beginning of the Chosôn dynasty, which was founded in 1392.

CHOSÔN PERIOD (1392-1910)

The Chosôn dynasty was founded on the basis of neo-Confucianism, which combined a strong political ideology with a practical ethics emphasizing the importance of the family. Neo-Confucianism was strongly antagonistic towards Buddhism, as Buddhist monks left their families and maintained strict celibacy. During the Chosôn dynasty Buddhism was not only suppressed by those in political power but also largely ignored by intellectuals. In terms of social stratification, monks were ranked in the same class as the servants and were not allowed to enter the capital city. Amidst such harsh circumstances, Buddhism became completely marginalized.

The Buddhists of this period used their adverse circumstances as an opportunity to systematize a harmonized perspective which reconciled the philosophical conflicts among neo-Confucianism, Buddhism and Daoism (the three systems were often called samgyo or the Three Religions.) This synthesis in turn served once again to set Korean Buddhism apart as a unique system of thought.

Kihwa (1376-1433), otherwise known as Hamhô Tûkt'ong, continued the syncretic view of Korean Sôn systematized by Chinul, and was also the first Buddhist monk to advocate Buddhism against the neo-Confucian attack. He was also the first Buddhist monk to assert the intrinsic unity of the three religions, Buddhism, Confucianism and Daoism. Kihwa's life and times are reflected in his philosophical system. He was a prolific writer of Buddhist exegeses, in which he freely used Confucian concepts as well as citations from Confucian texts in order to clarify Buddhist ideas: he saw Buddhism and Confucianism as supplementary and not contradictory systems. He objected not only to the exclusivist attitude of Sôn practitioners toward the doctrinal schools, but also of Confucianism toward Buddhism. Before he studied Buddhism he was educated, like most sons from upperclass families, in the Confucian classics. He often used poetry, both from his own pen and from the classics, as a means of elucidating Buddhist texts.

His syncretic approach is well demonstrated in his Hyônjông non (Treatise on Manifesting Righteousness). In this apologetic essay on the unity of Buddhism and Confucianism, he not only defends Buddhism using the language of Confucians, but he goes one step further and advocates Buddhism using scriptural evidence from the Confucian classics. In this treatise, Kihwa identifies the various mental functions, which he termed usually as the arising of dharma, with emotions, often described as the obstruction of the true nature of mind in neo-Confucianism. In so doing, he is pointing out the similarities between Buddhism and Confucianism in the sense that both attempt to eliminate the arising of dharma or obstructions of the mind so that the true nature will be manifested. Buddhists call this the 'enlightened state', while Confucians call it 'being a saint'.

Kihwa stressed that in terms of the final goal there is no discrepancy between them, and in fact there exists an intrinsic unity between the two. Further, as the title Treatise on Manifesting Righteousness implies, Kihwa saw that both ultimately reveal the truth. He also demonstrated that Buddhist cultivation does not differ from the Confucian principle of cultivating the mind, step by step, beginning with cultivation of the personal life, continuing with regulation of the family and national order, and finally ending with world peace (see Daxue). Moreover, he claimed that the Buddhist teaching allowed people to pursue different levels of practice according to their capacity, from the bodhisattva path to the merit-making of ordinary people. With this, Kihwa intended to demonstrate the superiority of the Buddhist teaching, which in his view embraces a universality that includes all kinds of people, in contrast to the soteriology of Confucianism, which is often limited to the highly educated.

Regarding the social aspect of the two systems, Confucianism was often considered to be superior to Buddhism. Kihwa believed otherwise. He felt that the Confucian system, by using tactics of reward and punishment in governing the people, enforced a mere superficial obedience. In contrast, as Buddhism based its teachings on the law of cause and effect, and as it further propagated the value of silence through meditation, it promoted a more spontaneous response.

Kihwa also developed the issue of social ethics, including filial piety, the most important aspect of Confucian ethics, into the greater context of truth itself, which he termed to (in Chinese, dao), or the Way. He defined the Buddhist perspective of the truth, the Way, as consisting of two aspects, the unchangeable principle and temporary expediency. According to him, only by both maintaining principle and adapting to change through the use of expedients can one achieve completion of the Way. However, the formalistic and family-centred ethics of Confucianism cannot achieve both of these goals. Similary, he felt that one who is still subject to passions is not able to be loyal to the state and, at same time, to be filial at home.

Only when one becomes free from one's own passions and conceptual boundaries can one extend oneself to universal altruism, as represented in the Confucian concept of humanity, in (in Chinese, ren), or the great compassion of Buddhism. Residing in the mountains away from home is neither unfilial nor disloyal, but is a greater form of filial piety and loyalty to the state, unimpeded by any particular phenonema. The Buddhist aim of achieving an unimpeded state between principle and phenomena, as well as among phenomena, was focused not on leaving society or the world, but rather on realizing the perfection of society.

Unlike the fourth and fifth century Chinese apologetic defenses of Buddhism, Kihwa defended Buddhism more positively and often advocated its superiority. However, before he became a Buddhist he was well known as a promising young Confucian scholar. One of his biographical accounts tells us that his interest in Buddhism was motivated by the sudden death of a friend, and also by a monk who questioned him about the Confucian practice of encouraging people to serve their parents meat, yet espousing universal affection toward all living beings. As this account illustrates, his spiritual and intellectual quest was more concerned with ontological and soteriological issues.

Although he seems to have found some insight through Sôn meditation, his quest did not stop there, but further impelled him to discern an intrinsic unity among the various philosophical and religious teachings of his time. His pseudonym was Tûkt'ong, which means attainment of interpenetration; it is an apt title, as he diligently pursued this goal not merely in regard to Sôn and the Buddhist doctrinal teachings, but also in connection to all the existing teachings of his time. Dismissing the question as to which of the three teachings, Confucianism, Buddhism or Daoism, was superior, he instead felt that they were intrinsically identical. For Kihwa, the Daoist teachings of non-action and the Confucian teachings of being responsive but always calm were no different from the teaching of Sôn

Buddhism, which espouses being: 'Calm but always illuminating; illuminating but always calm.'

Wônhyo's synthesis of the various doctrinal disputes was succeeded and developed by Chinul's syncretic view attesting to the unity of Sôn and scriptural teaching; this in turn was followed by Kihwa's harmonization of the three religious teachings. This tradition of the syncretic perspective in Korean Buddhism was further developed by Hyujông (1520-1604), known as Sôsan Taesa (Great Master of the Western Mountain).

Hyujông was not only the central Buddhist figure during the Chosôn period, but also one of the most influential figures in the entire history of Korean Buddhism. He not only continued to propagate the syncretic perspective of the unity of Sôn and doctrinal teachings as formulated by Chinul, but he also attempted to reconcile the three teachings in terms of their ultimate message of truth.

By Hyujông's time, the various doctrinal schools had been reconfigured into one unified school, called Kyo, or scriptural teaching, while the Sôn schools were categorized under the single, unified name of Sôn. The conflict between Sôn and the doctrinal teachings still existed as an active point of controversy among Korean monks. As the titles of his major works, such as Sôn'ga kwigam (The Mirror of the Sôn school), Sôn'gyo sôk (An Interpretation of Sôn and Kyo) and Sôn'gyo kyôl (The Secret on Sôn and Kyo), illustrate, Hyujông's major concern was to reconcile Sôn and the scriptural teachings by incorporating the doctrinal schools into Sôn. While generally agreeing with Chinul's syncretic teachings, Hyujông contrasted Sôn practice more sharply with Kyo and ultimately espoused Sôn's supremacy. He felt that since the intrinsic unity of Sôn and Kyo had already been clarified by the efforts of Chinul, his mission was not to reassert this point, but rather to establish a correct relationship between the two in terms of the means of attaining ultimate enlightenment.

According to Hyujông, the source of both Sôn and Kyo are the Buddha, but one refers to his mind and the other to his words. Regarding the relation between Sôn and Kyo, he asserted that Kyo is what reaches wordlessness from the word, while Sôn is what reaches wordlessness from wordlessness itself. Wordlessness means here the true nature of mind or the enlightenment state which cannot be reached through any verbal, logical description. By saying that both Kyo and Sôn reach wordlessness, however, Hyujông did not mean that one can reach the ultimate state through Kyo.

Rather, he meant that Kyo, beginning with the word (that is, scriptural teaching), should be applied and then continued ultimately for the purpose of attaining the state of wordlessness. In other words, one may begin practice by studying Kyo, but in the process of attaining enlightenment, Kyo must be discarded and Sôn must be practised. This relation between Sôn and Kyo is well elaborated in his theory of sagyo ipson, the principle of abandoning Kyo and entering Sôn, which is still followed in present day Korean Buddhism. In this way, Hyujông acknowledged the efficacy of Kyo as a part of Buddhist practice, yet he also asserted the supremacy of Sôn practice by postulating the limitations of intellectual understanding. Thus, he refused to recognize the possibility of attaining enlightenment through the use of Kyo alone. Of course, not every practitioner needs to follow both Kyo and Sôn practices successively. According to Hyujông, the person of high capacity may not find it necessary to follow both practices, but the person of middle or low capacity cannot omit doctrinal study, Kyo.

In his other work, Samga Kwigam (Mirror of the Three Teachings), Hyujông's purpose was to demonstrate that all of the three East Asian intellectual traditions, Confucianism, Buddhism and Daoism, ultimately lead to the truth, to, or the Way. The intrinsic unity of the three teachings was first expostulated by his predecessor, Kihwa. However, while Kihwa's approach can be said to incorporate Confucianism and Daoism into Buddhism, especially Sôn Buddhism, and thus ultimately to advocate the superior position of the Buddhist teaching, Hyujông's approach was different. He shows us the core or the essentials of the three teachings, and by doing so he reveals the similarities among the three, although he does not ignore their differences. He felt that to espouse the superiority of one teaching over another was to be guilty of sectarianism. In interpreting each teaching of the three religions, he used a higher perspective to reconcile their minor differences into the greater context of their intrinsic unity.

His approach, the synthesis of discrepancies into a higher perspective, immediately reminds one of Wônhyo's method of kae (unfolding) and hap (folding): by unfolding discrepancies, the various functions of the truth are displayed, and by folding them, the discrepancies are reconciled into the essence of the truth itself. In the epilogue of the Samga Kwigam, he mentions that his intention is to provide a communication channel while overcoming the limits of sectarian views. He called the three teachings 'three gates', indicating his perception of them as different means of attaining the ultimate goal. This goal, which is the realization of the ultimate truth, has often been termed to, or the Way, in the East Asian tradition, and carries no sectarian connotation. To realize this to, one's mind-eye, or wisdom, is the key. Hyujông's all-inclusive spirit, which perpetuates the long syncretic tradition of Korean religious thought, continues to have a great impact on contemporary Korean Buddhism.

CONCLUSION

Since Buddhism was introduced into the Korean peninsula during the latter half of the fourth century, Korean Buddhism has undergone three major paradigm shifts. The first occurred as a response to Korea's indigenous belief system, which may be characterized as shamanistic animism; this period extends from Buddhism's incipient stage to the Three Kingdoms period. The second shift represents the Korean effort to understand various doctrines and corresponds to the Unified Silla and Koryô periods. The third shift involved the defense of Buddhism from the criticisms of neo-Confucianism during the Chosôn period. Each paradigm shift represented a Buddhist response to challenges from either within or outside itself; in this way, Korean Buddhist philosophy developed continually. The new understandings which occurred at each shift did not disappear with the next shift, but rather remained as integral aspects of the Korean Buddhist tradition. Buddhism's first challenge came from the indigenous shamanistic beliefs which had helped to consolidate the various tribes of the peninsula into unified kingdoms.

The Korean Buddhist response was hoguk pulgyo, or state-protection Buddhism. Lectures on Buddhist sutras as well as ceremonies to ensure national security were held regularly during the Koryô period. Even during the Chosôn period, when Buddhism was suppressed, the tradition of hoguk pulgyo continued in modified form as armed monks organized into armies to resist the Japanese invasion. Although the concept of hoguk pulgyo was never elaborated into a sophisticated philosophy, it is nevertheless a pervasive element in the development of Korean Buddhism.

In the second shift characterizing the Koreanization of Buddhism, both Wônhyo and Chinul played pivotal roles. By Wônhyo's time, the major Buddhist texts, as well as the doctrines of the numerous Chinese Buddhist schools, had been introduced to Korea. Wônhyo, using his own hermeneutics of kae (unfolding) and hap (folding), and his hwajaeng (reconciliation of disputes) theory, attempted to reconcile the various doctrinal disputes. In doing so, he neither accepted nor denied any one sectarian perspective. While refusing to accept any one particular doctrine as the whole truth, he recognized all doctrines as the unfolding of one mind, or the Buddha-nature. On the other hand, by 'folding' the various disputes, he synthesized them into a higher perspective of the truth.

This approach reflected the fundamental spirit of Korean Buddhism, which preferred to emphasize the similarities rather than the discrepancies among Buddhist schools and among other religions. Thus the primary characteristic of Korean Buddhism, t'ong pulgyo, the Buddhism of total interpenetration, began with Wônhyo. It was Chinul, during the Koryô period, who attempted to reconcile the disputes between Sôn and Hwaôm, the latter representing the scriptural tradition in Korean Buddhism. To establish a new approach to Sôn, he assimilated the theoretical framework of Hwaôm, long considered to be the anithesis of the Sôn approach.

The third shift came from the challenge of neo-Confuciansm, which became the new state ideology of the Chosôn dynasty. Kihwa, and later Hyujông, attempted to maintain the tradition of Chinul's syncretic approach to Sôn while at the same time creating the theoretical framework for the intrinsic unity of the three major intellectual traditions of Korea and all East Asia: Confucianism, Buddhism and Daoism. Continuing the approach, begun by Wônhyo and Chinul, of reconciling disputes by way of a higher perspective, Hyujông suggested that each of the three teachings is a gate leading to the same goal, that is, the to, or Way.

In the early twentieth century Korean Buddhists, together with the rest of their countrymen, suffered from colonization by Japan. During this time, from 1910 to 1945, many Korean Buddhist monks such as Master Yongsông (1864-1940), Master Hanyông (1870-1948) and, most notably, Master Manhae (1879-1944) became engaged in a variety of political activities. These worldly involvements, which pulled them away from their practice in the mountains, were undertaken in the bodhisattva spirit, that is, as a means of helping to directly alleviate the suffering of others. Due to their participation in these activities, philosophical study was also undermined. Those monks who wished to study Buddhism on a scholarly level travelled to Japan and enrolled in universities there.

Japanese Buddhists in turn left their own country for Europe and absorbed the Western perspective from such countries as England, Germany and France. They gradually incorporated this new knowledge into their previous systems of understanding, and in the process Japanese Buddhist philosophy was significantly altered. The Korean monks who visited Japan were exposed to this new perspective and dutifully introduced it to their fellow Buddhists upon returning to Korea. From this time also, Buddhism began to be taught in the universities. This period marks the beginning of a bifurcation between monks and scholars, the significance of which became increasingly reflected in Buddhist scholarship.

In the 1970s and 1980s the philosophical study of Buddhism began to re-appear with renewed interest and energy. This was due to both external and internal factors: externally, Korean Buddhism faced new challenges from the West, primarily in the forms of Christianity and Western philosophy, while internally, the division between monks and scholars had become even more pronounced. In the 1980s a debate arose among monks and scholars over the issue of 'sudden' versus 'gradual'. Although this debate centred around the age-old conflict between direct experience and intellectual understanding, and thus between Sôn and doctrinal schools, due to the above-mentioned influences the conflict has become a new focus for modern Korean Buddhist thought. The debate itself has become well known not only throughout Korea but internationally as well.

Yet to this day, no satisfactory resolution has been reached: some emphasize the importance of direct experience while others stress the necessity of intellectual understanding. Perhaps the conflict cannot be resolved, and this may be a reflection of our modern times. Yet what seems to be called for is a new methodology with which to consider the problem. The t'ong pulgyo's perspective is unique to Korea and has served well in the past. Can Korean Buddhists find another way to embrace the understanding which it signifies, or do they need to discover an altogether different means of confronting the issue, one that stands outside of t'ong pulgyo? The times are unique; certainly any approach towards resolving the difficulties must be unique as well.

7

Significance of Buddhist Philosophy

'Buddhist' = Peçuliar to or originated from the Teaching of the Buddha, in the manifold forms it assumes, all however relating back to the same fundaments.

It will be more difficult to give a definition or even a description of the term 'Philosophy'. It is however very clear that 'philosophy' in its Western (viz. Greco-Christian) context shows a different 'content' than that in the East (predominantly Indian and/or Chinese). From almost every definition of philosophy it goes to show that Western philosophy centers around the question of 'being', the 'first (or last) cause' and the 'absolute'. It tries to find an explanation, analyzes the experiential data and attempts to develop a dialectic around it.

Western philosophy then will be mainly concerned with metaphysics, and especially with ontological questions.

Another facet of Western philosophy (and mysticism) is that it places itself outside the realm of religion, even in those cases where its use lies in giving a coherent structure to religion (viz. Scholasticism).

In the East, philosophy endeavors towards a coherent scheme around which multiple soteriological practices can be weighed, evaluated and structured. The search here is not the search for an explanation (the why-question) but for an efficiency (the how-question). It is not so much the 'absolute truth' that counts, but the effectiveness of a given system or practice.

It is therefore not the question of 'being' but the question of 'knowledge and knowing' (epistemology versus ontology) (viz. Wisdom) that will be the center of philosophical thought in the East. There is the search for understanding the connections and inter-relationships between phenomena and the ability to express them. It is an attempt to translate the non-conceptual (meditative or mystical) into concepts and words, with the clear purpose of describing the salvific process or way to liberation (Enlightenment or Nirvana,...), without however confusing the 'description' with the 'described'.

Emphasis therefore is put on psychology and epistemology as the basis for the development of a soteriology.

Thus, there is no search for the 'absolute' as there is in the West, but an uninterrupted input of relativism and self-critique. It is therefore the religious aspect that is dominant, integrating both philosophy and mysticism. A non-religious philosophy, while characteristic for the West, is conceived as an impossibility in the Eastern context. Even Confucianism, with its initial rejection of all things supernatural takes into account the concept of Heaven (T'ien) and its Virtue (working or effectiveness).

A Buddhist 'philosophy' will make no exception to this rule.

FUNDAMENTS OF BUDDHISM

The basic principles of the Teaching of the Buddha are found within the Four Noble Truths:

1. The Universality of Suffering
2. The Cause of Suffering
3. The Cessation of Suffering
4. The Way that leads to the Cessation of Suffering

(1) and (2) are situated mainly on the psychological level of the world of experience. Both the 'inner' and 'outer' world are seen as nothing more than a representation of the mind. Our knowledge originates in the subject. Not the world is illusory, but the glasses through which I see the world makes that the world as it appears to me is an ego-illusion.

If one looks at the meaning of these Four Noble Truths, one comes to the conclusion that the first three Noble Truths point to a theoretical model in which (1) can be taken as consensual, generally acceptable and not necessarily Buddhist; while (2) and (3) are causal: (2) as the cause of suffering, and (3) as the cause of the cessation of suffering. Truth (4) on the contrary is typically Buddhist in its referral to a praxis. The concept 'suffering' is usually misinterpreted, due to a Christian or materialistic point of view. The term 'duhkha', although mostly translated as 'suffering' reaches much further than our ordinary conception of the term suffering: it implies not just our bodily or social torments or vexations, but also-and primarily so-our mental torments. Therefore duhkha would be better described as 'universal unsatisfactoriness' or 'dissatisfaction with the existing situation'. In a certain sense we can also consult philosophers from the West for possible 'better' translations of duhkha. John Locke 1 (1632-1704) speaks of 'uneasiness', thereby remarking that this is the basic feeling, the drive behind every thought or action of humanity. Also found are terms such as 'Unerfülltheit' etc. It is through the use of these, that the term 'suffering' can be taken out of its physical-material context. In a certain sense we could look upon the Buddhist concept of 'suffering' as being the interval, the distance between the existentially experienced and our expectations, on the one hand 'desire' and 'attachment', on the other hand fear:

Suffering here, does not belong to the sphere of salvation or enlightenment-as is often the case in other religions-, but is a characteristic of the existential world in which existence unfolds. This 'suffering' stands loose from the sphere of nirvana: this becomes clear although paradoxically expressed in the 'Heart-Sutra' ("Here, there is no suffering, no cause of suffering, no cessation of suffering, no path that leads to the cessation of suffering."). Duhkha indeed is one of the universal characteristics of that which exists, viz. the 'experienced'. As the locus typicus goes:

- All forms of existence are characterized by suffering;
- All forms of existence are characterized by impermanence;
- All elements of existence are characterized by non-self.

The distinction between 'forms of existence' and 'elements of existence' is of the utmost importance.

All 'things' or 'beings' are compound: these are the 'forms' that existence takes on. (samskara = compound).

This 'compound' is characterized by its composing elements or components (dharma = principle, basic principle, characteristic,...).

If one would use the example of computer science as a metaphor, one could picture a dharma as corresponding to a unit of communication (bit) or a unit of transmission (baud). Samskara than would correspond with a 'message' or 'data'.

Both samskara and dharma have in fact a multitude of meanings that are not always clearly distinguishable. The Monier-Monier Williams Sanskrit-English Dictionary for example gives the following lemma for 'samskara': "...the faculty of memory, mental impression or recollection, impression on the mind of acts done in a former state of existence. Buddh.: mental conformation or creation of the mind (such as that of the external world, regarded by it as real though actually non-existent...". In the Pali Text Society Dictionary on the other hand we read for the same lemma: "1. Aggregate of the conditions or essential properties of a given process or result e.g. the essentials or 'elements' of anything;-essential conditions, antecedents or synergy (co-ordinated activity), mental coefficients, requisite for act, speech, thought. 2. One of the five khandhas, or constitutional elements of physical life...".

'Suffering' is unavoidable since all 'things' are impermanent (not-remaining = Skt. anitya). This impermanence has given rise to a lot of esthetical expressions such as the inevitable withering of a flower, or morning dew, etc. Often this theme of impermanence is emotionally interpreted as the 'transitory nature of all things' through which a sense of doom is evoked, e.g. in poetry. Yet anitya should be understood as objectively neutral: if things where 'doomed' to perish or to disappear, than enlightenment would not be a possibility. Even impermanence can become a factor of enlightenment !

Besides this it is clear that every change in a 'subject' at the same time means a change in the experienced 'object'. In this way anitya in fact becomes a universal experience.

Things are impermanent because there can be no 'permanent' substance ('soul', 'atman', 'self', 'ego'). The 'elements of existence' (dharma)-and therefore also the 'forms of existence' which are composed by these elements-are 'self-less' (P. anatta). All that exists (the world of experience) is self-less, without self, without permanence, without absoluteness. This is the main criterion of the Teaching of the Buddha.

But: if there is no 'self', than who is it that suffers?

That which we call an 'individual', a 'personality', 'ego' or 'psyche', is in fact no more than a convergence of events, impulses, thought constructions, volitional actions, etc. In short, all that is conventionally understood under the term "mental activity". This collection (khandha, skandha) has no permanent substance or essence (atman). Just as no permanent 'house-entity' is found in a constructed house, in the same way no permanent 'entity' can be found within the different forms of existence including sentient beings. This compound nature of the forms of existence explains not only their impermanence but also their 'artificiality', their com-positeness (together + to put) (sam-skri), their polymer character.

The term 'samskara' has, as was mentioned before, a lot of meanings that can not be confused with one another. Each of these possible meanings however point to a compound nature, an aggregate; yet, the context in which the term is used can differ.

Therefore it is necessary to make a clear distinction between its different uses: e.g. samskara is used to denote the fourth of the five skandha's (aggregates) in which case the connotations of 'karma' and 'will or volition' will be determining. When it is used as the second link of the pratitya samutpada (dependent co-origination), the emphasis will be put on the dynamic that runs from a (past) volitional action towards its (future) result, the fruit which conditions a future mental situation. Every momentous 'being' is a compound of a series of ever-changing and impermanent aggregates called the 'five aggregates' (pañca-skandha).

- *rupa*: form, corporeality
- *vedana*: feeling, perception
- *samjña*: cognition, conception
- *samskara*: volition, karma-formations
- *vijñana*: consciousness, discrimination

How difficult it is to give a proper translation or even an approach of these terms becomes apparent from the multitude of (sometimes contradictory) translations.

Author	RUPA	VEDANA	SAMJNA	SAMSKARA	VIJNANA
S. Bernard-Thierry	corporeite	sensations	representations	formations	connaissance
Edgerton	physical form	feeling, sensation	notion, idea, conception	predispositions	(practical) knowledge
H.V. Guenther	expressive form	feeling	sensation	motivation	discrimination, psychological process, mentalism
H. Inagaki	matter, form	perception	conception	volition	consciousness
J.E.B.D.	forms of matter	perception	mental conceptions and ideas	volition	consciousness of mind
D. Kalupahana	material form	feeling	perception	dispositions	consciousness
M. Monier-Williams	bodily forms	sensation	perception	aggregates of formation	consciousness or thought faculty
Nyanatiloka MT	corporeality	feeling	perception	mental formations	consciousness
PTSD	material qualities	feeling	perception	coefficients of consciousness	consciousness
W. Rahula	matiere	sensations	perception	formations mentales	conscience, connaissance
C. Rhys-Davids	the seen-thing, body	feeling	perception	activities, planning	mind, survivor
Soothill (CSB)	form, sensuous quality	reception, feeling, sensation	thought, consciousness, perception	action, mental activity	cognition
D.T. Suzuki	material existence	perception, sensation	mental perception and ideas	volition and other related activities	consciousness of mind
J. Takakusu	form	perception	ideas/conception	volition	consciousness, mind
comparative psychology	'stimulus'	'response'	'conception'	'drives'	'learning'

These five skandha's are stages of perception, cognition and volition. They are NOT ontological elements. They give an approach of the mental process that is active in the 'psyche'. We thus can look upon them as psychological/epistemological elements.

It would therefore be wrong to consider each of these skandha's as an 'entity', a 'being'. Not only are they compound (ad infinitum), they also can not exist by themselves but only in relation to and in function of the other skandha's. They are therefore without substance and without autonomy, the two prerequisites for the so-called 'atman'. Thus there is no 'atman'. Or to state it more clearly: concentrating on or around the idea of an atman is (according to Buddhist thought) an inefficient thought-error. Buddhism in all its forms and aspects is an-atman (anatta): non-self.

This strict norm is the main criterion to separate things Buddhist from things non-Buddhist.

Further: the fivefold classification of the personality into skandha's and the twelve-fold classification of karmic existence (see later) are not a "scientific neurological or neuro-psychological" analysis and make no statements concerning an objective, anatomical reality. We are to look upon these classifications as empirical 'expedient means' (upaya) used to gain an insight into the process which leads from an 'existence characterized by suffering' (samsara) to a state of 'non-suffering' (nirvana). We are therefore clearly dealing with a soteriological methodology and not with mere psychological data or metaphysical statements.

The illusion to have or to be an atman-or even to take it into consideration-is the deep origin of suffering. Suffering comes to an end through the destruction of the atman-delusion (avidya = ignorance, mis-conception). This delusion leads to desire (trisna, P. tanha = thirst) and hatred (dosa = aversion), out of which the whole world of dissatisfaction or unsatisfactoriness, in short 'duhkha' comes into existence.

The term 'desire, thirst' should not be interpreted to narrow, in the sense of merely emotional or psychological. Desire encompasses 'all beings'. So for instance we could say that 'the heart desires to beat' seeing that this is the hearts necessary function. We can even speak of a certain 'cosmic' desire, e.g. as is seen in the mutual attraction of two masses (Newton's Law). Seen as such, desire is not only the motive or drive of the individual, it can also be transposed to a collectivity, yes even cosmically as the drive or the motive of the universe.

This all leads us to conclude that 'suffering' has its origin in 'desire', which in its turn has its source in 'ignorance'. To often however this is interpreted as "my suffering has its origin in my desire which in its turn finds its source in my ignorance". Such an expression leads to irrelevant questions concerning e.g. the suffering of innocent children. This mistaken shifting of emphasis is based on the input of the concept of 'mine' there where 'it' is meant. The reduction to individuality is in contradiction with the presupposition of anatman or 'no-self' and leads to a methodological incoherence. In our discussion of causality (next chapter) we should continuously take this into account with every step in our train of thought.

This makes that the Third and Fourth Noble Truths should consequently be interpreted in a purely soteriological and pragmatic (i.e. effective) way. A further consequence of the anatman-idea is than that all concepts, all ideas, all forms of thought are anatman, and therefore have no absolute or adequate sense, i.e. they can only be understood as being relative (i.e. in relation to). Further: anatman is also applied to anatman, meaning even anatman is relative: it is only a form of expression in which the content is relative, interchangeable, impermanent. From this the concept of 'emptiness' (sunyata) originated. However, also the concept of sunyata is a mere concept..... therefore..... Buddhist philosophy than will primarily be an epistemology, a philosophy of knowing and Buddhist soteriology will be a wisdom of knowing: seeing things as they are in se, in their emptiness, and not as they appear to our existential consciousness.

In relation to this we could mutatis mutandis point to an analogy with "Gestalt Psychology", which has phenomenological data (Gegebenheiten) as its basis. "We do not perceive the world as it is, but as we are." The 'perceiver' organizes his/her own world of experience out of or around his/her own attitude.

To give a structure or a soteriological efficiency to such "emptiness-thinking", we can make use of several keys or paradigms with which we can solve the apparent unacceptability's or paradoxes. Most used in relation hereto are:

(1) the logical tetralemma, which forms the basis of the Buddhist fourfold logic:

a. A is

b. A is not

c. A is, and is not

d. A neither is, nor is not

In which the final and definitive emphasis is put on (d.). Where paradoxes occur (e.g. in the question of self/no-self) the thought process should-if possible-extend to the fourth lemma (d.) i.e. "neither self, nor no-self".

(2) the threefold level in relation to 'person', based on a centrifugal perspective:

a. personal

b. transpersonal

c. impersonal

CAUSALITY

Causality is another important key-concept found within the Teaching of the Buddha. To understand it one needs to make a clear distinction between two forms of causal relations:

Hetu is the determinant 'root'-cause that acts as a necessitating force; a cause without which nothing can come to origination (causa necessitans).

Pratyaya (P. paccaya, Skr. also pratitya) is a conditioning circumstance, viz. a non-necessitating, but correlative inclining cause (conditio causalis). This cause is non-determinant and therefore leaves a chance for the expression of a 'free' (but in itself conditioned) will (cetana).

"Dependent Origination" (pratitya samutpada, P. paticca samuppada), literally "co-origination of causal conditioning" is worded as a conditioning and is therefore by no means deterministic. This has its repercussion on the Buddhist concept of karma: karma is neither deterministic nor fatalistic, but offers room for the conscious or unconscious volitional activity of man.

1. avidya	(avijja)	ignorance
2. samskara	(sankhara)	volitional activity, karma-formations
3. vijñana	(viññana)	consciousness
4. namarupa	(nama-rupa)	personality
5. sadayatana	(salayatana)	sense-functions
6. sparsa	(phassa)	contact, impulse
7. vedana	(vedana)	perception
8. trisna	(tanha)	desire
9. upadana	(upadana)	attachment
10. bhava	(bhava)	process of becoming
11. jati	(jati)	birth
12. jara-marana	(jara-marana)	aging and death

The stereotyped expression of Pratitya Samutpada is as followed:

"[...] By and large, Kaccayana, this world is supported by (takes as its object) a polarity, that of existence and non-existence. But when one sees the origination of the world as it actually is with right discernment, 'non-existence' with reference to the world does not occur to one. When one sees the cessation of the world as it actually is with right discernment, 'existence' with reference to the world does not occur to one. By and large, Kaccayana, this world is in bondage to attachments, clingings (sustenances), and biases. But one such

as this does not get involved with or cling to these attachments, clingings, fixations of awareness, biases or latent tendencies; nor is he resolved on 'my self'. He has no uncertainty or doubt that, when there is arising, only suffering is arising; and that when there is passing away, only suffering is passing away. In this, one's knowledge is independent of others. It is to this extend Kaccayana, that there is right view. 'Everything exists': that is one extreme. 'Everything doesn't exist': that is a second extreme. Avoiding these two extremes, the Tathagata teaches the Dhamma via the middle:

"From ignorance as a condition come karma formations;

From karma formations as a condition comes consciousness;

From consciousness as a condition comes personality;

From personality as a condition come the six senses;

From the six senses as a condition comes contact;

From contact as a condition comes perception;

From perception as a condition comes craving;

From craving as a condition comes attachment;

From attachment as a condition comes becoming;

From becoming as a condition comes birth;

From birth as a condition, then aging and death, sorrow, lamentation, pain, distress and despair come into play.

Such is the origination of this entire mass of stress and suffering." (SN, XXII 90-12)

The importance of this formulation is that there is no mentioning whatsoever of a permanent entity, of a concept such as atman, 'soul' or 'ego'. The unceasing individuation process that runs through Pratitya Samutpada is none else than the further-becoming or the further-flowing of the pañca-skandha.

The enumeration in addition has no chronological meaning but is a purely causal explanation of existential phenomena. One can therefore picture the 12 nidana's as arising simultaneous and/or overlapping one another.

One could also observe that the first six nidana's form an epistemological structure, while the six latter ones show existential characteristics. This clearly situates the relationship between the functioning of the 'mind' and its effect on 'existence'. In this sense it is understandable that the philosopher Nagarjuna concludes his discussion of the Pratitya Samutpada with upadana, attachment, which he views as the direct cause of suffering in the aspects of the process of becoming, birth, aging and death. After all, attachment has as its objects the five skandha's, which supply the building bricks for the experience of suffering. Hence the mentioning of the term 'pañcopadana-skandhah (P. e.g. Buddhaghosa: pañc' upadanakkhandha) literally the 'five aggregates of attachment', for the relationship that links upadana to the five skandha's. This relationship however also implies that the five skandha's are not only the object of attachment, but that through attachment these five aggregates are made into subject time and again.

The relationship 'ignorance-suffering-enlightenment' often reminds us of the metaphor of the cave, used by Plato to indicate the relationship between the world of shadows and the world of ideas. The beings in the cave, who only see the shadows, are then people chained to ignorance. If they could turn around towards the entrance of the cave, they would experience the light and true reality. But as it is with metaphors and parables, we should not infer to much from the cave-metaphor.

The great importance that Buddhism has laid on Pratitya Samutpada, becomes apparent from the multitude of text referrals which are intended to show that Dependent Origination forms the central core of the Teaching:

- He who sees pratitya samutpada, sees the Teaching; he who sees the Teaching, sees pratitya samutpada." (MN I, 191)

- He, monks, who sees pratitya samutpada, sees the Teaching; he who sees the Teaching, sees the Buddha." (Salistamba-sutra)
- Whoever perceives dependent arising also perceives suffering, its arising, its ceasing and the path [leading to its ceasing]." (Nagarjuna, MMK XXIV, 40)

DIVERSIFICATION

The diversification of the Buddhist streams-reaching several climaxes between the 2nd Century BCE and the 5th Century CE-did not so much result from schisms concerning the fundamental doctrines-such as the Four Noble Truths or the doctrine of Dependent Co-Origination-as from the additions of elements not mentioned by the Buddha, or even elements which the Buddha refused to discuss.

At first, these additions remained peripheral, later however they became more far-reaching and radical (e.g. in the Pudgalavada-tradition where the concept of anatta was 'bypassed'). The diversification on the philosophical level concerns mainly two themes:

- dharma: principle, supporting characteristic, basic element of cognition;
- buddha: as historical figure, as transcendental being, as cosmic principle.

It is and remains agreed upon however that both are in fact identical, and thus interchangeable: "He who sees the Buddha, sees the Teaching; and he who sees the Teaching sees the Buddha", the Buddha more than once proclaimed. (e.g. in SN, IV-120)

Broadly speaking however, it could be said that the 'dharma-theme' was more emphasized within circles of monks and philosophers, whereas the 'buddha-theme' (certainly at the outset) was more appealing to lay-people, preachers and artists-as is apparent from the oldest archeological Buddhist findings in India. Also a lot of the early 'biographical' literature, e.g. Lalitavistara, Jataka's and Buddhacarita, refers mainly to the exemplary function of the 'buddha-theme'. The diversification can (but therefore doesn't have to) happen by way of diverse, interactive points of view, coming from diverse angles, which will require us to look upon it in the light of a multidimensional complexity.

Apart then from disciplinary and/or soteriological problems, we can determine the following important points of view concerning the Teaching of the Buddha, without however being able to pinpoint in how far they are simultaneous or consecutive. Their chronology remains very uncertain.

Diversification According to the "Addressee"

In the scriptures of the different schools we see that the Buddha addresses a great diversity of social and spiritual categories of listeners, thereby each time adapting his use of language and terminology in function of the social and/or educational level of his audience.

Grosso modo we can reduce this to three main groups of listeners:

- the monks: with a strong emphasis on meditative states and levels;
- lay-people: mainly concerning ethical questions;
- the "specialists" (e.g. brahmins, sramana's, muni's, etc.): questions regarding worldview and metaphysics.

A strong and definitive demarcation between these three groups is however impossible, since the Teaching of the Buddha starts out with the anatta-criterion, a criterion that covers all further consequences.

Tensions between (1) and (2) have led to the first known 'schism' (during the so-called Second Council at Vaisali, be this historically correct or not...) whereby-for purely disciplinary reasons-the Elders (Sthaviravada) who strongly held to the letter of the Vinaya, parted with the Greater Community (Mahasanghika) which consisted for a great part, if not the majority, of lay-people. Tensions between (1) and (3) could have been the cause for the origination of the "pre-Mahayana".

Diversification According to Abhidharma

The Abhidharma (Pali: Abhidhamma) in its broadest meaning is the "Extended Teaching", viz. the systematically and philosophically structured envelopment of the actual soteriology. This later 'extension' differs strongly from school to school as becomes apparent from the transmitted Abhidharma-pitaka's. Certain schools even went as far as rejecting every form of Abhidharma. (e.g. Sautrantika)

The two extremes of this diversification according to importance given to, or rejection of the Abhidharma are:

- Buddhist 'Scholasticism', is most strongly represented by the Sarvastivada (e.g. their discussion concerning the dharma's, their classification, their existence and their time-value). Mostly practiced by monks and based on scriptural texts and commentaries. Leads towards abstraction and reduction to conceptual forms (e.g. buddha (buddhata)
- 'Devotion' and especially 'popular devotion', most strongly emphasized by the lay. Traces of this can be found back in the oldest Buddhist archeological monuments (e.g. Bharhut and Sanchi) and in the Edicts of Emperor Ashoka. Institutionally they are mostly represented in the Mahasanghika-stream (e.g. Lokottaravada, with its emphasis on the transcendence and the "deification" of the historical Buddha)

The synchronicity of diversifications A and B leads to new perspectives apart from the distinction between the Smaller Vehicle (Hinayana) and the Greater Vehicle (Mahayana). (Philosophically very artificial at first). The distinction between the two streams is in fact much more complex than conventionally presented. Many correlations and interactions have played an important role in this process.

Further we see an evolution in the thinking and living of the Teaching, in which the distinction between Smaller and Greater Vehicle has given way to the emphasis of either Buddha or Teaching (Dharma).

Diversification According to Dharma and Buddha

In connection to A and B we see the inclination towards an emphasis on either the expression of the Teaching or the 'person' of the Buddha:

Dharma: The historical Buddha is 'only' the bringer of the Teaching, which makes him 'subordinate' to the Teaching. This emphasis will be expressed the strongest in those currents that give importance to discussion and polemics, to scholasticism, ethichs and psychology, such as there are

- Sarvastivada and Theravada (i.e. Smaller Vehicle)
- The Prajñaparamita schools in India and China (i.e. Greater Vehicle) E. Conze uses the term "Wisdom-schools".

Buddha: The Teaching is the manifestation of Buddhahood, with its inherent, open to human experience, characteristics of Wisdom and Compassion. Here we notice however again a distinction between:

- Gautama Buddha as exclusive Buddha, be it as a historical figure or as manifestation of an "Eternal Buddha": e.g. Theravada (Smaller Vehicle); Lotus-sutra, Zen (Greater Vehicle).
- Non-historical (so-called 'meditative') Buddha-figures who assume a cosmic scale (up to present only Mahayana): e.g. Vairocana in Avatamsaka and Tantra; Amitabha in Sukhavativyuha.

We need to underline however that within this complexity the actual soteriology remains centered around the Four Noble Truths, of which the coherence should be looked upon as exclusively soteriological, certainly not ontological. Most 'additions' or 'extensions' are of a cognitive and explanatory nature. Within Mahayana philosophy they are regarded as 'expedient means' (upaya-kausalya), as are all forms of appearance of the Teaching.

NIRVANA

If there is one term in Buddhism that has given rise to a lot of confusion and misunderstanding, it must be nirvana.

Nirvana, "the Great Nothing or Void as Supreme Bliss", is such an image that has more become-from Schopenhauer until present-a western pseudo-myth than the central concept of Buddhist soteriology.

The negative appreciation of nirvana as destruction of existence is in fact the result of a dichotomous approach. Although it is true that nirvana is in a sense a negative expression, it must be said that that which is negated does not belong to the domain of ontology, not even the domain of general metaphysics. It is most certainly not a negation of "being", nor of "non-being". In Buddhism, 'being' and 'non-being' can neither be affirmed nor denied: they are concepts that do not belong into the soteriology. Sakyamuni Buddha himself classified questions of this nature in the category of theoretical irrelevancies.

The sense of nirvana therefore must be searched for within another domain. Time and again, the Buddha-and many masters after him-has emphasized that nirvana should be approached and interpreted in an (in a certain sense) epistemological, and primarily in a pragmatic-soteriological sense.

If we look at the etymology of the term we find that nirvana is a compound of the prefix ni[r]-(ni, nis, nih) which means "out, away from, without", and the root vâ[na] (P. vâti) which can be translated as "blowing" as in "blowing of the wind", but also as "smelling, etc"

The compound 'nirvâna' therefore undeniably has the meaning of "blowing out, putting out, extinguishing (of a lamp or of fire), setting (of the sun)". Used as an adjective it can mean "quiet, stilled, tamed, departed". MMW adds to this lemma that for Buddhists and Jains the term means "the absolute extinction or annihilation of individual existence or of all desires and passions". Nirvana thus means the "settling of the wind, the extinguishing of the fire". As a medical term it is also used as "stopping of the fever or stress".

Although all Buddhist schools in a way agree on this basic meaning of the term, diverse interpretations and connotations appear. Grosso modo we can make a distinction in interpretations between those of the Hinayana (especially the Sautrantika and Sarvastivada schools) and those of the Mahayana schools.

The Smaller Vehicle sees nirvana primarily-and almost exclusively-as an ethical event, attainable in this life (at least in theory) through the practice of morality, contemplation and insight. It is only within the Abhidharma-literature that the meaning of nirvana will somehow extend to a certain realm of existence of passionlessness, peace, etc.

Such an approach must necessarily lead to a strictly negative formulation, e.g. that of Udana viii. There, nirvana is described as the realization of the fourth proposition of the logical tetralemma: "neither [this]....nor [not this]....", with by the way a truly Nagarjunian sense for expression.

This negative formulation will be less the case in Mahayana-texts. Often, nirvana is here equated with sunyata (emptiness), which-one should keep in mind-for a Buddhist is a positive term, equivalent to 'availability' and even-especially in later Mahayana-'totality'. Nirvana in this sense can be approached in a positive way as 'Enlightenment' (bodhi), Buddhahood (buddhata), etc.

The situation becomes more clear when nirvana is in the first place seen as the opposite of samsara: the world of suffering as the cycle of birth-and-death. Since samsara is in a sense "propelled" by karma-formations (volitional activity conditioned by desire, aversion and delusion), nirvana means-as the opposite of samsara-the halting of these (causative) karmic formations and therefore also the exhaustion of their karmic 'fruit' (results of volitional actions). The realization of nirvana is therefore the cessation of the karma-causality.

Mostly the commentators agree when it comes to the 'attributes' that can be ascribed to nirvana, this despite the fact that they-paradoxically enough-keep stressing that nirvana is "inconceivable, unthinkable, indescribable'. So, it is said that nirvana is the 'unconditioned' (asamkrita), peaceful (santa), unarisen (anutpada), etc.

Moreover distinctions were made between a 'temporal, created nirvana' (nirvana seen from the human condition, and therefore as a relative truth), and the 'perfect, definitive, uncreated nirvana' which belongs to the experience of ultimate (absolute) truth.

Or, a distinction is created between a 'place bound' nirvana (pratisthita-nirvana), which is realized in this existence and with this present body, and the 'nirvana of no-abode' (apratisthita-nirvana). Only this nirvana is complete as the realization of Buddhahood.

D.T.Suzuki (in his translation of the Kyogyoshinsho, note 90) says that nirvana "....is the annihilation of the notion of ego-substance and of all the desires that arise from this erroneous conception. But this represents the negative side of the doctrine, and its positive side consists in universal love or sympathy (karuna) for all beings."

Nirvana then is not an 'individual' event or state, but the cessation of every illusion or conceptual form of (individual) personality. The Lotus Sutra states: "But he (the Buddha) does not teach a particular Nirvana for each being; he causes all beings to reach complete Nirvana by means of the complete Nirvana of the Tathagata."

Among the Buddhist philosophers there were-and still are-those who held/hold different, sometimes diverging opinions concerning the nature of nirvana. Yet, there remains a unanimity concerning the 'nirvanic' nature of the cessation of the condition of suffering. Remarkable however is the fact that it is exactly the European Buddhologists (among whom we find names as de la Vallée-Poussin and Theodore Stcherbatsky) who have started the polemics on the subject.

RELATIONSHIP HINAYANA/MAHAYANA

Taking into account the different diversification criteria, we can conclude that the Smaller Vehicle (Hinayana) and the Larger Vehicle (Mahayana) have (1) a lot of themes in common and (2) that they overlap each other on a number of topics. It should be noticed here however that to look upon these two streams as 'whole units', viz. completed and closed-off systems, is a fiction.

1. A lot of the so-called 'typical' Mahayana doctrinal points appear in the Pali-Canon, which is seen without a doubt as the Hinayana document par excellence. A great number of these doctrinal points are found in the oldest layers of the Pali-Canon and cannot be taken to be later interpolations.
2. Another remarkable fact is that within Indian Buddhism there rarely is any mention (not until very late) of separate Mahayana communities. Apparently the monks of the divers streams lived among one another, following more or less the same Vinaya rules. Witness to this are the writings of the pilgrim monk Hsüan-chuang (600-664) who gives a detailed description of the situation of Buddhism in India. There is therefore no reason to speak of a 'schism' in the Christian sense of the word. It is impossible, given the present archeological research, where India is concerned to draw a sharp demarcation line between the two streams. It is only in China that the institutional separation of Hinayana/Mahayana becomes truly noticeable.

Also remarkable is that, on the doctrinal level, we notice an evolution (or better yet, an extension) of the original anatta-teaching. With the transmission of the term from Hinayana to Mahayana, we notice that the emphasis on its non-ontological character is preserved, whereas the dualism between self/non-self is transcended in the sense of the logical tetralemma (viz. the fourth lemma 'neither-nor').

At first, the term 'Mahayana' did not have the implication of being sectarian or schismatic, but it referred to a 'different approach' of the salvific problem.

The adjective maha(n)t, in compounds 'maha', does not just mean 'great', but also 'broad' or 'large'. It is exactly this meaning that lies at the basis for the term 'Mahayana': the 'broad or large vehicle'.

In this sense 'Mahayana' points primarily to a soteriology that is 'broader' [than for monks alone]; namely, that there is also a possibility for salvation outside of the strict observance of the Vinaya rules or the monastic discipline. The 'Way' (or path, Skt. Marga, Ch. Tao) is 'Broad' ! It is in this sense that the term appears, probably for the first time, in Asvaghosha's "Mahayana-sraddhotpada-sastra" 1(The Awakening of Faith in the Mahayana).

In a somewhat later evolution, the Mahayana evolves towards a stronger contrast in regards to the 'Smaller Vehicle', which emphasizes the effort towards individual salvation "Diligently strive towards your own salvation". In contradistinction to this the Mahayana posits "the salvation of all beings, regardless their numbers". This will go as far as the Mahayana accusing the 'Smaller Vehicle' of mere self-concern and a lack of compassion.2

This polemic will appear most clearly in the controversy Arhant/Bodhisattva as the proposed ideal set to be followed by the 'adept'.

Arahant (P.)-Arhant (Skr.)

It is stated that the adept meditator has to transgress four stages on his way to enlightenment:

- sotapanna: the 'stream-enterer'
- sakadagami: the 'once-returner'
- anagami: the 'none-returner'
- arahant: the 'praiseworthy' or the 'holy one'

The arahant, the final stage of this evolution, is the one who is no longer subject to the cycle of birth-and-death. By overcoming the fundamental ignorance he has become desireless and has been freed of every ego-illusion. Because he gives no more rise to desire, no more karma-formations (volitions, acts of will) arise and he is no longer reborn.

He has reached this state through his own efforts by practicing the Dharma, the Vinaya and the "Four Levels of

Meditation" (P. jhana; Skt. dhyana). When he experiences suffering as a result of past karma, there is no more mental reaction against this suffering in him. He lives in a state of 'emotional non-reaction'3, equanimity an invulnerability, a state to which every being should strive.

This ideal state is difficult to describe, and even more difficult to realize. The subject in any case brought along a lot of discussion within the different Hinayana-schools (e.g. concerning the question whether the Arahant can 'regress' to a lower state or not).

In the Mahayana-schools the Arahant-ideal was mostly the subject of sharp attacks. He was blamed for working exclusively towards his own salvation. It is true that he functions as an example and that in this way he arouses the desire in others to walk the same way, but besides this he is inactive. He sits alone in a 'small vehicle' and lacks the element of Compassion.

Difference between Arahant/Buddha

- The arahant needs the Teachings (Dharma) set forth by the Buddha, whereas the Buddha discovered the Dharma.
- The arahant puts the Teachings into practice, whereas the Buddha established the practice.
- The arahant has put an end to the causes of suffering, but is not necessarily capable of transmitting this experience to others; whereas the Buddha necessarily shares his experience with others.
- The arahant has a passive knowledge (jñana) of the Teaching, but lacks Wisdom (prajña); whereas the Buddha has (is) active Wisdom.
- The arahant misses compassion (karuna); whereas the Buddha has (is) Great Compassion (maha-karuna).

Pratyekabuddha (P. paccekabuddha)

At a certain moment, another distinction between a Buddha or 'Sammasambuddha' versus a 'pratyekabuddha' is introduced.

A pratyekabuddha or a 'solitary Buddha' discovers the Teaching by himself, and fathoms its Wisdom, but he dies without having proclaimed it (viz. the Compassion-element) to others. A lot of interpretations concerning the pratyekabuddha are possible ! (e.g. the possibility of enlightened beings outside the realm of Buddhism).

Bodhisattva (P. bodhisatta)

Enlightenment-being-Being towards Enlightenment-Being focused on Enlightenment.

This term is difficult to translate, even more difficult to describe.

Evolution of the Term

The term bodhisatta is already found in the Pali Canon, be it with a limited meaning: Bodhisatta is Siddharta Gautama before he realized Enlightenment. Therefore we see two phases in his biography: bodhisatta before, and Buddha after his Enlightenment.

Therefore Bodhisattva is the stage that precedes Enlightenment; however, the way of the arahant excludes Perfect Enlightenment (sammasambodhi). The arahant realizes Complete and Final Nirvana5 at the moment of his death, not being reborn again he does not pass through the stages of the bodhisattva. The way of the bodhisattva leads towards Enlightenment; not just his own enlightenment, but the Enlightenment of all beings indiscriminately.

In the Mahasanghika-school a more liberal interpretation of the bodhisattva-idea will come to light and gradually the ideal of the bodhisattva will become the Mahayana counterpart of the arahant ideal in the Hinayana. The bodhisattva is a 'being' that refuses to remain (some would say 'enter') in Nirvana because of its vow to help others; the bodhisattva chooses to remain in the world of suffering and rejects Complete and Final Nirvana (in the sense as stated before).

This will become the 'leitmotiv' for Mahayana Thought: the bodhisattva chooses Enlightenment for himself and all other beings over his own, individual Enlightenment (cfr. the anatta-doctrine). Besides this, every being (and therefore every human being) has within itself a conscious or unconscious drive towards Enlightenment: the Mind of Enlightenment (bodhicitta), through which it has the potential to realize the bodhisattva within itself.

Different 'Kinds' of Bodhisattva's

It doesn't hold to classify bodhisattva's into different 'kinds' or 'categories'. If we do so, than it is exclusively with the intention to smoothen the approach of the problem. Because, every distinction lies exactly within the approach. So it goes that the Buddha-characteristics of Wisdom and Compassion in se are not different, and yet we experience them as two separate characteristics. It is important to keep in mind that the bodhisattva does not have a separate existence; he is mainly an ideal-projection of-and in-our mind.

BODHISATTVA-MAHASATTVA

The "Great Being Bodhisattva's" traditionally number about 10. They are in fact manifestations of a Buddha 'quality'. The two most important 'qualities' we ascribe to a Buddha are 'Wisdom' (prajña) and 'Compassion' (karuna). Thus we see two kinds of manifestations:

'Wisdom Bodhisattva's' such as Mañjusri (cognitive wisdom) or Mahasthamaprapta (intuitive or emotional wisdom). The Wisdom Bodhisattva's have multiplied almost infinite in number, especially in Tibetan Buddhism.

'Compassion Bodhisattva's' such as Avalokitesvara (the most popular, spread over the divers Buddhist cultures, very important in popular devotion); Samantabhadra (active compassion); Maitreya (the Peaceful, Buddha of the future).

'Human' Bodhisattvas

Since all beings have bodhicitta within them, human beings are also potential bodhisattva's. Here we distance ourselves from the metaphysical structure of the term and emphasize more the emotional element: every human being can be bodhisattva in the perception of every other human being. In this way a human relationship can through the capacity of wisdom and compassion rise above ordinary human standards.

Some typological examples:

* The sages and teachers that brought new insights to the Teaching and thus brought human beings closer to Enlightenment, are often called bodhisattva. E.g. we speak of the philosopher Nagarjuna as Nagarjuna Bodhisattva.
* A strong, spiritually colored relationship through which a normal human relationship is elevated towards a higher level. E.g. Shinran Shonin (1173-1262) saw in his wife Eshin-ni the embodiment of Kannon Bosatsu (Avalokitesvara Bodhisattva). On the other hand, Eshin-ni, after Shinran's death mentioned in a letter to her daughter Kakushin-ni, that-although she had never told him-she always was convinced of the fact that Shinran was an embodiment of that same Kannon Bosatsu.
* Meritorious people who have made a continuous effort for the spiritual, mental and physical welfare of other people are at times-by way of silent consensus-titled as bodhisattva's. E.g. In Hiroshima's Peace Park there is a sober almost inconspicuous monument in memory of a doctor who died of the effect of radiation, after treating other victims of the atomic bomb for 3 or 4 days. The inscription calls him 'bosatsu' (bodhisattva).

This 'seeing' of a bodhisattva in another human being is a religious act.

The 'Cosmos' as Bodhisattva

When all beings can become bodhisattva, the term bodhisattva will gain an strong expansion. So the feeling of interaction will arise through which all beings out of their true nature are inclined to bring all beings to Enlightenment. Through contact with all beings, any being can experience the Teaching of the Buddha.

From the limited understanding of 'bodhisattva as manifestation of Buddhahood' we will arrive to the embracing of the totality of human occurrences and from there to the embracing of the totality of existence in all its manifest forms. All beings and things participate in each others bodhisattvahood. Certainly in Chinese Buddhism this thought has found a vivid expression, maybe through interaction with Taoism.

DIFFERENCE BUDDHAHOOD/BODHISATTVA

Buddhahood surpasses the existential and is related to 'true nature': availability, totality, sunyata.

The bodhisattva stands in relative existence and is subject to anatta. He has no objective 'being'. He is the existential reflection of Enlightenment; he outlines and objectivates Enlightenment in this relative, relational existence. Besides this he offers man a kind of spiritual ideal, in which man can project him/herself as a being on the way to Enlightenment.

His function, both in Buddhist popular devotion as in the doctrinal development and experience, is therefore not to be underestimated. But also in the personal, intimate approach of the Dharma, the bodhisattva-on whatever level he is situated-is an important element.

MADHYAMAKA AND NAGARJUNA

The philosopher Nagarjuna is the first Buddhist thinker with a vision that transcends the "theological" i.e. the Abhidharmic. He implements the convergence of the various Mahayana-streams and unites them in one coherent system, without neglecting elements from Hinayana-literature.

The starting point of his philosophy is the return to the main tenets of the Teaching as they were proclaimed by Gautama Buddha, thereby thoroughly rejecting the Abhidharmic elaboration. His basic point of view is-just as the historical Buddha's view-mainly empirical, epistemological and not ontological (as e.g. De la Vallee Poussin and partially also Stcherbatsky had claimed), emphasizing the 4th lemma of the Logical Tetralemma (see before), by which it obtains a negative aspect. His point of view is that the Mahayana-acquisitions continue the original themes of the Middle Way (Madhyamaka is the equivalent of Madhyama-pratipad).

Biography: Legend has made itself master of Nagarjuna's biography and is therefore highly unreliable. He is supposed to have lived during the 2nd or 3rd century, as a Brahmin or the son of a Brahmin, in the Middle and/or Southern India. It is even suspected that several "Nagarjuna's" are processed in the legend. Nagarjuna ('snake-white') is a very common name in India.

Works: A great number of works are attributed to Nagarjuna, but textual criticism (already in India, China and Tibet) has rejected the authorship by Nagarjuna of several of these works.

According to the latest research results1 the following works could be authentic:

Mula-madyamika-karika

Sunyata-saptati

Vaidalya-prakarana

Catuh-stava

Suhrillekha

Yukti-sastika

Vigraha-vyavartani

Ratnavali

Pratitya-samutpada-hridaya

Sutrasamuccaya

Some important other works attributed to Nagarjuna are less certain, e.g. Maha-prajñaparamita-sastra and Dasabhumika-vibhasa. All other works are unanimously considered to be inauthentic.

Controversy: Nagarjuna, Hinayana or Mahayana?

Nagarjuna reverts to what he sees as the original teaching of the Buddha, and certainly not to the 'Hinayana'-developments of it. It is by means of original data that he systematizes the pre-Mahayana and Mahayana themes and that he refutes the propositions characteristic for the Sarvastivada and Sautrantika-schools.

We can thus determine notable differences between Nagarjuna and the traditional Hinayana doctrines. So, e.g. Nagarjuna emphasizes sunyata (emptiness) over anatmya (P. anatta-non-self); he posits dharma-sunyata instead of dharma-svabhava (Sarvastivada) and pudgala-sunyata (Sarvastivada, Sautrantika, Theravada).

Yet, it is claimed by some that Nagarjuna is not a "factual Mahayanist" (Warder), or even that he is a Theravadin (Kalupahana). Against these opinions we can bring up the following arguments:

1. The presupposition that only the Pali-canon reflects the 'original' Teaching of the Buddha cannot be maintained. The final redaction of that Canon dates from Buddhaghosa, ± 2 centuries after Nagarjuna.
2. Kalupahana's argument that in MMK only the Katyayanavada is mentioned as a reference; and that this agama appears in the Pali-canon as Kaccayanagotta-sutta, is not convincing, since that same text is also found in the Chinese ("Mahayna") canon.
3. Kalupahana states that "Assuming that Nagarjuna was a Mahayanist and, therefore, must have rejected any literature that came to be preserved by the Sthaviravadins,...). This is contrary to the reality that Mahayana has integrally absorbed the Hinayana-texts into its own scriptural canons.
4. Nagarjuna introduces-also in his MMK-themes that are completely strange to both the Pali-canon and the Hinayana-tradition, e.g. upaya (expedient means) or the Three Levels of Truth with the impossibility to attain absolute truth by way of discursive thought.
5. The traditional transmission within Hinayana rejects the propositions of Nagarjuna (not withstanding the

influence they had on their teachings); in Mahayana on the other hand, Nagarjuna is looked upon as the 'second Buddha' who "set the Wheel of the Dharma in motion for the second time." In some cases Nagarjuna was even deified!

6. We should not take MMK out of the context of other undeniably Nagarjunian works, but should recognize their mutual interrelation.

Nagarjuna is without doubt the systematizer of the Mahayana and the starting point of Mahayana philosophy. This is probably why J. Takakusu in his 'Essentials of Buddhist Philosophy' describes Madhyamaka as 'Quasi-Mahayana'.

It is generally accepted that Nagarjuna was especially inspired by the Prajñaparamita literature. This is undeniably so, but also a link with the Avatamsaka way of thinking can not be denied. Typically 'Nagarjunian' sayings can often be found in the Garland-Sutra, e.g.:

"Samsara and nirvana are both ungraspable. Deceiving teachers preach a difference between samsara and nirvana." Or,

"The bodhisattva clearly sees that all existence has only a non-self nature and therefore he understands that it is completely empty and without substance. There is neither body, nor is there no-body, neither thought nor no-thought. There is neither being nor no-being. The entire existence is without possession and without being. It is neither being nor no-being."

One cannot get more 'Nagarjunian' than this...

Emptiness, Concepts and the knowledge of Truth.

Already the historical Buddha stated that:

all forms of existence are characterized by unsatisfactoriness;

all forms of existence are characterized by impermanence;

all elements of existence are characterized by non-self.

Within the existential experience we can therefore not speak of permanent or autonomous values.

But how then should we interpret this existential experience?

In Buddhist terms this is samsara, the 'world of suffering'. 'To exist' is what each separate being perceives for itself. Existence is that which takes place-again for each separate being-between the moment that has passed and the moment that is not yet here, i.e. the transitional process from past (karma = the acts of the past) towards future (phala = karmic results). The present therefore is always a 'becoming'. This 'becoming' is none other than pratitya samutpada, namely, a process of causal conditions.

That which is 'true' therefore remains beyond being (permanence) and non-being (annihilation).

Nagarjuna consequently extends this train of thought.

He calls this 'neither being nor non-being' sunyata (emptiness). Emptiness is not a negative concept (as in 'nothing'), but affirms the possibility, in function of eventual relational conditions, of manifesting all imaginable characteristics.

Since all that is knowable (the phenomenal world) is 'empty', also all our knowing which is made relative by the relation (subject/object) is 'empty'. We reduce the perception into elementary concepts (dharmas), who in their turn can be again regarded as cognitive objects. Nagarjuna stresses the 'emptiness' of each dharma on every level of our cognitive abilities.

Concepts (dharmas) are empty, i.e. without substance. Our discursive thought, which uses language to attach concepts to what is perceived, is therefore irrelevant when it comes to adequately knowing reality in-itself, i.e. independent from perception.

The only thing that can be said with sense, is that all experience and expression of that experience, is 'emptiness'. 'Emptiness' is, where our powers of cognition are concerned, the only reality that all things (subjects and objects) have in common.

But also this concept of 'emptiness' is 'empty' and in the final analysis irrelevant-yet, it remains the ultimate point of what is expressible.

Conceptual thought is necessarily dualistic since-when reduced to its simplest expression-it can only exists in the mutual relationship of a 'conceiver' (as subject) and a 'concept' (as object). Neither 'conceiver' nor 'concept' can be regarded as separate entities. By way of discursive thought, which works with concepts and their language expressions, we therefore can never go beyond what is relative (or relational).

Here, Nagarjuna manifests himself clearly as an empirical epistemologist. He comes to the conclusion that there are three levels of truth. The first two are mutually related and form a bivalence: something is untrue/something is true. Which gives us:

1. asatya-untruth (lie or mistake), e.g. "a hare has horns"
2. loka-samvriti-satya-'world speech truth', 'relative truth', e.g. "a hare does not have horns" the third level of truth is non-conceptual:
3. paramartha-satya-'ultimate truth, absolute truth'. Since this third level can neither be conceptual nor discursive, it is a truth which is inconceivable and inexpressible.

Traditionally these three levels of truth are illustrated by the metaphor of the snake:

At dusk a man walks along a path in the forest. Suddenly on the road in front of him he sees a snake. He is terrified and runs off. Next morning he walks the same path and discovers that what he took to be a snake is, in broad daylight, just a rope.

1. the perceived 'snake' is untruth
2. the 'snake that is a rope' is a relative truth.

   Nagarjuna adds to this that both 'rope' and 'snake' are only concepts and concludes:
3. in 'absolute truth' there exist neither snake nor rope, only the empty concepts of them.

Concepts that are untruth, belong to the world of ego-illusion (aham iti = I am) and are characterized by ego-thought: subject 'untrue' object 'untrue'

Concepts that are relative truth, are forms of expression from a non-ego perspective. They are 'true' in the system in which they appear: subject 'untrue' object 'true'

Concepts can never be 'absolute truth', since on this level every duality falls away. Every knowledge of absolute truth therefore has to be non-conceptual i.e. 'im-mediate' (without mediator)

In the forms of mediate knowledge, which makes use of ideas, thoughts, words, etc., things are only knowable as concepts, i.e. within the relations in which they appear. Subject and object are reducible to dharmas, thus, 'emptiness' is the only 'true' nature we can attribute to them.

Where there is dualism present, the "true nature of things" or "true reality" remains beyond knowing; the "knower"-at best-remains at the level of relative truth.

Some examples of dualisms or dichotomies: good/evil, creator/creation, the Enlightened One/the foolish being, transcendent/immanent, suffering/joy, duality/unity, samsara/nirvana.

Applied in relation to the Buddhist teachings this gives:

- untruth: adharma, the non-teaching
- relative truth: buddhadharma, the teaching as it was proclaimed by the historical Buddha Sakyamuni.
- absolute truth: saddharma, the Teaching seen beyond time and space.

What then, is the relation between the Four Noble Truths and the levels of truth established by Nagarjuna?

To the level of relative truth belong the first two Noble Truths (Suffering and the Cause of Suffering), since they take place on the samsaric level. They form as it where the transition from (a) to (b) and their result is relative knowledge (jñana: knowledge).

To the level of absolute truth belong the last two Noble Truths (Cessation of Suffering, and the Noble Eightfold Path), since they take place on the nirvanic oriented level. They form as it where the transition from (b) to (c), and their result is absolute knowledge (sarvajña: omniscience or prajña: wisdom).

We can note here that each of these transitions is nothing else than a process of dependent causation, which takes place according to the paradigm which is pratitya-samutpada.

Nagarjuna's point of departure is clearly negating. The introductory verses to his MMK e.g. are (from the Sanskrit Version):

> *"I salute him, the fully enlightened, the best of speakers, who preached the non-ceasing and the non-arising, the non-annihilation and the non-permanence, the non-identity and the non-difference, the non-appearance and the non-disappearance, the dependent arising, the appeasement of obsessions and the auspicious."*

The Chinese translation of the introductory verses by Kumarajiva is even more powerful, and is known as the Eight Negations.

No Arising,

No Extinction,

No Annihilation,

No Permanence,

No Unity

No Diversity,

No Coming,

No Going.

NAGARJUNA AND BUDDHIST SOTERIOLOGY

Nagarjuna's thought reflects itself mainly on the soteriology. For, only this is truly important to the being subject to suffering, impermanence and delusion. In a nutshell we can say that Nagarjuna-just as the historical Buddha-was before all an empiricist and a pragmatic, whose goal it is to free man from [wrong] views.

The problem of conceptual dualism and the rejection of it has several consequences:

> *It is not through conceptual, discursive thought that Enlightenment can be realized. Intellectuality (including philosophy...) cannot offer a perspective on Enlightenment; only direct or immediate experience, among others on the meditative level, whereby the activity of the ego-forming consciousness (manas) is neutralized, offers access to absolute truth, which in turn stands for nirvana.*

Good and evil are dualistic, i.e. relative concepts which can only be used on the level of relative truth. Salvation or Liberation lies beyond these concepts. Nagarjuna here emphasizes the subordinate function of morality and moral discipline (sila) in relation to the soteriology. He however underlines the input of concepts as 'wholesome' (kusala) and 'unwholesome' (akusala), certainly on the level of relative truth, as actions that are carried by the karmic law. This law stands in function of volition. In this perspective the pairs 'good' (punya) / 'wholesome' (kusala) and 'evil' (papa) / 'unwholesome' (akusala) are only 'expedient means' (upaya kausalya).

In the end, even samsara and nirvana are only concepts and therefore only applicable on a relative level, e.g. in relation to each other or in relation to the situation of the suffering being. Seen from the 'absolute', they are both sunyata, both with the identical characteristic of emptiness. Their difference resides in the wisdom-approach. As is stated in the MMK, XXV.19-205

> *There is no difference at all*
>
> *Between Nirvana and Samsara,*
>
> *There is no difference at all*
>
> *Between Samsara and Nirvana.*
>
> *What makes the limit of Nirvana*

Is also then the limit of Samsara.
Between the two we cannot find
The slightest shade of difference.

Should therefore be seen in its proper context of MMK, XXV.23-24:

What is identity, and what is difference?
What is eternity what non-eternity?
What means eternity and non-eternity together?
What means negation of both issues?
The bliss consists in the cessation of all thought,
In the quiescence of Plurality.
No (separate) Reality was preached at all,
Nowhere and none by Buddha.

The difference and/or equality that we ascribe to samsara and nirvana are thus in no way to be interpreted as an ontological difference, as if this world of suffering would be different or identical to the world of enlightenment. Difference and/or equality are empirical, epistemological statements: we regard an eventual 'objective' world only through experiential data. Discriminating between, and conceptualizing about samsara and nirvana are therefore constructions of our consciousness and thus only valid on the level of relative truth.

Nagarjuna has prevented that Buddhism would end up as a static teaching. That risk was real, e.g. in the Sarvastivada school with its leaning towards scholasticism. Also, through relativating philosophical and even soteriological concepts (ideas) he has opened, from an originally a-metaphysical Buddhism, a way towards a wider-and in a certain sense even a metaphysical-research, even towards a so-called horizontal mysticism.

Through the rejection of all dogmatic interpretations he offers the Mahayana the possibility of numerous non-conflicting ways as long as they remain relative 'worldly speaking' expressions of a "inconceivable, unthinkable and inexpressible

Teaching". It is therefore only fair that Nagarjuna is looked upon as a founder and patriarch by almost all Mahayana and Vajrayana schools, be it sometimes for quite different sayings from the Master.

It probably happens that an exclusively negativistic view is ascribed to Nagarjuna. This is however countered by his stand in relation to the possibilities that man is offered towards the realization of Enlightenment. Because what Nagarjuna has refuted in the first place is the possibility of realizing Enlightenment by way of conceptual thought.

Opposite to that however he puts the so-called Three Gates towards Liberation (trini vimoksa-mukhani, Ch. san-chieh-t'o-men, J. sangedatsumon), namely the meditations on:

- emptiness (sunyata, Ch. k'ung, ku)
- the non-substantiality of phenomena, their signlessness (animitta, Ch. wu-hsiang, J. muso)
- the undesirability of things (apranihita, Ch. wu-yüan, J. mugan), i.e. the being-free of desire and meaning.

In this way Nagarjuna gives his philosophy a positive direction, even when this is aimed against conventional, worldly 'knowledge'. We could look for analogies in Lao-tzu.

MADHYAMAKA AFTER NAGARJUNA

Nagarjuna's way of thought was undoubtedly a great influence and has been carried on by a great number of philosophers after him. Thus it could be said that his philosophy (together with the Prajñaparamita-literature and the Lankavatara-sutra) has laid the foundation for the later Ch'an-schools, be it however with a strong influence from Taoism and Yogacara-thought. Yet, the impact of Nagarjuna goes further, and it is no miracle that he is recognized as a patriarch in practically all Mahayana-schools.

In the 5th century Madhyamaka was split up in two currents who each attempted to represent the 'true' Madhyamaka. It is undeniable that also the blooming of Buddhist Logic-e.g. Dinnaga7-was unthinkable without the impulse given by

Nagarjuna. The two schools in which the Madhyamaka was divided are:

Svatantrika: 'School of the Independent Grounds', most known representative is Bhavaviveka (6th century). 'Svatantra' refers to a more positive position: the negations characteristic for Nagarjuna are exclusively the refutation of wrongly held views. The pratitya-samutpada is the middle position between affirmation and negation.

Prasangika: 'Teaching of the Undesired Outcome'. The origin of this school is attributed to Buddhapalita (5th century), but its most important exponent is without doubt Candrakirti (6th-7th century), also the most famous commentator on MMK. According to him Nagarjuna aimed at a polemic reductio ad absurdum, a demonstration that each statement, each conclusion must lead to the falling away of any/every presupposition. Emphasis is put on the pratitya samutpada as the proces of the origin of suffering. Often this school is associated with 'radical empiricism'. It is this current that has had the most success in China (thanks to Kumarajiva 344-413 and Chi-tsang 549-623). To this day it remains the dominating philosophy of the Tibetan Gelug-pa.

But also outside of Buddhism Madhyamaka had a great influence:

- on Hinduism, and especially on the 'New Vedanta' (Nava-Vedanta) of Sankara (8th-9th century). Even a century earlier a certain Gaudapada was accused by Kumarila, a Mimansa-master, of conceding too much to Buddhism. Ramanuja (± 1050-1137), the main exponent of theistic Vedanta, accused even Sankara of being a crypto-Buddhist...
- More recent however we can note the great interest of present-day philosophers and physicists for Madhyamaka. In this way, Nagarjuna had no small influence on existentialists such as Karl Jaspers and Martin Heidegger, or theoretical physicists such as Heisenberg and Schrodinger.

Yogachara and Vasubandhu

Yogachara: Teaching in Discipline Vijñanavada: Path of Consciousness Also the name Vijñapti-matratā is sometimes used: "System of Consciousness-Only". This name was mainly used in China (Wei-shih) and in Japan (Yuishiki).

This current follows both chronologically and logically on Madhyamaka.

Nagarjuna postulated the double negation: negation even of negation. Religiously seen this is an attitude which is difficult to manage, since it forces the adept to go to the most extreme possibilities of his (everyday) thought. Opposite this conceptually negativistic attitude of Nagarjuna, one will however keep on striving (empirically) towards something affirmative. It was thus to be expected that there would follow a psychological reaction against the philosophical negation.

This however is not a step back; only a shifting towards an empirically more understandable realm: from the 4th lemma back towards the 3rd lemma, in the form of "being and non-being".

The Yogacara will then not systematically refute Nagarjuna, but on the contrary, will apply some of his thought to come to a stage where a positive formulation becomes possible and useable.

Yogacara, just as Madhyamaka, accepts the impossibility of an adequate formulation of an 'absolute' truth. On the other hand however we have to our disposal the use of cognitive elements (whether they are objectively-realistic or subjectively-idealistic...). This presupposes that we have cognitive experiences, even if these are limited by the limits of our consciousness. And it is within this consciousness that logical and critical inquiry belong to the possibilities.

A clear sign of this idea we find for example in Dhammapada (I, 1-2):

"Everything (all dharmas) has mind in the lead, has mind as a forerunner, is made by mind (...)"

The Lankavatara Sutra (of which the date of origin is not clear, but which was already translated in Chinese by Gunabhadra in the 5th Century) is one of the texts on which Yogacara-philosophy will be based. The first figure that in a certain way can be related to the Mind-Only School is Asvaghosa in his work 'The Arising of Faith in the Mahayana' (Mahayana-sraddha-utpada).

The definitive formation of the school however rests with Asanga, in his 'Clarification of the Teachings of the Mahayana' (Mahayana-sutra-lamkara) and his 'Exposition on the Stages of the Practice of Discipline' (Yogacara-bhumi-sastra').

It is his brother, Vasubandhu, who firstly from a Hinayana point of view (Sautrantika, and not Sarvastivada as is sometimes claimed) wrote the impressive Abhidharma-kosa-bhasya ('The Treasury of the Abhidharma'), but later went on to the Mahayana-thought of his brother and than wrote the Vimsatika-vijñapti-matrata-siddhi ('The Exposition on Consciousness-Only in 20 volumes') and the Trimsika-vijñapti-matrata-siddhi ('The Exposition on Consciousness-Only in 30 volumes').

The two brothers, Asanga and Vasubandhu, are dated somewhere between 280 and 500 (?) CE.

Starting Point: It is a fact that we cannot 'know' in an absolute way, but even our relative thought presupposes an 'instrument of thought'. This 'thought-instrument' is called vijñana, mostly-but unjustly-translated as 'consciousness'. This 'consciousness' is therefore the only reality that is undisputable.

To situate the concept of 'vijñana' more clearly, we have to take into account the etymology of the word. The prefix "vi-" points to separation (according to MMW vi = *dvi = two), to discrimination or distinction, and sometimes it even has a meaning opposite to the thought expressed in the word that follows it. The Lankavatara-Sutra describes it as "The cutting of the whole in its parts and than applying a selection to it". It becomes clear that we have to approach the term 'consciousness' with great reserve. This will certainly be the case in the compounds of vijñana in the sense that they are used by the Yogacara.

Every progress in mind-concentration (i.e. a 'single-mindedness') is an approaching of absolute reality.

Things are nothing but convergences of perception. Consciousness is the ability to take in sense-impressions and by sifting through them come to the formation of concepts. The activity of consciousness has its origin in a beginningless drive. All skandhas and sense-functions (ayatanas) are reducible to vijñana.

Being-in-itself is denied, but not so the possibility of introspection.

The accepting of the reality of vijñana is by the way an empirical necessity, for without consciousness the universe would fall into a state of complete 'blindness' (not 'blinding'!), and every form of knowledge-even of wrong or relative knowledge-would be impossible.

Only vijñana exists and functions and is knowable; its 'objects' ('consciousness-content') however are delusional through the working of ego-activity. The point concerning the objective 'being' of the world outside of the experiencing consciousness however was never stated very clearly, neither by Asanga nor by Vasubandhu. The Hindu Nava-Vedanta will extend this point in deciding that the world outside of consciousness is a total illusion (maya).

The Structure of 'Consciousness'

First we have to remind that vijñana only partly corresponds to what we call 'consciousness'. The compound vijñana does after all point to a 'split knowing'. As a technical term, vijñana applies to all stages or phases that modern psychology categorizes as 'sub-consciousness', 'waking-consciousness', 'dream-consciousness', 'ego-consciousness', 'supra-consciousness', etc.

Thereby comes that according to the context, vijñana can both relate to 'consciousness as a function or organ'; or/and as the 'actual consciousness-content'. Buddhism then sees different stages in what is called 'consciousness':

1. In function of the 'object', we can make a distinction according to the five skandhas (see previous):

rupa-vijñana	corporeal consciousness consciousness of corporeality
vedana-vijñana	perceptive consciousness consciousness of perception
samjña-vijñana	cognitive consciousness consciousness of cognition
samskara-vijñana	volitional consciousness consciousness of volition
vijñana-vijñana	centripetal consciousness consciousness of consciousness

2. it is however more common to integrate the first 4 skandhas in the 5th skandha (vijñana), i.e. to interpret consciousness in function of the 'sources' (organs, 'gates' to the external world). In this sense, vijñana comprises the whole of the consciousness-content:

   - *caksur-vijñana*: eye-consciousness or visual consciousness, the consciousness that stores and recalls visual images.
   - *srota-vijñana*: ear-consciousness or auditory consciousness, the consciousness that stores and recalls sound images.
   - *ghrana-vijñana*: nose-consciousness or olfactory consciousness, the consciousness that stores and recalls images of smell.
   - *jihva-vijñana*: tongue-consciousness or gustatory consciousness, the consciousness that stores and recalls images of taste.

- *kaya-vijñana*: body-consciousness or sensual consciousness, the consciousness that stores and recalls images of touch.

  Besides these there is also a sixth ('mental') sense:

- *mano-vijñana*: thought-consciousness or intellect, the consciousness of psychic formations which also includes the psychic activities of vedana (perception); samjña (cognition); and samskara (volition).

Mano-vijñana than functions as the centralizing factor for thought and experience, but not without the interaction (feed-back) with the other consciousness aspects. This stage of consciousness is the working of discursive, conceptual, discriminative thought, which not only processes data from the 'outside' according to a 'manas' program, but which also continuously adds its 'own interpretation' to this experiential data.

We can thus ask ourselves in how far our consciousness-content accords to 'objective reality'.

The Vijñanavada answer to this is negative. Mano-vijñana encloses the mind within itself. Only that which is in the mind is knowable, but the mind is enclosed within its own limits and therefore can only come to a knowledge of what is within its consciousness-content.

The term vijñapti-matrata literally means: "being non more or less than information".

In this context we can search for an analogy with the empirical idealism of e.g. Locke, Berkeley and Hume. Yet, we should not to easily come to the conclusion of an identity of vision. Once more, we should point out the fact that the Empiricists' conclusion ends up on the level of metaphysics there where the Buddhist Yogacara's conclusion is situated on the level of epistemology and soteriology.

Asanga and Vasubandhu will in their writings consequently extend the classical Buddhist structure of 'consciousness'. In this way the intellect (mano-vijñana) will lead towards self-reflection (vijñana-vijñana), i.e. the knowing subject will look upon itself as the knowledge-object.

The personality experience that culminates through this in our consciousness is nothing other than the consciousness of 'being ourself'.

This is where the fundamental 'error' known as avidya (wrong-knowing, ignorance) is situated: the consciousness of consciousness is interpreted as 'being-ourselves'.

Out of this distortion originates manas, the 7th form of consciousness, that function of the mind by which we experience the nama-rupa (viz. 5 skandhas) as an atman, a permanent entity that constitutes our "self-ness".

Manas is therefore the source of ego-thought (aham-kara), of the "I am" illusion (asmi-maya). In relation to modern psychology the manas-activity will be mainly situated in the sub-conscious, which makes it so difficult to point to or to fathom.

Manas is different from mano-vijñana because it is 'stained' by discrimination. It is then a 'sense' which is more discriminating and thought-constructive than intellectually perceptive; because of this manas is the source of ego-centeredness and individualisation, and from there also the source of all illusion arising necessarily from the thought-error that appearance is reality (or in Buddhist terms "to take the unreal to be real").

Skandha-vijñana-Forms of consciousness in function of object

1. rupa	rupa-vijñana	consciousness related to corporeality
2. vedana	vedana-vijñana	consciousness related to perception
3. samjña	samjña-vijñana	consciousness related to cognition
4. samskara	samskara-vijñana	consciousness related to volition
5. vijñana	vijñana- vijñana	consciousness related to consciousness

Forms of consciousness in function of "gate"

1. caksur-vijñana	eye-consciousness	visual consciousness
2. srota-vijanana	ear-consciousness	auditory consciousness
3. ghrana-vijñana	nose-consciousness	olfactory consciousness
4. jihva-vijñana	tongue-consciousness	gustatory consciousness
5. kaya-vijñana	body-consciousness	sensual consciousness
6. mano-vijñana	thought-consciousness	psychic forms of consciousness
7. manas	ego-forming consciousness	
8. alaya-vijñana	storehouse consciousness	'collective unconscious'

Summary Tabel

1. RUPA	2. VEDANA	3. SAMJNA	4. SAMSKARA	5. VIJNANA	
A. Eye	A1	A2	A3	A4	Visual Consciousness
B. Ear	B1	B2	B3	B4	Auditory Consciousness
C. Nose	C1	C2	C3	C4	Olfactory Consciousness
D. Tongue	D1	D2	D3	D4	Gustative Consciousness
E. Skin	E1	E2	E3	E4	Sensual Consciousness
F. Mind	F1	F2	F3	F4	Mano-Vijnana
Vijnana	Rupa Vijnana	Vedana Vijnana	Samjna Vijnana	Samskara Vijnana	Vijnana Vijnana
					MANAS

In reality manas is only the individualization-process that originates in the storehouse consciousness (alaya-vijñana) through the working of karmic activity. This is the impersonal, unconscious consciousness (cfr. Jung's Collective Unconscious) which is part of the experiential consciousness that stands outside of the individualization-process, and should be looked upon as beyond our knowing. It stretches across and beyond all manas-boundaries, it is common to all beings and that which constitutes their only true nature. Therefore we could also call it the "Cosmic or Universal Consciousness".

A great part of Vasubandhu's writings strives towards an approaching description of alaya-vijñana as a stage of consciousness in which there is no distinct ego-thought present.

The most clearly is comparing it to a boundless ocean:

Alaya-vijñana is the endlessly vast and deep water in which the karmic formations float as 'seeds' (bija), which form the potential for karmic results (vipaka); the surface of the ocean is moved by the 'wind' of the Karmic Law, which forms waves; each of these formed waves is 'manas'; but just as a wave (which has only local, i.e. relative movement) this manas has no selfness...it is a momentous (ksanika) form of appearance of a dynamic.

Manas is therefore an ego-differentiated and differentiating aspect of alaya-vijñana, just as a wave appears to be distinct from the great ocean. The bijas are 'perfumed', i.e. they receive impressions through knowing and acting, through which they are manifested within the karmic process, i.e. they take on form in manas; this leaning towards formation of karmic results lays the 'seeds' in a 'seedbed', from which they 'spring' at the 'appropriate moment', i.e. when a causal condition (hetu pratyaya) creates the possibility for it to arise.

There are those bijas that are present from time immemorial (the so-called 'primal or original' bijas), and there are those that are newly acquired, which are re-perfumed, i.e. re-activated. Both kinds together create all manifestations of the existential delusion and are therefore cause of the 'defilements'.

But, there is also an 'unstained seed', that through sprouting and growing absorbs and suppresses the delusional and bewitching nature of alaya-vijñana and so leads towards ultimate enlightenment. This unstained seed is none other than Buddha-nature. When this seed has transformed the totality of alaya-vijñana into Buddha-nature (= Enlightenment !), there arises-at least according to the later Vijñanavadins-a 9th form of consciousness: the 'Stainless Consciousness' (amala-vijñana), which is identical to Suchness (tathata). Once alaya-vijñana is freed of itș defilements related to its content, it becomes the source of Buddhahood: the "Womb of the Tathagatas" (Tathagatagarbha).

A lot of commentators and authors have attempted to describe the nature of this 'storehouse-consciousness'. As the basis from which all bijas of consciousness spring. As the container-intellect; as the basic consciousness seen as totality of both the absolute and the relative, impersonal and personal; as the fundamental mind-consciousness of sentient beings who as it where confiscate all experiences of individual existence; as the seedbed of all events; as the root of all experience, i.e. of the skandhas on which all beings are dependent for their conscious existence; as the source of the cycle of birth-and-death, etc. Each of these descriptions are at the same time right and wrong.

Concerning the complexity of 'consciousness' and 'total-consciousness' we could refer to the holographic model of consciousness in the holistic theory developed by e.g. John R. Battista.

THE THREE TRUTHS

Following Nagarjuna the Yogacara also knows a threefold structure of truth, viz. untruth, relative truth and absolute truth. Nagarjuna, however, did not show a lot of interest in the relative truth, since this is merely situated on the level of conceptual thought. Yogacara on the other hand thinks that it is exactly through this relative truth that the possibility exists to arrive at the absolute truth.

This absolute truth is called parinispanna by Asanga: the complete fulfillment, not subjected to impermanence.

The relative truth (samvriti), also called laukika-satya or worldly truth' by Dharmapala (439-507), is however subdivided in:

- parikalpita (established in the mind, imagined): purely subjective, without self-existence, yet empirically experienced as truth, however by the yogin recognized as untrue since it is not-adequate, i.e. leading towards enlightenment.
- paratantra (dependent on other things): resulting from causality (hetu-pratyaya), what arises and is recognized as the subject/object dichotomy; "the manifestation is in fact untrue, but that which causes the manifestation is true". From there also the connotation of 'consensual truth', i.e. a truth which is valid within a certain 'consensus', a certain 'system of coordinates'.

Absolute truth stands beyond every subject/object dichotomy and is therefore subjectless and objectless (= emptiness). Paratantra is the overlapping of parinispanna by an infecting parikalpita. By removing this infection from paratantra, parinispanna is realized.

We can mention here that this teaching of Three Truths (Trayasatya) has given rise to the formation of a full-grown Buddhist Logic.

TRIKAYA: THE THREEFOLD BUDDHABODY

The three levels of truth reflect in the three 'body' forms of Buddhahood.

At first Buddhism knew of two so-called 'Buddha-bodies':

- buddhakaya: the corporeal manifestation form of the historical Buddha.
- dharmakaya: the spiritual message as it was proclaimed by the Buddha.

Slowly these concepts developed however, e.g. through the abstraction procedure in the Sarvastiva, and through the import of the concept "Eternal Buddha" (e.g. in the Lotus Sutra).

Asanga states in his Mahayanasutra-lankara and in his Mahayana-samgraha that a threefold body can be attributed to Buddhahood:

1. Nirmanakaya (also nairmanika-kaya): an appearance-body, manifestation-body or transformation-body, the body that can assume an infinite number of worldly forms and which mainly exists for the benefit of all beings. This body can be historical, e.g. Buddha Gautama. It is then the manifestation in time and space of Infinite Buddhahood. This form appears within the samsara/nirvana duality and therefore is sometimes called the 'nirvana-body' (nirvanakaya). In later centuries (in China, and probably under the influence of Taoism) the nirmanakaya comprises the whole manifested world.
2. Sambhogakaya (also sambhogika-kaya): the 'glorification-body', the 'bliss-body', 'reward-body': the ideal image of Buddhahood conceivable to beings. It is in this way that bodhisattvas 'see' Buddhahood. The glorification-body is a) the radiance of Absolute Buddhahood in a conceivable form, and b) the projection of the human ideal ('the ideal human') in the glorified forms of bodhisattvas and Buddhas. It is certainly in this sense that the sambhogakaya can be seen as a 'transitional' object', an 'expedient means'.
3. Dharmakaya: (also svabhavika-kaya = body of own-nature): The Body of the Teaching, Absolute Body of Wisdom/Compassion, Principle Body: the ultimate reality as Suchness (tathata), Enlightenment, True Reality (dharmata). According to the later Vijñanavadins the Absolute Self. The Dharmakaya is totally situated beyond the conceptual (after all, dharmata equals sunyata or emptiness) and is consequentially "formless, colorless, inconceivable, unthinkable, inexpressible".

The Trikaya-doctrine does not attempt to be an ontological explanation of Buddhahood; it should be looked upon as a paradigm in which the human mind can fit in the different levels and consciousness-data of its soteriological thought.

This paradigm can be used in various ways, e.g.:

Nirmanakaya	**Sambhogakaya**	**Dharmakaya**
Gautama	Avalokitesvara	Amitabha
historical	spiritual	cosmic
parikalpita	paratantra	parinispanna
Enlightened	Enlightener	Enlightenment
existence	interaction	essence
personal	transpersonal	impersonal
avidya	dharma	prajna
Namu (=Bombu)	Amida Butsu	Namu Amida Butsu

We also should take into account that although these "Three Bodies" conceptually appear as different concepts, they are essentially a unity. Metaphorically we can see them as the three sides of a prism, of which the volume remains undefined since it has to remain a-conceptual.

This clearly comes to expression in the later evolution of the Trikaya-doctrine. So, e.g. we see that in the so-called 'developed' (Ch. shan-chia, J. sange) current of the T'ien-t'ai-school (out of which also Jodo-Shinshu originated) it is taught that the three kayas are in fact identical, as three ways in which the 'absolute' reveals itself to the world. In the last stage of the evolution of the Trikaya the three bodies are not as much seen as doctrinal formulations, but as upaya-adjustments to understand an indivisible unity. This makes that the Tri-partition of the Trikaya is not defined by the number 3, but that it is possible to import other divisions; e.g. T'an-luan who opts for Four Kayas by dividing Dharmakaya in two aspects: a static aspect (the 'essence' = dharmata) and a dynamic aspect ('compassion' as 'expedient means' = upaya).

A three-dimensional scheme is presented by K.T.Tsuji (An Outline of Buddhism), as a three-sided pyramid, in which each side represents a different aspect of Buddhahood, while Buddhahood itself is represented by the volume of the pyramid

Avatamsaka-Hua-yen

"Avatamsaka" (Flower Wreath) is the name for both the scriptural cycle and the philosophical current based on this literature. The sutra cycle probably dates from the 2nd or 3rd century CE. It mostly deals with the mystical teachings concerning Maha-Vairocana-Buddha, i.e. the "Cosmic Buddha". As scriptural source we know mainly the Buddha-Avatamsaka-Sutra (Discourse on the Buddha Flower Wreath), a collection of texts of which most of the Sanskrit originals have been lost. Still extend are:

Gandavyuha-sutra: The story of the young man Sudhana who goes on a quest for the absolute (dharmadhatu). Determined to find it he becomes the student of 51 (or 53?) teachers (kalyana mitra, lit. "good friends") all of a distinguished character: sages, kings, men, fools, women (even a prostitute), gods, bodhisattvas, etc. After many kalpa's of searching throughout an innumerable number of universes, he ends up with Manjusri Bodhisattva, the Supreme Wisdom of Buddhahood. Manjusri shows him to a place where "the" Wisdom can be found: a tower high upon a steep mountain. After a journey full of dangers Sudhana arrives at the tower: it is empty!

Also the Dhasabhumika-sutra (Sutra on the Ten Stages) is traditionally counted among the Avatamsaka texts.

In India there doesn't appear to have been a separate Avatamsaka school. The story of Sudhana is however also told in Divyavadana (preserved in the Sanskrit and Tibetan translations) and it is depicted on the Boro-Budur temple complex in Java. The entire Avatamsaka cycle is preserved in Tibetan and also in several translations in the Chinese Canon.

It is in China that the Avatamsaka doctrine will receive its factual philosophical systematization, in which the acquired teachings of both Madhyamaka and Yogacara are integrated in to one "holistic" system. The foundation for this is laid by Tu-shun (557-640) and Chih-yen (602-668). The actual systematization belongs however to Fa-tsang (643-712). His works include: Chin-shih-tzu-chang (Essay on the Golden Lion); I-hai pai-men (One Hundred propositions on the Ocean of Thought); Hua-yen ching chih-kuei (Essential themes of the Avatamsaka Sutra). For the final touch-up Ch'eng-kuan (738-838) was also important.

The main ideas of Avatamsaka-thought are found in the Hua-yen ching I-240:

The One is the Many.

The Many is the One.

In the word the meaning is to be found.

In the meaning the word is to be understood.

Non-being is Being. Being is Non-being.

Formlessness is Form. Form is Formlessness.

Non-being is Being. Being is Formlessness.

Avatamsaka philosophy wants to provide an affirming answer to Nagarjuna's attitude of negation. It also manages to clarify some of the problems that had not or unsatisfactorily been answered within the Yogacara, e.g. the relationship between manas and alaya-vijnana (storehouse-consciousness). In this sense Hua-yen forms an organic whole of all essential elements of Mahayana Buddhism. In the Avatamsaka-and even more so in its Chinese form-the Hua-yen we will for the first time encounter a metaphysical approach, be it in a very subtle form. Up until then Buddhist philosophy had refused to venture along the path of metaphysics, e.g. by asking the question concerning the nature of the Absolute.

Hua-yen (maybe influence by Taoism?) dares to take the step to a "being outside of consciousness' (li = noumenon) and in doing so breaks through the limitations of consciousness, by which it became possible to conceive of a worldview.

Identity and Totality

In their true nature all things are identical.

Starting from a syllogistic structure

If A equals X

And B equals X

Than A equals B

we can exchange the terms A and B for 'dharma's' and X for sunyata (emptiness):

If dharma 1 = emptiness

And dharma 2 = emptiness

Than dharma 1 = dharma 2

Or, as Fa-tsang expressed it, exchanging the term dharma with the term "thing" or "phenomenon" (shih):

If shih 1 = k'ung (emptiness)

And shih 2 = k'ung

Than all things in their true nature, in their emptiness are equal to one another. Things only differ from one another through the relational context in which they find themselves.

In their unity "things" are identical. This identity leads towards a "totality" (the absolute, chen), the "suchness of beings" (Skt. Bhuta-tathata, Ch. Chen-ju). Seen from the point of view of the phenomenal it the "realm of phenonema" (dharmadhatu, fa-chieh). But seen from an Absolute point of view this is the "essence" or "suchness", the ultimate principle that lies at the basis of all beings, the "element of elements" (dharmata, fa-hsing). Soteriologically this absolute reality is the source of enlightenment, the "womb of the tathagatas (tathagata-garbha, ju-lai tsang); all beings therefore have Buddha-nature.

Bhutatathata, dharmadhatu, dharmata, tathagata-garbha are various aspects of the inexpressible absolute. Also alaya-vijnana is none other than such an aspect. To the Hua-yen, alaya-vijnana is the "Great Ocean Mirror" (ta hai yin), in which the countless drama's of the universe spontaneously and simultaneously reflects each other, in a harmonic play of mutual, multi-dimensional projections and interpenetrations.

R. Grousset (in Sur le Traces du Bouddha) describes this absolute as: "un absolu non plus supérieur aux phénomènes, mais entièrement inherent à eux...l'absolu en tant que processus même des choses." ("An Absolute not superior to phenomena, but entirely inherent in them...the Absolute as the process of things themselves.")

This leads us to a second remarkable point:

INTERPENETRATION

Not only are "things" in their true nature identical to each other or do they form a "totality", they are also present in one another. Each separate thing does not only reflect all other things but also reflects the Absolute in its totality. (cfr. Holographic model).

All things interpenetrate each other, contain each other:

All is in One-One is in All.

All things are present in Oneness,

Oneness is present in all things.

My ego-ness is present in the Absolute,

The Absolute is present in my ego-ness.

All beings are present in the Buddha,

The Buddha is present in all beings.

Nirvana is present in samsara,

Samsara is present in Nirvana.

The cosmos is present in each separate thing,

Each separate thing is present in the cosmos.

We have to be careful though not to lose sight of the 4th logical lemma!

In this context it is not inappropriate to quote Leibniz: "Infinitum continuum vel discretum proprie nec unum, nec totum, nec quantum est." In other words, we should not quantify this interpenetration.

An expression such as: "All is Buddha, Buddha is All" is wrong in the sense that from this one could conclude that all beings are Buddha, or that "I am a Buddha". This of course could never be the intention of the Hua-yen.

What we can conclude from this is that the totality of Buddhahood is present in each and every element of our personality (nama-rupa), i.e. the 5 skandha's (aggregates). As within a hologram the total picture is present within each part of that picture, so it is that within each part of our mind (and body...) enlightenment is present. In this way we partake in the Buddha-Body that manifests itself in the three (or more...) Buddha-Bodies.

But only an enlightened one sees this enlightenment.

The total interpenetration of things makes that also contradictions are present. However these do not exclude each other. This is the doctrine of "non-hindrance" or "all-embracing", also called the "total freedom of things in their true nature".

"Here we find that both time and space have lost their meaning and power as we understand and experience them. Here is not merely a realm-embracing-realm ad infinitum, but a total change-over, a thorough liberation from all obstructions. Here is a perfect melting and merging of all realms, the all-in-one and the one-in-all, the dissolving of being and non-being, the convergence of Voidness and existence, the "simultaneous abrupt arising" and the "perfect mutual solution". All these mysteries of Totality consist, however, in one basic principle; namely, all things of dependent-arising (pratitya-samutpada) are void....

To stress the "ego-less" aspect of this great mystery of sunyata, we have Hinayana Buddhism; to stress the void-aspect of this mystery, we have Madhyamaka Buddhism; to stress the non-clinging, non-abiding aspect we have Zen; and to stress the non-obstructing and all-embracing aspect, we have Hua-yen.

...we have found that the Totality and Non-obstruction of Buddhahood are expressed in these terms:

- That the universe can be infinitely vast or small depending on the scale of measurement, or the position from which a measurement is made.
- That the "larger" universes include the "smaller" ones as a solar system contains its planets, or a planet contains its atoms. This system of higher realms embracing the lower ones is pictured in a structure extending ad infinitum in both directions to the infinitely large or the

infinitely small. This is called in Hua-yen vocabulary the view of realms-embracing-realms.

- That a "small" universe, (such as an atom) not only contains the infinite "lesser" universes within itself, but also contains the infinite "larger" universes (such as the solar system), thus establishing the genuine Totality of Non-obstruction.
- That "time" has lost its meaning as merely a concept for measuring the flow of events in the past, present and future. It has now become an element of Totality which actualized the total interpenetration and containment of all events of past, present, and future in the eternal present.
- Upon the grand stage of the infinite Dharmadhatu, countless various dramas of religion are being enacted in numerous dimensions of space/time throughout eternity. (G.C. Chang, The Buddhist Teaching of Totality, 1971, p. 11-13)

Empress Wu Tse-T'ien (T'ang-dynasty, 684-705, first concubine of Emperor Kao-tsung) invited Fa-tsang to clarify to her the Hua-yen teachings of Totality and Interpenetration. The master adorned a hall of the palace with mirrors and in the center of the hall he placed a Buddha-image with a lamp beside it. The image reflected itself infinitely in all directions, the image was present everywhere. Then the master, standing in the center of the hall, held a small crystal ball in his hand. All of the mirror images where now captured in this one small ball.

Obviously these scenario is only a metaphor in which we should remind ourselves that it is only concerned with "images", that in fact there is neither a Buddha-image nor a lamp, that the mirrors only reflect their own emptiness to each other, that there is no-one looking into the mirror. And finally, that there "are" no mirrors!

In the Vows of the Bodhisattva Samantabhadra an image is projected of the "infinite" and the "interpenetration" of worlds.

All the innumerable separate is contained in the innumerable One. We have to remark here that things, although present in each other, are not necessarily identical. They are after all identical in their "true nature", not in their relative appearance.

THE TRUE SELF

Avatamsaka-thought is covered by the necessity to eliminate all forms of duality. So, e.g., the problem of self/non-self or the dichotomy of samsara/nirvana can be eradicated through the ascend into higher dimensions of the One Totality that is the "true nature of things".

The True Self (svabhava) hereby becomes identical with Enlightenment, Buddhahood (buddhata), Suchness (dharmata). The intellectual and emotional tensions associated with time/space fall away. Enlightenment is experienced as an "event" beyond any temporal/spatial context. Since traditionally samsara has no beginning ("it exists from the beginning of beginningless time"), while nirvana has no end ("it lasts until the end of endless time"), the transfer from the world of suffering to nirvana "happens" at the "moment of enlightenment" as long as samsara-and-nirvana are regarded as a "personal" event. Enlightenment "spans" both views and therefore has no beginning nor end.

With this Avatamsaka-thought also provided a solution to another Mahayana problem that had occupied Buddhist minds throughout several centuries: "Can Enlightenment still be realized by every being" (Ch. Shi-chüeh, J. shikaku: lit. "Entering upon Enlightenment")? Or, is Enlightenment already realized for all beings (Ch. Pen-chüeh, J. Hongaku: lit. "Original, Primal Enlightenment")? Also for this dilemma Avatamsaka will provide a solution: the tension between the "still to be realized" and the "already realized" Enlightenment is a purely dialectical one. Given that, from the perspective of Wisdom, Enlightenment is situated beyond any temporal/spatial context; from the perspective of Compassion, Enlightenment is to be realized in every moment by all beings. Indeed, time and history-as relative concepts-start anew in every moment (eka-ksana).

Since in Enlightenment Wisdom and Compassion are One, the difference between the two aspects of Enlightenment are solely epistemological and methodological, but in no way absolute.

PHENOMENON / NOUMENON

From Avatamsaka-thought in convergence with themes from the Lotus Sutra and Nirvana Sutra emerged the synchretistical view of the T'ien-t'ai school characterized by its strong mystical imprint. The metaphysical basis for this school was largely formed from Hua-yen philosophy. During the Sung Dynasty there arose a dispute within the T'ien-t'ai concerning the relationship between the relatively experienced (the phenomenal) and the all comprising Absolute (the noumenal).

The dispute started between two chief-disciples of the 11th T'ien-t'ai patriarch (Ch'ing-sun). One disciple, I-chi, later followed by Chih-li, proclaimed that the object of right meditation should be focused on the unenlightened within the mind and not on the pure and undefiled aspect of the mind, as was claimed by Chih-yen.

This disputatio, which started on the practical level of meditation, soon evolved into a dispute on the metaphysical level and is known as the shan-chia-shan-wai discussion (J. sange-sanrai). The "orthodox" T'ien-t'ai interpretation, which called itself "[The Teaching] on the Mountain", remained with the assertion that all phenomena (shih) are mutually and indifferently comprised within the absolute (li) with which they are identical. This is the shi-shi-wu-ai: phenomena are mutually unhindered and interfused. Contrary to this stands the doctrine of which it was said that it was too much "Avatamsaka" and therefore stranger to T'ien-t'ai; hence the name "Outside the Mountain". This teaching stated that phenomena are indirectly equal because they are with the all comprising Absolute. This than becomes: phenomena are not separated from the Absolute: (li-shih-wu-ai).

It is this kind of questions that have contributed to the need for extension of Buddhist thought in China (and later also in

Korea and Japan). Namely the necessity to overcome new historical situations. It is for example the broadness of the scope of thought within the T'ien-t'ai that provided the basis for later evolutions. T

he characteristic evolution of Japanese Buddhism during the Kamakura Era would have been inconceivable without the input of Avatamsaka through T'ien-t'ai. The fact that great reformers such as Eisai (Rinzai-zen), Honen (Jodo-shu), Shinran (Jodo-shinshu), Dogen (Soto-zen), Nichiren (Nichirenshu) all started their spiritual career within the Tendai (J. for T'ien-t'ai), is self-evident.

BUDDHIST LOGIC

Buddhism has from the beginning emphasized a logical structure. Examples of this can be found in the structure of the (midwifery) talks and discourses of the Buddha.

The basic structure can be found in the logical tetralemma:

- A is true
- A is not true
- A is both true and not true
- A is neither true nor not true

This formulation, which is very often found back in the oldest texts, provides the 'key' to most 'typical Buddhist problems' towards their 'understanding' or their 'inconceivability' (e.g. the anatta-doctrine, the conception of sunyata, or the teaching of Totality within the Avatamsaka-teachings [see later]). What seems 'illogical' according to the binary logic (the so-called Aristotelian logic), becomes clear through the perspective of this tetralemma.

With its dissemination Buddhism unavoidably came into contact with other Indian spiritual currents. From this arose the necessity of having a set of polemic instruments at its disposal with which it could answer the argumentations of the formal-logically structured Hindu darsanas (especially Nyaya and Vaisesika).

In relation to this J. Takakusu says in his 'Essentials of Buddhist Philosophy': "Buddhist Logic is not a formal logic of thought, but is rather a logic of dispute or debate which lays stress on the investigation of cause, relations and possibility and is therefore an art of argumentation and refutation." We can see this need strongly represented in Nagarjuna, but even more decidedly with Vasubandhu, who by way of his view on the trayasatya (Three Truths) gave rise to the implementation of a clear Buddhist formal logic.

It is however Vasubandhu's disciple Dinnaga who is generally accepted as the factual founder of this logic. In his Nyaya-pravesa (also called Nyaya-mukha), 'Introduction to Logic', he explains the new lines of thought based on the 'knowledge of causality' (hetu-vidya). He supports his claims on the 'three forms of causality' (lingasya trini-rupani) by way of the 'nine necessitating causes' (hetu), in which he replaces the-until then-usual comparative method with a sharp method of deduction which expresses itself in new syllogistic formulations. His works are-except for the aforementioned Nyaya-pravesa and some Sanskrit fragments-mainly preserved in Chinese and Tibetan translations.

A next important step in Buddhist Logic was taken by Dharmakirti (7th Century ?). Concerned about the decline of the Teaching in India, he searched for new structures of argumentation. In his works Pramana-varttika, Pramana-viniscaya, but especially in his Nyaya-bindu he points out that names and relations are only instituted by mind, whereas the sense-functions represent their objects of experience accurately, unless of course they are distorted and perverted.

Other important Buddhist logicians are Agotra, Dharmapala, Dharmottara, Silabhadra, Sthiramati...

8

Buddhism in China

Although Buddhism is already mentioned in China in the beginning of the 1st century, the beginning of any Chinese form of Buddhist philosophy can only be situated after the Han-Dynasty, i.e. during the period of division (the Three Kingdoms 220-265; the Six Dynasties 265-589; and the Northern Dynasties 385-581).

This period is characterized by the flourishing of Religious Taoism and so-called Neo-Taoism. It is especially within the circles of the latter that we can notice a remarkable likeness between on the one hand the teachings of Lao-tzu and Chuang-tzu and on the other hand Buddhism, with the main focal point being Prajñaparamita and Madhyamaka. Translations of Buddhist texts during this period are characterized by the frequent use of Taoist terminology.

In this way there arose a initial symbiosis-or at least a certain sympathy-between the Neo-Taoist thinkers and Buddhism. So, for example, we see:

- Sun-ch'o (301-380) who in his Tao Hsien Lun (Treatise on Buddhist Monks and Taoist Sages) compares seven 4th century Buddhist monks with the famous Seven Sages of the Bamboo Forest (3rd century Taoists).
- Fan-yüeh (398-445) who in his Hou Han Shu (History of the Later Han Dynasty) writes: "when we carefully study the [Buddhist] teachings concerning the purification of mind and the liberation from the shackles [of existence], and thereby putting an emphasis on the

setting aside both 'emptiness' and 'being', we [come to the conclusion that the Buddhist teachings] belong to the same current as those of the Taoist scriptures.

- Liu-ch'iu (438-495) writes (quoted in Seng-yu's 'Extracts from the Tripitaka'): "East of the K'un-lun Mountains the term 'Great Unity' is used. Towards the west of Kashmir cheng-chüeh (sambodhi) is used. When one aspires for 'non-being' (wu) or attempts to 'emptiness' (k'ung), it is the same principle."

Newly imported terms such as sambodhi, sunyata, bhava/ abhava are experienced as Taoist equivalents. This terminological equation (ko yi = method of analogy) combines the 'internal writings', i.e. the Buddhist sutras, with the 'external writings', namely Lao-tzu, Chuang-tzu and even I-Ching.

BEGINNING OF CHINESE BUDDHIST PHILOSOPHY

The beginning of Buddhist schools in China is shrouded in great obscurity. There is talk of the 'Six Houses and Seven Schools' (liu-chia ch'i-tsung), but original texts are very fragmentary and we have to refer to works of centuries later. Yet, it is clear that they were all strongly tinted by philosophy and that they based themselves on both Madhyamaka and Yogacara thought.

The first figure that stands out clearly and originally is Seng-chao (384-414). After his Taoist studies he became a disciple of the translator Kumarajiva, who introduced him to Madhyamaka-thought. Seng-chao however gave great importance to the Vimalakirti-nirdesa. His work was collected under the general title Chao-lun, yet its chapters are clearly conceived as separate entries.

Seng-chao is regarded as the founder of the San-lun tsung (School of the Three Treatises, also the Madhyamaka-School), which bases itself on two works attributed to Nagarjuna: Madhyamika-sastra (MMK plus a commentary T 1564) and Dvadasadvara (the 'Twelve Gates', T 1568); and a work attributed to Nagarjuna's disciple Aryadeva: Sata-sastra ('Treatise in One Hundred Verses' T 1569).

Seng-chao's main interest focuses on the problems of time, space and movement. So, e.g., he states that dharmas are "neither in motion, nor in rest", but that their characteristic is pu-ch'ien, literally 'unchangeing': they have such a short momentary existence that they are more as static images following on each other in a tremendous speed.

The San-lun school mainly emphasizes three themes:

1. A polemic attitude towards all discursive claims and the refutation of all affirmative prepositions; absolute truth, which is the only ideal, is after all nisprapañca: 'inexpressible and unthinkable'.
2. A sharp distinction between relative truth and absolute truth: relative truth leads to 'knowing', absolute truth is wisdom. "Wisdom is no-knowledge" is by the way the title of Seng-chao's 3rd chapter.
3. The eightfold negation of Nagarjuna (introductory verses of MMK) which translated in Chinese state:

No Production

No Extinction

No Annihilation

No Permanence

No Unity

No Diversity

No Coming

No departure

Some quotations from Seng-chao:

"The true nature of dharmas is that they are neither in motion, nor at rest. Or, to state it differently: they are both in motion and in rest. To use the formulation of the Path of the Middle: by stating that there is both motion and rest, we fall into one of the two extremes. By stating that there is neither motion nor rest, we follow the Path of the Middle."

"All dharmas are truly non-existent in one sense and not non-existent in another sense. In the first point of view they are although apparently existing, de-facto non-existing. In the second point of view they are although apparently non-existing, de facto not non-existing."

"That is why the Holy Man is as a hollow void. He cherishes no-knowledge. He remains in this world of impermanence and usefulness, however he abides in the realm of non-action (wu-wei). He is situated within the walls of what is expressible, and yet he lives in the open space that transcends all speach. He is silent and alone, empty and open; his form of existence cannot be covered in words. There remains nothing further to be said about him."

A second important figure is Tao-shêng (360-434), just as Seng-chao he is a disciple of Kumarajiva. Later he also becomes a follower of Hui-yüan (334-416, more about him later). Besides a profound knowledge of Madhyamaka, Tao-shêng also had a special interest in the Nirvana-sutra (Nieh-pan ching, T 374-7), especially concerning the problem of Buddha-nature and the icchantikas (Ch. [I-]ch'an-t'I, literally 'those who follow their own [desires and impulses]'), those beings who are without any merit and who, according to general tradition, cannot or don't wish to realize Enlightenment. According to the Nirvana-sutra also these beings will realize Enlightenment because of the presence of Buddha-nature in all beings, no matter who or what they are.

Tao-shêng, who was also familiar with Confucianist and Taoist teachings, is said to have provided a philosophical foundation to this vision of the sutra, making ample use of Chinese insights. Although only small fragments of his work remain by way of quotations, fact remains that he was discussed extensively by his contemporaries and even by the next generations.

Although Buddha-nature is present in all beings, it can not be expressed by words. Words are traps, 'bow-nets that are left behind once the fish is removed'. True insight is therefore without (beyond) words. Also in this sense Tao-shêng can be regarded as a precursor of the Chinese Ch'an School.

From this same vision on Buddha-nature, Tao-shêng concludes that Enlightenment is a 'sudden' event. As long as the mind remains captive in the chains of existence, no true, definitive Enlightenment is possible. The falling away of the last ties to existence (e.g. to the insight of 'being' and 'non-being') is a unique fact that has the duration of a single thought-moment (eka-ksana, Ch. I-nien), i.e. the limit value of the shortest possible time-experience. This notion of 'Sudden Enlightenment' stands against the notion of 'Gradual Enlightenment' in which enlightenment is seen as realizable by way of passing through a gradual series of levels or stages (bhumi). From Tao-shêng on forward this will become one of the most occurring themes of discussion within Mahayana Buddhism and a criterion for the (later) division into 'schools'.

RESISTANCE AGAINST BUDDHISM

Right from its first introduction in China, Buddhism has met the resistance of Confucianist schools. It is after all clear that Buddhism stands in opposition to a great number of notions held by Confucianism, such as e.g. the 'celestial ruler', 'society', etc.

Thereby comes a growing Chinese nationalism during the 5th century as a reaction against the 'barbarian' rulers who conquered Northern China, and who generally where in favor of Buddhism. In these northern states there often developed a kind of cooperation between the Sangha, the Buddhist community, and the political powers, through which a great deal of corruption entered the monasteries and temples. To strengthen their influence, ambitious monks did not hesitate to attribute themselves with magical powers or perform impressive rituals.

Despite the initial sympathy from the Neo-Taoist thinkers, we can see a hostile reaction from the 'religious Taoists' around the beginning of the 5th century. To them, Buddhism was clearly the 'competition'. In the also divided South of China the relations were different. Buddhist institutions and thinkers there profiled themselves as more independent in regards to the political powers and focused themselves more on meditation and study.

Ignited by the Confucianists and Taoists the first persecution of Buddhism in China took place during the Northern Wei (from 446 until 454), in which a great number of temples, statues and texts were destroyed.

But even after the persecution had lifted, the Confucianists kept an antagonistic attitude towards Buddhism. Most distinguished in this regard are especially Seng-yu (445-518) and Tao-hsüan (596-667). Fan-chen (450-515, also called Tzu-chen) attacked mostly the doctrine of karma and rebirth, which in the eyes of the Chinese was the most striking characteristic of Buddhism: ("the body is the soul and the soul perishes with the body" [sic]). It should be mentioned here that Hui-yüan, for the sake of propaganda, supplied a more simplistic, popular version of the karma and rebirth doctrine, in which he even introduced the non-Buddhist concept of a 'soul' (shen).

Besides this rejection of karma and rebirth, the attacks of Confucianism were mainly directed at:

At the unprovability and uncontrollability of the sutras, against the 'clear' objectively controllability of the Five Classics (Wu ching: namely 'Shu ching' (Canonical Book of Documents); Shih ching (Canonical Book of Songs); I ching (Canonical Book of Changes); Li Chi (Canon of Rites) and Ch'un-Ch'iu (Spring and Autumn Annals)); and the Four Books (Ssu Wu: Lun-yü (Analects of Confucius); Ta Hsüeh (The Great Learning); Chung Yung (The Teaching of the Middle); and Meng-tzu (the works of Mencius).

At the fact that Buddhism was insulting toward authority, in conflict with tradition and Chinese customs.

At the fact that Buddhism would disrupt the social system.

Also Taoism will gradually react more sharply against Buddhism, be it mainly through an attempt to imitate its outward appearance.

From the 5th century onwards Taoism will try to structure itself by building monastic communities and hierarchies, by establishing a collection of scriptures (the Tao Tsang in 1120 volumes) and by taking into its pantheon popular bodhisattvas and Indian deities. It never made it into a firm and lasting organization though.

SUKHAVATI: PURE LAND BUDDHISM

Pure Land Buddhism-just as Tantric Buddhism-should primarily be regarded as being more of a praxis than a doxa. Over the centuries it has attracted more and more philosophical and even mystical Mahayana-elements to arrive at a climax in the 13th century Jodo-Shinshu, a school of which even Christmas Humphreys (who by the way had no sympathy whatsoever for Shin Buddhism!) had to admit that "it seems to be twofold, the frank confession that the older Buddhism is too difficult for the masses, and must therefore be 'simplified', and at the other extreme a doctrine so lofty, so subtle that only the rarest minds could understand and use it." (Buddhism, 1952, p. 164).

Also D.T.Suzuki, mainly known for his works concerning Zen Buddhism, stated that it is "Japan's major religious contribution to the West" (Shin Buddhism, 1970).

Already early in the history of Buddhism, we notice a tendency towards regarding the historical Buddha Gautama Sakyamuni as being more than THE teacher who by his own effort realized Enlightenment and passed on the Dharma to his fellow-beings.

The tendency to mythologize 'The Teacher' is a deeply human almost unavoidable characteristic, something which even Islam and its prophet Muhammed could not avoid. The Buddhist teachings concerning anatta and nirvana however do not offer the possibility of a mystical devotion (bhakti), in which the person of the devotee is absorbed in or merged with the person of the adored deity.

Doctrinally we see-already within the early Hinayana-the establishment of a 'shifting towards abstraction'. The Mahasanghika, and especially the school of the Lokottaravadins, state e.g. that the Buddha is an 'outer-worldly' being. In the Lotus Sutra, of which the oldest parts date back to the 2nd century BCE, we can read the tendency to regard the historical Buddha as a manifestation of eternal-beyond space/time-Buddhahood.

Not only within popular devotion, but also doctrinally the Buddha-figure will gradually receive the aspect of a "Savior". His Wisdom and Compassion helps beings to walk the way towards liberation. He forms the natural force-field-a 'Buddha-field' (buddha-ksetra) or 'Buddha-land'-through or in which beings are drawn towards enlightenment. Together with the emergence of the Greater Vehicle, the number of Buddha-figures multiplies infinitely, and with it also the number of Buddha-lands in which each Buddha forms the central point of attraction. Within religious practice however it appeared that one Buddha-land was more successful than the other. In the popular view only a few Buddha's and Bodhisattva's were effectively experienced as "Saviors". The most 'successful' Buddha-land is undoubtedly Amitabha's Pure Land Sukhavati (the 'Realm of Bliss') which in the course of the centuries eclipsed all other Buddha-lands.

The reason for this can most probably be found in the name of this Buddha-figure itself. Amitabha (amita-abha = 'who's light is immeasurable') means after all 'Immeasurable Light'; besides this he carries a second name: Amitayus (amita-ayus = 'who's life is immeasurable'), which means 'Immeasurable Life'. This led (especially in China) to the adoption of a series of comparisons which gave this Buddha-figure a unique aspect, which is in a way compressed in the name by which this Buddha became known in China and other countries within the Chinese cultural sphere of influence:

Amitabha = Infinite Light = Wisdom = Infinity in space

Amitayus = Infinite Life = Compassion = Infinity in time

Amitabha-Amitayus thus becomes A-mi-t'o-Fo, the Infinite Buddha, the Infinity of Enlightenment (prajña), which is identical to the Infinity of Compassionate Activity (karuna), and which can only metaphorically be experienced as a 'person'.

The special place that this Buddha will occupy in the Far East becomes apparent from the fact that the sutras related to him where among the first to be translated and disseminated into Chinese.

Basically there are three sutras that are regarded as the basic texts for classical Pure Land Buddhism:

1. The Larger Sutra on the Adornments of the Pure Land (Sk. Sukhavati-vyuha-sutra, Ch. Wu-liang-shou-ching, Jap. Muryoju-kyo, from now on referred to as Dai-kyo or 'Larger Sutra', T 360-364)
2. The Sutra on the Meditation on Amitayus (Sk. Amitayur-dhyana-sutra, Ch. Kuan-wu-liang-shou-ching, Jap. Kanmuryoju-kyo, shortened to Kan-gyo or 'Meditation Sutra', T 365), and
3. The Shorter Sutra on the Adornments of the Pure Land (Sk. Sukhavati-vyuha-sutra, Ch. O-mi-t'o-ching, Jap. Amida-kyo, T 366-367).

It is especially the first text, the Larger Sutra, which is important for our exposition. It contains after all the mythological image out of which the salvific structure of Pure Land Buddhism becomes apparent. The first chapter relates the story of a king who lived a very long time ago-in times immemorial-who, strongly moved by the suffering of beings, forsakes his throne and becomes a monk named Dharmakara. As a monk he meets the Buddha Lokesvararaja. This meeting moves him so much that he decides to become a Buddha himself, creating a Buddha-land in which all the limitations characteristic to other Buddha-lands would be overcome, and in which all the 'benefits' of all other Buddha-lands would be gathered. After meditating on all the Buddha-lands for a period of 5 kalpas, he formulates his insights in 48 special vows. After practicing his vows for an innumerable length of time he finally realizes enlightenment and becomes Amitabha Buddha, thus establishing his Buddha-land Sukhavati, the Land of Ultimate Bliss, in Chinese translated as ching-t'u: the Pure Land (Jap. Jodo).

The beings who sincerely entrust themselves to Amitabha and say his Name, are born in this Pure Land, despite their heavy karmic burden. Conventionally this Pure Land was regarded as a transitory stage from which it became possible to realize enlightenment. The beings who are born there in a lotus find themselves in the most beneficial and effective circumstances to hear and live the True Teaching (Saddharma).

Faith in Amitabha's Pure Land increased strongly and continuously in India; we find reflections of this in the numerous works, both sutras and sastras, such as e.g. in the Dasabhumikasastra attributed to Nagarjuna, or the Ratnagotra-vibhaga of Sthiramati. The authors of these works express their sincere aspiration for birth in Sukhavati.

Pure Land Thought in China would take a different course. Not only did Amitabha receive a soteriological function, he also received a clear cosmological/philosophical structure; the texts were approached through a kind of close reading through which more dynamic connotations became apparent.

The first person in China of whom it is known that he aspired for "Birth in the Pure Land" is a certain Ch'ueh Kung-ts'e (Ts'e, Duke of Ch'ueh) who lived during the Eastern Tsin dynasty (317-419). From this Ts'e onward more and more people are mentioned as Pure Land devotees.

The most known, besides Chihtun (314-366) and Taoan (312-385), is without doubt the learned monk Huiyüan (334-417), who is regarded by later Pure Land masters as their very first patriarch. It is with him that the Pure Land movement becomes an important religious current. On Lu-shan, a mountain in the South of China, he established the 'White Lotus Society' (Pailien she), a community of monks and lay-people who devoted themselves to meditation and visualization on e.g. the appearance of Amitabha, in order to realize what is called nien-fo sanmei (Jap. nembutsu zammai) or the concentrated practice whereby the aspirant realizes a unity with Amida Buddha. This emphasis on meditation will for a long time characterize Pure Land Buddhism in China (and also in Japan, at least until the Kamakura period).

From the Liu-Sung-dynastie (420-479) onward Pure Land Buddhism will spread throughout the whole of China. This is also the Era of the great translators: Kumarajiva, Punyayasas, Paoyun, Bodhiruci, Bhuddhabhadra, Kalayasas. During the Chou and Sui dynasties (557-618) we see the arising of numerous works and commentaries on the Pure Land Sutras-also by famous monks of other traditions, such as Chitsang, Fa-ch'ang, Chih-I, Chih-yen. This all testifies to a vivid interest for Pure Land Buddhism, even if the interpretations were mostly very divergent.

The more 'exclusive' Pure Land masters, who are also decisive for the later evolution of Pure Land Buddhism in Japan, (T'an-luan, Tao-ch'o, and Shan-tao) will lay the foundations for the exclusive nien-fo practice.

So, e.g., T'an-luan (476-542) reads that one should make a distinction between on the one hand the contemplation-and-recitation of the Name of Amitabha Buddha (nien-fo, Jap. nembutsu) and on the other hand the attitude of the devotee: the deep mind of unconditional entrusting (Ch. hsin-hsin, Jap. shinjin) in the Infinite Compassion of Buddha-Power.

He differs from Hui-yüan in the sense that where the former claims that one should visualize (see) the Buddha in samadhi, T'an-luan states that the Pure Land is solely based on Amida's Salvific Power. The sutras however do not tell us how to see Amida, they do tell us what Amida promised us in his vows. It is therefore not man's practice that is required by Amida, but his sincere entrusting.

Tao-ch'o (596-645) emphasizes the distinction between the 'self-power' (jiriki) of the adept who walks the "Path of Sages", and the 'Other-Power' (tariki) of the Infinite Compassion of the Buddha as the dynamic which leads beings to Enlightenment. According to him the beings "in these decadent times of the decline of the dharma" are incapable to walk the difficult path towards enlightenment by their own efforts, and therefore should entrust themselves exclusively to the "Pure Land Path", the salvific power originating from Buddhahood itself.

Shan-tao (613-681) on the other hand will put more emphasis on the verbal expression of the Name. The other traditional 'right practices' in the Chinese Pure Land temples are, according to Shan-tao, to be regarded as secondary. Those practices include:

1. Reciting of Sutras;
2. Meditating on Amida and his land, to which Shan-tao strangely enough devoted about half of his Commentary on Kan-gyo;
3. Worshiping Amida through services;
4. Reciting the Nembutsu
5. Praising and making offerings to Amida.

Saying the Nembutsu (practice 4) is according to Shan-tao the "right practice among right practices", it being the most efficient act towards the right assurance of Birth in the Pure Land.

In the early years of the T'ang-dynasty Pure Land Studies reach an intellectual climax throughout the whole Far East, because next to the Chinese authors, also a great number of Korean masters became involved.

Yet, the appreciation of Pure Land Teachings was far from unanimous. The Ch'an-schools involved themselves in strong polemics, e.g. concerning the nature of the "Pure Land": was it an 'internal land', only existing in the mind; or an 'external paradise' within a certain geographical or astronomical reach? These discussions led to an internal reinforcement of the 'attacked' party and to the formation of a separate Pure Land School, the Ching-t'u. Up until then Pure Land practices had not been limited to a certain current.

Within all these polemics Pure Land adepts showed that the nien-fo sanmei was an ineffable, deep and wondrous meditation. But also from certain Ch'an-temples arose voices that wanted to work towards a doctrinal reconciliation between

Ch'an and Ching-t'u, e.g. by Hsuan-shih, a disciple of the 5th Ch'an patriarch, and by Nan-yang Hui-chung, a disciple of Hui-neng, the famous 6th patriarch of Ch'an who taught the simultaneous practice of "practice and meaning", wherein 'practice' was understood as the recitation of nien-fo and 'meaning' as the insight which was gained through Ch'an-meditation.

This same syncretistic way of thought became dominant after the great Buddhist persecutions of the later years of the T'ang-dynasty, and has remained a characteristic of the whole of Chinese Buddhism in the centuries to follow.

Ch'an and Ching-t'u were able to survive the persecutions (including the 'big one' of 845) for several reasons:

- because of their 'aloofness' from the temples in the capital (these temples were more closely involved in the political arena and to a certain extend were even dependent on it).
- because of the breadth of their basic following;
- through their lower material vulnerability.

It is therefore very 'logical' that they were prone to grow towards each other, in such a way that-up to this present day-Chinese Buddhism is more or less a convergence, if not a symbiosis/synergy/syncresis, of Ch'an (especially for monks) and Ching-t'u (aimed at the laity), perhaps with a little pinch of T'ien-t'ai added.

Pure Land practice arrives in Japan together with the introduction of Buddhism. Fairly soon it becomes an established practice in almost all schools, especially however in the Tendai-school, which is the by Japan adopted and adapted form of T'ien-t'ai thought. The Pure Land practice as seen in the Tendai is based on Shan-tao's interpretation: "The practice for Birth is the saying of the Nembutsu 'Namu Amida Butsu'", an easy but efficient self-power practice, entirely in the spirit of the Smaller Pure Land Sutra (Amida-kyo). It is also out of this Tendai that the concern will grow to proclaim Buddhism as a soteriology to 'ordinary, ignorant beings'. Those beings who, as it where per definition, lack the power or will necessary for the performance and fulfillment of meditative and/or non-meditative practices.

Such a Tendai monk was e.g. Kuya (also named Koya, 903-972) who roamed the marketplace dancing, singing and juggling, encouraging people to recite nembutsu.

Of greater influence was Genshin (942-1017), whose major work Ojoyoshu, "Essentials for Attaining Birth" made a deep impression in both Japan and China. Yet, the practice of recitation-often in the sense of the mechanical recitation of a mantra-remained being looked upon as a practice for the illiterate, with the 'provisional' result of the lotus-birth in Amida's Western Paradise, out of which one could then realize Final and Definitive Nirvana.

It was up to another Tendai monk to detach the recitation of the Name Namu Amida Butsu from this provisional and somewhat pejorative connotation, and in the same instance to form an autonomous-i.e. apart from the existing temples-"Pure Land School" (Jodo-shu), in which the nembutsu was seen as the central and exclusive practice for both monks and laity.

Honen (also called Genku, 1133-1212) emphasized the fulfillment of the 18th Vow from the Larger Sutra, which he calls the "Primal Vow":

> *"If, when I attain Buddhahood, the sentient beings of the ten quarters, with sincere mind entrusting themselves, aspiring to be born in my land, and saying my Name perhaps even ten times, should not be born there, may I not attain the supreme enlightenment. Excluded are those who commit the five grave offenses and those who slander the right dharma."*

According to Honen this implies that Amida Buddha himself guarantees Birth in the Pure Land for all beings who meet the minimum of requirements, i.e. to entrust themselves completely to Other-Power and to concentrate (samadhi) on the recitation of the Name. Honen is a charismatic figure and a pragmatic reformer; in his view, beings in these times of the Decadent

Dharma benefit more from a single practice, than from all the intellectual and buddhological theorizing. This simple practice assures Birth in the Pure Land for all, whether they are wise or foolish, men or women, rich or poor, monk or lay, good or "bad"...

His success was overwhelming. The doctrine that anyone, without having to rely on intellectuality or intensive meditative practices and/or rituals, could realize enlightenment, aroused the jealousy and envy of the established temples and monasteries. In 1207 this resulted in the ban of the nembutsu-teaching, during which some of Honen's disciples got executed. Honen, together with his most important students, is exiled. In 1211 however the ban is lifted, which marks the beginning of the actual flourishing of Japanese Pure Land Buddhism, which up to the present day still occupies a predominant place, although it is now divided into three doctrinally diverging branches.

It would be Honen's disciple Shinran who would draw the consequences from his master's notions, making them correspond more with the main ideas of Madhyamaka and Yogacara-thought. Shinran emphasized:

- The identity of the Pure Land and Nirvana (Enlightenment): The Pure Land is not a transitory phase but is identical to the Final Perfect Enlightenment. Also, the Pure Land is no longer seen as a "Paradise in the West", rather, it is seen as an "abstraktes Gebiet". Amida is not a ruler or god that rules over this 'land'; he has no form and is not a person. Besides this, in the light of the merit-transference (eko), nirvana is not different from samsara, so that Realization (sho) is nothing else than the 'return' towards the world of suffering as 'Other-Power'.
- The absoluteness of Amida's Other-Power as Dharmakaya, manifested as Great Compassion (dai-jihi: Sk. maha-maitri-karuna) in the Name Namu Amida Butsu (the myogo), which is verbalized in the nembutsu. Saying the nembutsu, especially after hearing the myogo,

is not a petition, not a 'good work' through which man can be liberated, no, it is an expression of gratitude for the salvation offered by Amida.

- Shinjin therefore is the natural activity of karuna (Amida's Primal Vow) within the human mind. It is the settlement of Birth in this existence: through shinjin man is as it where 'born anew', with his passions intact, yet without their karmic implications. Shinjin is as it where the reflection of the Pure Land in this samsaric existence.
- All Buddha's and Bodhisattva's are contained in Amida, which means that all practices are contained in Amida, the Infinite Buddhahood.

KYOTO SCHOOL OF PHILOSOPHY

Ran-gaku or "Dutch Knowledge" developed during the Tokugawa Era, more precisely in the beginning of the 18th century. This form of imported science-in contradistinction to the revival of "National Science" (koku-gaku)-furthered rationalist thought in Japan. This led to a compromise, in which koku-gaku was seen as a superior (i.e. Confucianist) teaching necessary for the moral and social education of man, whereas ran-gaku, with subjects such as medicine, biology, astronomy, architecture, etc. was considered to be a 'practical', i.e. technical knowledge. The actual 'modern' period of Japan starts from 1868. At first, the Meiji regime aimed at a cooperation between the western forms of technology, science, and even 'knowledge' on the one hand, and the official State-Shinto thought (plus a large dose of Confucianism...) on the other, to thus establish the foundation for a modern, but national socio-moral and cultural life.

Young intellectuals however laid a greater emphasis on the imported philosophical systems than on the own Shinto-Confucianist heritage. From the 1870's onward their main interest went to August Comte, J. Stuart Mill, Darwin; in the 80's it extended to an interest in the French, e.g. Voltaire and Rousseau. In the 1890's it were however the German philosophers that occupied their main interest: Kant, Hegel, Schopenhauer-although also Nietzsche, Bergson, Tolstoi and William James were actively studied.

In most intellectual circles, however, it wasn't so much the "adoption" of foreign systems that was aimed at, but their comparison with familiar Buddhist and Confucianist values, towards which goal they used e.g. 'categorical' methods and criteria characteristic to western philosophy. This point of view did not lead to an imitation but to a more sharp and often more critical insight. Often, however, the Japanese intellectuals of the 2nd half of the 19th century were presented with a superficial image of European and American philosophy. All this changed in the beginning of the 20th century thanks to the endeavor towards a synthesis of both eastern and western worlds of thought. Characteristic of this phenomenon is the publication of Hatano Seiichi's (1877-1950) study on Spinoza in 1904, which was-remarkably enough-written in German only to be translated in Japanese in 1910.

The breakthrough came with the informal foundation of the "Kyoto School of Philosophy" within the lap of the faculties of philosophy and religion of the Kyoto State University, mainly under the impulse of Nishida Kitaro (1870-1945), known as Japan's most important philosopher since the Meiji Restoration.

The Kyoto School is in the first place a renewed way of applying philosophy, "more of a philosophical ethos than a unified system of thought". As a basis for this we see:

1. a profound respect for the own religious traditions;
2. a definite openness towards that what western thought has to offer;
3. the intention of arriving at a synthesis of what the West has to offer (e.g. Christianity) and of the eastern heritage (e.g. Buddhism)

This basis can only be realized through a thorough, competent knowledge of both sides of the problem. It can not be characterized by missionary intentions or proselyte polemics, but should on the contrary move across contradictions and paradoxes, which is expressed by Nishida as a "self-identity of absolute contradictories".

Among the most important representatives of the Kyoto School we find-besides Nishida-Tanabe Hajime (1885-1962), D. T. Suzuki (1870-1966), Nishitani Keiji (1900-1990), Takeuchi Yoshinori (1913-..), and Abe Masao (1915-..).

For this essay on the Kyoto School of Philosophy we will limit ourselves to the two main currents: that of Nishida Kitaro, which is clearly inspired by Zen philosophy, and that of Tanabe Hajime, which is mainly based on Shinran (1173-1262: Founder of Jodo-Shinshu).

Nishida Kitaro

(A Study of Good, 1911, English translation 1960)

Through his Zen-experience, Nishida's thought is based on Prajñaparamita-literature and Madhyamika-philosophy. His remarkable point of view on the topos of Nothingness is directly derived from the intuition to which he gave the meaning of 'pure experience'.

Topos (Greek 'place'; J. basho) has-for Nishida-a broader significance than usual, e.g. in Plato's Timaeus or with Aristotle. Also the modern concept of 'force-field' or 'cosmic field' (Einstein) is said to have influenced Nishida. To approach his understanding of topos, we must keep in mind that our everyday word 'place' is neither a merely non-existing 'nothing' nor an existing 'something'. According to Jan Van Bragt "it is more in the nature of what Jaspers calls an "encompassing" (Umgreifendes) that allows things to exist where they are: each on its own, and yet all together in a sort of oneness."

Also the term "Nothingness" clearly refers to sunyata ('emptiness'), although also here Nishida gives a broader interpretation than is usual, namely a "no-thingness" (Undinglichkeit). His attitude is in the first place "to see the form of the formless and to hear the voice of the voiceless":

> *"By intuition (or seeing) I mean our way of seeing things in the world through which we see a 'being', but also*

our own act of seeing, as a shadow image of the Self-reflection of Nothingness-I mean the shadow of Self-reflection of Nothingness that fulfills its function by projecting itself on one point within its topos."

To philosophically clarify the Topos-nature of Nothingness, Nishida introduces his three key-ideas of 'action-intuition', the 'Eternal Now' and the 'historical world in its identity of contradictories'.

Action-intuition

Nishida here expressly refers to the Oriental methods of thought such as the Zen-koan and the art of Archery. Action-intuition is both the structure and the dynamic of all creative activity. Here there is a mutual process as e.g. with the cutting of a wooden image, whereby the sculptor sees anew and recreates his image with every move, in such a way that with every new 'seeing' of the form of the image, he is inspired to cut further. Thus, human creativity only becomes possible when the self-reflecting world expresses itself within the human being, which in its own turn expresses itself and reflects itself by way of its work in the mirror of the world. By way of this mutuality or interdependentness both the world and man realize their synthesis in the historical world.

Eternal Now

The being-present of all things in the world is a "presence in time", namely in the present, in contradistinction to the past and the future. Only in the present one becomes self-conscious as an individual. This way of being-present-in-time is an immediate or direct event, out of which the endeavor for truth can start.

In this, one's whole being is involved, but also the being of all other things in the world. Nonetheless, this kind of being-present is ephemeral and transient: "it appears as being only to disappear again; and it disappears only to let a new being-present appear." Being and non-being are in their true structure interrelated to each other. Because of this the present is a unity of contradictory moments.

Although brief and ephemeral, the present envelops the totality of the time-experience, since past, present, and future all belong to that same present. It is in this way that the endless series of moments, from the incalculable past until the incalculable future, are dependent on the brief presence of the 'here-and-now'. The present is as a time-monad which contains in itself the whole width of past-present-future, despite the fact that it itself belongs to this series as an infinitely small part of the whole. From this follows that the present determines itself: it is 'the present of the present'. Out of this flows the time-experience, as it where from present to present. This characteristic of time explains the nature of man's direct (immediate) self-consciousness and feeling of freedom.

Yet, this experience of self-being and of freedom is closely tied to man's awareness of impermanence. How then is it possible that the fleeting moment can in itself contain the infinitely long series of time-moments? According to Nishida, this is possible because the present is rooted in the Eternal. The Eternal reflects itself and the focus of this self-reflection is the 'present-of-the-present'.

That the Eternal is topologically equal to the present is, according to Nishida, not a simple identification in the mystical sense of the word. Nishida's notion is more dialectic. According to him the fleeting present and the Eternal are on the one hand each others opposites; on the other hand however, one can interchange these both poles, since both are tied to each other through their ultimate self-identity. The Eternal, the Absolute-in-time as topos of Nothingness, can within itself summon each separate moment and bring it to life. The Eternal thus establishes each moment as a true (i.e. autonomous and self-determining) individuum: the present. Through this the Eternal and the present are interconnected in an identity of contradictories.

The Historical World in its Identity of Contradictories

The Creative Now is not only a synthesis in time, but also in space. The world itself is the self-reflection of the existence in which all individua are con-cluded. The world is the embodiment of the Eternal Self, or rather: Non-Self, since each individual existence in this body is only the manifestation of this individual. Each present has therefore the characteristic of a time-synthesis in space.

Because of this, time is determined in two ways: linear and spatial circular. Both time-dimensions converge at every time-moment, be it in an individual existence or in the entire world. This, thus, becomes a historical world, wherein time and space are intertwined; it is, in a sense, the same as the religious world since the Absolute Nothingness is the principle of both the historical world and religion. Since Absolute Nothingness is the life-principle in the world, it should be realized in the world. Its transcendence in relation to the world can only be realized through its immanence in the world. Through the unceasing consecutive manifestations of Absolute Nothingness in the world, the real historical world is unceasingly sanctified, i.e. religiously penetrated.

This can be explained by the double aspect that Nishida gives to his notion of Absolute Nothingness: on the one hand the Christian notion of Absolute Being, on the other hand the Buddhist vision of Absolute Enlightenment.

This does, however, not automatically mean that the world is the domain of religion. Nishida here makes a clear distinction between culture and religion. Religion should be regarded as being qualitatively different from the socio-cultural value-determining actions of humanity. The true ground of the world, however, is religious, just as our existence in the world is religious. But what does it mean when we say that we are religious? It is because we realize our restlessness, our brevity, that in our mind we discover the religious as factuality.

What is typical in Nishida's vision on religion is revealed in what he calls the disjunction/conjunction in the relationship between God and man. 'God' stands opposite to man as the divine Will stands opposite to the human will. To man, 'God' is a transcendence, and although he is immanent, man can not see him, can not meet him, can not immediately experience him. He is at the same time Absolute Being and Absolute

Nothingness in his true identity of contradictories. In each moment in time and at each place in space he both is and is not, in the sense that his absence for the enlightened mind is the proof of his omnipresence.

Tanabe Hajime

Tanabe was originally a student of Nishida but because of his different outset-i.e. different from the Zen-experience-his thought was for a great part a reaction against Nishida. Tanabe was greatly influenced by the teaching of Shinran (1173-1262) and by the works and the life of Kiyozawa Manshi (1863-1903), who-mutatis mutandis-during the turn of the century fulfilled the role within Shin Buddhism that Kierkegaard had fulfilled within the Danish Lutheran Church.

According to Tanabe the only possibility to transcend the noetic (i.e. Metaphysics as speculative philosophy on the level of the subject/object relationship), is the undergoing of a total turning of the mind (J. e-shin), a metanoia in the "death-and-resurrection-experience". According to him, the true dialectic is neither the "and-and" speculative synthesis of Hegel, nor the "or-or" ethical concern of Kierkegaard; but the "neither-nor" double negation in our immediateness through the Compassionate activity of the Absolute. Our awareness of 'sin', i.e. of our religious non-worth, means than at the same time the abolishment of 'sin' through the graceful activity of the Absolute (zettai), since 'God' or 'Buddha' is Absolute Nothingness, and therefore the power and mercy of absolute self-surrender.

For Tanabe the Absolute is only absolute as Nothingness. Absolute Nothingness is qualitatively different from the world and thus transcendent in relation to the relative world. The Love-Compassion of the Absolute is embodied in this world by the bodhisattva, the teacher who proclaims the message of the metanoic truth and who through his "fire" (i.e. his own experience of death-and-resurrection) ignites his disciples to action-entrusting. The Compassion of Absolute Nothingness is thus transmitted from teacher to disciple.

As mentioned before, Tanabe bases himself on Shinran's Kyogyoshinsho. The 'being born in the Pure Land' was already greatly demythologized by Shinran, who was convinced that the essential experience of death-and-resurrection was fulfilled at the moment of e-shin, of the metanoia that is the 'moment of shinjin', the 'settlement of birth', i.e. the samsaric aspect of Birth in the Pure Land, of which the nirvanic aspect-the fulfillment of Buddhahood (Absolute Truth)-remains shifted to "the other life". Tanabe uses the image of the bodhisattva who makes all preparations to meet the Buddha, fulfills his path until the end and than goes and visits the Buddha in his room. He, however, discovers the Buddha's absence (the Buddha-room is after all emptiness) and realizes that at this moment the Buddha is in the world; therefore the bodhisattva returns to the world of suffering to work side by side with the Buddha. It is in and through this return that the bodhisattva becomes a Buddha, which in fact is a non-reachable goal because of its utter paradox: Buddhahood is after all a 'state' in which even the noble goal of becoming a Buddha is surpassed.

Against Nishida's action-intuition, Tanabe emphasizes action-entrusting. According to him, Nishida's topos still belongs to the domain of contemplative speculation. To him (as with Kierkegaard) religious truth in this life is fragmentary and certainly not a continuum. If this truth is a whole, than Being is and it would make no sense to call this Being 'Nothingness'. Absolute Truth-for Tanabe, Amida's Light-penetrates us in an intensive manner, not as an extensive totality. Tanabe uses the image of a figure-skater, who only keeps his balance on the ice as long as he is moving. In 'entrusting' there is always the presence of a certain anxiety and an existential uncertainty, but the more uncertainty there is, the more certain becomes our awareness of our limitation and our (karmic) awareness of 'sin' (i.e. our 'nothingness'), which can only be lifted through e-shin. The mind of entrusting, as the transformation of our nothingness to Absolute Nothingness, is-according to Tanabe-'uncertain certainty'. It becomes established in the repetition of the Name, which is the decisive action. In the 'here-and-now' of this religious act there is also present the Absolute Truth, not so much as an eye-to-eye revelation, but as a veiled, i.e. hidden from our consciousness, Truth.

Nishida and Tanabe

1. Nishida emphasizes action-intuition; Tanabe emphasizes the meaning of action entrusting in the religious existence.
2. Action-intuition sees our existence as a creative element within the creative, historical world. Tanabe sees the dialectic only in function of the historical world.
3. Nishida places his creative element in each new moment, in such a way that the whole can continually be seen from a different perspective. To Tanabe, the historical world is at any moment and at any place a dead end street which has to be broken through with entrusting and determination. Nishida emphasizes the integrating aspect (each moment as integrated within the course of time), Tanabe emphasizes the infinity-aspect (mugen = infinite, unconditional light, infinite compassion, infinite wisdom).
4. The fundamental experience according to Nishida is the immediate realization of Absolute Nothingness as the Dharmakaya in Zen Buddhism. With Tanabe, the ethical standpoint dominates. It is out of his ethico-social concern (cfr. Kiyozawa Manshi) that he focuses on the study of religion, in an attempt to unite the truth of the Buddhist Zen and Pure Land traditions and the truth according to Christianity.

Despite these differences, both philosophers share a number of notions which became characteristic of the Kyoto School of Philosophy:

1. The absolute should be seen as Absolute Nothingness.
2. The essence and value of philosophical thought rest in our religious existence.
3. The representations of the Eternal Now and Nothingness as disjunction/conjunction.

9

Influence of Buddha and Buddhism in Bengali Literature

Lord Buddha taught that selfishness is the chief evil of human life. His preachings known as Buddhism, was a religion of proper moral conduct and not a religion of priests, temples, gods, sacrifices or rituals.

Gautama said that to achieve salvation by starvation and self denial had no meaning. Rather a clear mind nourished by a healthy and well cared for body was essential for attainment of Bodhi (enlightenment). He realized that man is evil when he tries to achieve physical pleasure, power, fame and riches.

Buddhism was a revolt against social injustice, parochialism and selfishness. A Marxist Soviet writer rightly said, "Buddhism strove to replace Brahminism, the religion of early slave-owning society in ancient India".

> *"Brahminism, as is well-known sanctified the estate structure of society (its division into the varnas) and the dominant position of Brahmans declared themselves to be above all other men. They taught that in this as well as in the next world happiness could only he obtained through sacrifices of cattle, food, and melted butter to fire."*

> *"Buddhism rose against these senseless sacrifices and in the first place, against him to whom the sacrifices were offered against God Brahma declaring him to be non-existent."*

T. W. Rhys David in his Hubert Lectures said, "for the first time in the history of the world, it proclaimed a salvation which each man could gain for himself, and by himself, in this world, during this life, without the least reference to God or to gods either great or small."

It is now an established fact that the Buddhism is a religion for common man while it is being philosophical guide for an intellectual. Buddhism succeeded in winning the support of many oppressed people suffering from lack of rights, poverty and hunger. In referring to early Buddhism, it should be noted that it succeeded, under the definite socio-historical conditions of the times, in expressing in a special form the aspirations of the people for a better life.

The Buddhistic thoughts cast a new light on the socio-economic and intellectual life of Bengal since 3rd century BC. Teachings of Buddha were not known or practiced all over the sub-continent and outside India during his life time. But by the middle of 3rd century BC. Emperor Asoka sent his son Mahendra daughter Sanghamitra and a large number of monks and scholars to different countries to preach the teachings of the Buddha. Thus the thoughts of the Buddha spread almost all parts of the world: Japan to Victnam, Sri Lanka to Mongolia.

The Most brilliant Bengali scholar is Atisa Dipankara (980-1053) who preached the teachings of Buddha in Tibet for 13 years. While in Tibet he wrote 79 books or discourses, of which 30 are original works and the rest are translations. In one of his books "Bodhi Patha Pradipa", which has been translated into several languages including English, he dealt with the theory of knowledge and practice. According to him, one attains the enlightenment not by mere knowledge but by proper practice. Atisa also opined neither the mere knowledge of Buddhism nor the meaningless practice of it is useful. One must have adequate knowledge of teachings of the Buddha and should utilize it in practice.

The rulers of Palas, Chandras and some other dynasties of medieval Bengal were Buddhists. The Palas and other dynasties were Mahayanists but they were very liberal. All sects of

Buddhism flourished during their reign. They were great patrons of art, literature, sculpture, philosophy and other intellectual works.

Bengali language originated in the hands of Buddhist monks and Siddhacharyas from crust of Prakrit. The first ever songs and lyrics in Bengali language were composed by these Siddhacharyas during the reign of Pala Kings in ancient Bangladesh from 8th to 12-13th centuries.

Bengali writers and thinkers of the modern times owe a great deal to Buddhist philosophy. The greatest thinker and reformer of early 19th century in India, Ram Mohon Ray (1772-1833) founded the Brahmo Samaj in 1828 to reform orthodox traditional religion of the Hindus. Son of the Hindu Brahman, Ram Mohon Ray studied history, philosophy and was greatly influenced by the liberal thoughts of Buddhism and Islam. His Brahminism was a revolt against the Brahman and a protest against caste, idolatry and other religious and social superstitions.

Though a great student of Vedanta philosophical system, Ray was an objective idealist. He was greatly influenced by Buddhistic teachings and differed from traditional Hinduism and bitterly criticized the caste system of the Hindu community. He said, "the present system of religion adhered to by the Hindus is not well-calculated to promote their political interest. The distinction of castes introducing innumerable divisions and sub-divisions among them have entirely deprived them of patriotic feeling, and the multitude of religious rites and ceremonies and the laws of purification have totally disqualified them from undertaking any difficult enterprise." He was also moved by the humiliating condition of the oppressed classes. For all these reformative and revolutionary activities he owed much to the teachings of Lord Buddha and Prophet Mohammed.

A large number of Bengali writers, thinkers and intellectuals of the 19th century wrote on the life, philosophy and religion of the Buddha. Many creative writers-poets, novelists and playwrights were directly or indirectly influenced by the rationalistic philosophy of the Buddha. Among the notable

Hindu writers who devoted to Buddhism are Rajendra Lal Mitra (1822-91), Ramda Sen (1845-81), Satyendranath Tagore (1842-1923), Krishna Kumar Mitra (1851-1935), Rajanikanta Gupta (1849-1900), Bijoychadra Majumdar (1861-1942), Sharat Chandra Das (1849-1971), Haraprasad Shastri (1853-1921), Chandra Ghose (1844-1922) and Girish Chandra Ghose (1844-1922).

Founder of Buddhist Text Society (1892) and great scholar in oriental languages, Sarat Chandra Das spent many years in Tibet investigating on ancient Buddhist literature. It was Mr. Das who made familiar Atisa Dipankara to the Bengali readers. He also visited many Buddhist countries including Sikkim, China, Japan and Thailand for the search and study of Buddhism and Buddhist culture. His contribution in the study of Buddhism in Bangladesh could not be measured. In his invaluable books like: Journey to Lasha and central Tibet, Indian Pandits in the land of snow and "Bodhisattavadana Kalapalata" (Bengali), he devoted to delve deep into the Buddhistic studies.

Rajendra Lal Mitra's outstanding books on Buddhism include: An Introduction to the the Lalitavistara (1877), Buddha Gaya the Hermitage of Sakyamuni (1878) and the Sanskrit Buddhist Literature of Nepal (1882).

Akkhay Kumar Datta (1820-86), a great prose--writer and thinker and editor of the famous monthly "Tattabodhini" devoted a chapter in his brilliant book "Bharatbarshio" Upashak Sampraday" (The Worshipers of Indian sub-continent).

Haraprashat Shastri is a great figure in the field of ancient Bengali language and Buddhist culture. He discovered some oldest mystic songs of Buddhist monks from Nepal. The script is known as "Charyacharjabinishchaya." The scholars are of opinion that these songs were composed between 8th and 12th century AD.

The most outstanding playwright of Bengali literature Girish Chandra Ghose published his "Buddhadeva-Charita" (1887). The play depicted the life of the Buddha. His another historical play "Asoka" (1911) is based on the life of Buddhist emperor Asoka (273-232 BC).

One of the greatest Bengali novelists and thinkers Bankim Chandra Chattapadhya (1838-94) paid tributes to the Buddha in his treatise Samya (Equality), (1879). He described the Buddha as the greatest liberal humanist and democrat who liberated the oppressed common man from the curse of caste-system of the Vedic period. In his literary journal "Bangadarshan" he published a number of valuable treaties and essays on the philosophy of the Buddha written by eminent persons.

Keshab Chandra Sen (1838-84) a leader of "Bharatbarshio Brahmo Samaj" was greatly inspired by the liberal humanism of the Buddhistic thoughts. His brother Krishnabihari Sen (1847-95) wrote "Buddha Charita" an authentic biography of the Buddha.

By late 19th century, study of Buddhism took a new dimension in the then Bengal. Several associations and learned bodies were established in Calcutta for the promotion and study of Buddhism. Among them are Mahabodhi Society of India (1891), The Buddhist Text Society (1992), and the Bengal Buddhist Association (1992). A good number of scholars were associated with these Associations and devoted themselves for the study of Buddhist philosophy and culture.

Dr. Benimadhab Barua (1888-1948) who obtained his D. Litt from London in 1917, first among the Indians had some remarkable works on Buddhism. His books include: A History of pre-Buddhist Indian Philosophy, A Prolegomenon to the History of Buddhist Philosophy, Inscriptions of Asoka (three volumes), Prakrit Dhammapada, Buddhokosh and Bouddha Parinay Paddhaṭi. He was an authority in ancient Buddhist culture and civilization.

A great poet Nabin chandra Sen (1847-1909) wrote "Amitava", an epic on the life of the Buddha. A major poet Satyendranath Datta (1882-1922) composed several poems on Buddhist theme: the poems are Buddhapurnima, Buddhabaran and Susheta etc.

The rational and humanistic aspects of the teachings of the Buddha and Buddhist culture had attracted Nobel-laureate

Rabindra Nath Tagore (1861-1941). Contributions of Buddhist rulers and Buddhism in Indian civilization and the role of Buddhist philosophy and culture in art, literature and intellectual life of India were recalled by Rabindra Nath in his poems, plays, essays, travelogues, treatises and lectures. Buddhism had a great impact in the thoughts and reflections of the poet.

Rabindra Nath was highly impressed to see the Buddhist culture and civilization in different countries like Burma, Thailand, Indonesia, Japan, Sri Lanka and China which he had visited and there he exchanged views with the noted scholars on various matters including art, literature and world peace. He had not only written a lot on Buddhistic thoughts but also encouraged others to write on the teachings of Buddha. A Brahmo-Hindu Rabindra Nath was against all sorts of idolatry and superstitions, but he had a lasting regard for the Buddha. His reverence for the Buddha has been expressed in the words of Acharya Kripalini, "Only once in his life, said Rabindra Nath, did he feel like prostrating himself before an image, and that was when he saw the Buddha at Gaya."

A great scholar, philologist and linguist of Bengal literature Dr. Muhammad Shahidullah (1885-1969) was an authority in oldest ancient Buddhist mystic songs known as Charyapadas. His first book "Les Chantas Mystique" is in French and was published from Paris. The book deals with the language, contents and history of the oldest (900-1200 AD.) Buddhist mystic songs. One of his other major works "Buddhist Mystic Songs, (1940) was English translation of the Charyapadas. He was two other books on Buddha Charyapada and Doha. Besides, he published several articles on oldest Buddhist songs which played a great role in the developed of Bengali language and literature.

After the partition of Indian sub-continent in 1947 a good number of works on Buddhism have been published in the then East Pakistan, now Bangladesh. An idealist philosopher and Professor of philosophy of the Dhaka University Dr. Govindra Chandra Dev (1906-1971) published a book "Buddha, the Humanist" (1969) and a good number of articles on Buddhism.

In the preface of the book Dr. Dev said, I look upon Buddha as a cementing force that can bring together advocates of warring, opposite paths and make for a world understanding on a durable basis. In this crisis of history when a wanton use of power might as well efface the very existence of man, Buddha's cult of universal love and friendship will. I am sure, forge a bond of unity between materialists and spiritualists, secularists and their adversaries, advocates of spiritual values, free thinkers and traditionalists and draw them closer together to ensure a better future for the common man. Dr. Dev was brutally killed during the War of Liberation of Bangladesh in 1971.

Bangla Academy, the highest body of art, literature and culture, published a number of books on Buddhism during the last 35 years. Besides, many discourses on Buddhist philosophy have been published by different authors in Bangladesh.

BUDDHISM AND THE BRAHMA CONCEPT

The term Brahma occurs fairly frequently in Buddhist literature. There are many terms that are prefixed with the word Brahma. Some of the well-known are Brahma-cariya, Brahma-vihara, Brahma-kaya, Brahma-danda, Brahma-jala, Brahma-cakka and Brahma-sara. Even the Brahma world as well as denizens of such worlds known as Maha-brahma, Brahma-sahampati, Brahma-sanankumara are also mentioned.

In phrases such as 'Brahmati matapitaro', the term Brahma is used to give it a special ethical connotation. What we propose here is to examine how this pre-Buddhist word came to be used in Buddhist literature and to discuss the changes it has undergone in this process of adaptation.

The 6th century B. C., the period to which the Buddha belongs is a period in which Indian religious and philosophical scene underwent a radical change. By this time the Brahmanic religious tradition had reached a very high stage of development. It began with the Vedas and developed through the Brahmanas, Aranyakas and reached its climax in the Upanishads.

It was at such a time that the Buddha appeared on the religious scene of India. During this period there were two distinct groups of religious thinkers: one group advocating the belief that salvation had to be attained through Karma marga or Yajan marga, i. e. through the path of sacrifice; and the other holding that salvation is possible only through the path of wisdom or Jnana-marga.

Besides these two religious paths, both put forward by the Brahmins, there was the path to salvation through ascetic practices put forward mainly by such groups as Ajivakas, Paribbajakas, and Niganthas. The latter group belonged mainly to the Sramana tradition which was opposed to the Brahmana tradition. Even the Buddha belongs to this Sramana tradition.

The Buddha who had mastered all the religious traditions of the time not only rejected the prevalent views on salvation, but presented a novel philosophy of emancipation. He discarded such views as divine creation, belief in a permanent self, determinism and annihilationism, and presented his teaching basing it on the fundamental doctrine of paticcasamuppada or dependent co-origination.

This fundamental doctrine formed the foundation for his other basic teachings such as karma, rebirth and freedom. Even the theory and practice of Buddhist ethics is founded on this doctrine of paticcasamuppada, which is the central philosophy of Buddhism.

The oldest scriptures that record the teachings of the Buddha are referred to as the Tripitaka (Three Baskets) written in the Pali language. When one examines the Tripitaka, it becomes quite clear that the Buddha's teaching is basically different from Vedic and Brahmanic teachings.

Yet, it becomes also clear that in spite of this difference, the Buddha himself had to adapt and use certain cherished beliefs, concepts and terms that were in vogue among the Brahmins, in order to put across his own teachings. Among such pre-Buddhistic concepts, the Buddha adopted the concept of Brahma occupies an important place. As mentioned before, the word Brahmao ccurs frequently in pre-Buddhist as well as in Buddhist literature indicating a wide variety of senses and context.

(1) The technical terms used in Buddhist literature can be classified into three groups.

(2) The terms that are common in form as well as in meaning in both Brahmanic and Buddhist literature.

(3) The terms that are common in form, but different in meaning.

Terms that denote completely a Buddhist meaning.

According to this classification the term Brahma falls into the second group. In Buddhism it is used in a sense quite different from the sense in which it is used in Brahmanism. Both Brahma and Brahman connote the idea of the Highest. In the earliest stages the term Brahman meant the universe. Hence the first beginning of the Brahma ideal could be traced to the Purusa Sukta which occurs in the 10th Mandala of the Rgveda.

It alludes to some kind of primordial universal matter. Gradually this idea developed and finally it came to be accepted that the Brahman or Brahma is the source of the whole universe. In the early Brahmana period Prajapati is considered more important and he is considered the primordial being and Brahma occupies a secondary place.

In the Satapatha Brahman it is clearly mentioned that Prajapati created the Brahma. But in later Brahmana texts their positions were reversed, Brahma superseding Prajapati, with Brahma being considered as the foundation as well as the source of the universe.

This idea reached its culmination in the Upanishad literature, where reference is made to the undifferentiated unity of Brahman and Atman, that is the Universal Soul and the Individual Soul, in other words, the macrocosm and the microcosm.

Brahman as the Cosmic Soul is universal, permanent, indestructible, unique; it is the primordial essence, the ultimate ground of existence. The final goal came to be considered as the realization of the unity between Brahman and Atman; the realization of "oneness" between the universal soul and the individual soul. The attainment of this undifferentiated unity is considered in the Upanishads as the goal and ideal of all Brahmins. It was said that there are two paths open to this goal. One is the path of Sacrifice (Yajna or Karma-marga) and the other the Path of Knowledge (Jnana-marga). The latter was followed by the Upanishad sages, the munis who practised severe ascetic practices.

The Buddha's attitude towards this long-cherished concept of Brahmais two-fold.

- Complete rejection of the Brahma concept.
- Giving new meanings to certain ideas connected with the Brahma concept.

Both as religion and philosophy, Buddhism is based on the "no soul" view. Therefore, the Buddhist attitude to the Upanishadic view of reality needs no examination. In the Vasettha-sutta of the Dighanikaya, the attempt to reach the Brahma that no one has seen is compared to the effort of a line of blind men. The Buddhist teaching that everything is impermanent rejects the belief in a permanent substance that underlines everything in the universe.

The Buddhist theory of causality shows that if there is a Brahma, he cannot be uncaused and similarly cannot be eternal. According to the Buddhist doctrine of paticasamuppada the universe is not the creation of a personal God or impersonal Godhead, but the outcome of causes and conditions.

Though the Buddha rejected this Brahma concept which was prevalent in pre-Buddhistc times, it is clearly seen that he used some aspects of this concept to put across his own philosophy.

Buddhism does not deny the existence of Brahma. It speaks of Brahma-lokas, refers to Maha Brahama as the Lord of the Brahama-lokas. In many suttas this supreme Brahma is referred to as Sahampati. He is represented as one who has cultivated his mind and as one who honours and pays reverence to the Buddha. This shows that Buddhahood is higher than Brahmahood. The Buddhist texts also refer to many instances when Brahma came to meet the Buddha. Among these Brahmas are Sanamkumara, Ghatikara, Narada.

Reference is also made to the path leading to the Brahma World. The Tevijja Sutta says that the path to the Brahma World is through the development of jhanas pertaining to the five material spheres. The Brahma Worlds are known as Suddhavasas, the Pure Abodes.

It is said that the attainment of the First jhana leads to the Brahma Worlds called "Brahama-parisajja", "Brahma-purohita" and "Maha Brahma"; the Second Jhana to Parittabha, Appamanabha and Abhassara; the Third Jhana to Parittasubha, Appamanasubha and Subhakinna.

The Fourth Jhana is said to lead the non-Anagamins to Vehapphala and Asannasatta Brahma-lokas and the Anagamns to Aviha, Atappa, Sudassi and Akanittha Brahma-loka. This shows that Buddhism too has a parallel concept of the attainment of companionship with Brahma. But this, however, does not mean that Buddhism, like Brahmanism, admits the possibility of eternal companionship with Brahma.

What is meant by this jhanic attainment is the experiencing of a very high level of mental development through the jhanic process.

The teaching on the four Brahma-Viharas (four Sublimes States) is another instance which shows how the Buddha adopted another important aspect of the pre-Buddhist Brahma concept. Many scholars are of the opinion that the teaching on Brahma-Vihara is purely Buddhist. Perhaps this is more likely to be an adaptation of a pre-Buddhist concept to suit the Buddhist point of view. This becomes clear from Buddhaghosa's definition of Brahma-vihara:

> *"Why are these called Brahma-viharas? It is because they are supreme and faultless. These states constitute the best mode of conduct towards others. The Brahmas live with their minds freed of the five hindrances. The Yogins who are endowed with these states also live with faultless minds like the Brahmas".*

As the parents have these mental attitudes towards their children, they too can be called Brahmas. In fact in comparing the parents to the Brahmas, the Buddha appears to have added a new dimension to the Brahma concept.

The Buddhist path leading to Nibbana is called the "Brahma-faring" (Brahmacariya). The Buddha addressing the first disciples who grasped his teaching said, "Come O! monk, the doctrine is well taught. Practise this Brahma faring for the perfect ending of suffering".

The five ascetics who were the first disciples of the Buddha were already following some kind of a restrained noble life. By inviting them to lead "Brahmacariya" a new Buddha seems to have made clear that his interpretation of the Brahma faring meant something different from what they were already engaged in. The Varnasrama dharma followed by the Brahmins divides the life into four stages.

These four stages are studentship (brahamacriya), householder (grhastha), forest entry (vanaprastha) and renunciation (sannyasi). Here, Brahmacariya meant merely the studentship, limited to the student days of one's life. But Brahmacariya in Buddhism is not limited to any particular period of life. It is valid for all stages of life and can be commenced by renunciation of the worldly life.

It is somewhat parallel to the sannyasi stage in the "varnasrama dharma" of the Brahmins. From this it becomes clear that the Brahmacariya in Buddhism, which developed from a pre-Buddhist idea, was identified as the path leading to the ending of defilement resulting in the destruction of suffering. In general the term Brahma is used in the sense of Supreme, Noble, Highest, Holy and so on. This shows how important the idea of Brahma had been to the Brahmins and how much influence it exerted on Buddhism. It is also seen that in the canonical texts, the two terms Brahma and Dhamma are at time used co-terminously.

Terms such as Brahma-cakka, Dhamma-cakka, Brahma-bhuta, Dhamma-bhuta, Brahma-kaya, Dhamma-kaya, illustrate such synonymity of the two terms. This clearly shows that the

Buddha used the pre-Buddhistic Brahma concept to give a new dimension to certain important Buddhist concepts.

THE BUDDHIST PARADOX

Anyone familiar with the ancient religious philosophy of Buddhism has no doubt come across one of the most puzzling paradoxes in any spiritual study: the apparent conflict between the "no soul" doctrine (anatta) and belief in reincarnation. If one has no soul,who or what is reincarnated, and how?

If one has no soul,who or what is reincarnated, and how?

This paradox has been the source of endless speculation and has spawned varying interpretations of Buddhism. A solution to the puzzling paradox would no doubt lead to a more uniform understanding of the teachings of Buddha. The effort to find such a solution, however, faces challenges.

The primary challenge lies in the nature of Buddhism; it is a study equally weighted between theory and practice. Lacking the firsthand experience that comes with hands-on practice, most will find the Buddhist texts obscure. Readers distant from the practice face even greater difficulty when confronted by the apparent conflict between the anatta doctrine and reincarnation. In spite of this challenge, an attempt to explain the paradox is worthwhile for a number of reasons:

1. Practice follows theory, theory follows practice. If one starts with incorrect theory, practice will suffer. Thus it is worth considering whether or not a theory is correctly interpreted.
2. Buddhism has an important role to play in today's world. Confusion arising from conflicting views, however, threatens to diminish and obfuscate the Buddha's message. If the conflict between the doctrines of anatta and reincarnation can be solved, the confusion will diminish.
3. Hidden within challenging paradoxes one often finds a path to greater understanding. A paradox often masks a new paradigm, a new way of looking at the world, that

provides invaluable rewards to those who persevere in their attempts to resolve the apparent contradiction.

A paradox often masks a new paradigm, a new way of looking at the world.

The effort begins with an analysis of the thoughts shaping the paradox. Many interpret the anatta (no soul, no self) doctrine to mean there is no soul or spirit within the composite person that is the human being.

They argue the Buddha taught that only the aggregates (khandhas or skandhas) make up the person. These are 1) material processes, 2) feeling, 3) perception, 4) mental formations, and 5) consciousness. (Consciousness in this context refers to sensations, what one might call sentience, as distinguished from the consciousness to which I later refer.) Those who argue this viewpoint claim all aspects of a person are impermanent, transitory. Therefore nothing is eternal, nothing survives the dissolution of the aggregate; no self exists apart from the temporary arrangement of material factors. This view echoes the philosophy of materialism which claims all phenomena are simply emergent properties of building-block matter.

On the other hand, Buddhists speak of reincarnation. Tibetan Buddhists counsel the departed individual in the stages after death called Bardos. (See Tibetan Book of the Dead.) Most people have seen movies or read books about the Tibetan search for reincarnated leaders who survive from life to life. The Buddha himself spoke of his many past lives. How can such beliefs be compatible with a version of anatta which holds nothing survives, that no soul continues on past body death? The two lines of thought contradict one another.

Attempts to explain away the paradox with talk of streams of consciousness forming from old aggregates make little sense. This line of reasoning mirrors the materialistic concept that consciousness emerges out of matter and has no existence in its own right. These arguments focus solely on the impermanent and thus become circular. As long as we restrict the discussion to the phenomenal world of impermanent forms, we will not find anything permanent. This is a given; a self-fulfilling prophecy. By definition, nothing of the impermanent, transitory realm constitutes a permanent self.

...others believe Buddhism takes the opposite position and supports a supernatural, transcendent realm.

The important question, however, is whether or not consciousness transcends the impermanent world. Some argue the anatta doctrine dictates against such a transcendent reality; others believe Buddhism takes the opposite position and supports a supernatural, transcendent realm. It is across this divide that the argument regarding the true meaning of anatta takes place.

Matthieu Ricard (The Monk and the Philosopher) hints at a partial solution in an alternative view of the self, which, with deceiving subtlety, can slip past a reader. Ricard acknowledges the idea of a stream of moment-to-moment consciousness-awareness of a series of impermanent states-then advances the idea of an individual stream of consciousness with integral continuity. This "individual stream of consciousness" comes close to being a description of a conscious, immaterial being-perhaps this is the missing "self" or "soul" that escapes notice when one considers only material aggregates.

Upon close inspection, it appears the Buddha himself also did not support the strong version of the anatta doctrine. At the same time he taught there was no self or no soul (anatta), he also stated it was not correct to argue there was no self, no soul. How could both views-a) there is no soul and b) it is incorrect to say there is no soul-be accurate? What new distinction was he offering for his students' consideration? Any analysis of Buddhism must unravel this conundrum. A concept of what it is that reincarnates or experiences rebirth must be developed.

How was it possible for the Buddha to recall past lives if nothing of self remained in existence over the span of those lifetimes? How was it possible for the Buddha to recall past lives if nothing of self remained in existence over the span of those lifetimes? It would seem a continuity of consciousness is necessary for such recall. Not the consciousness of sensation tied to the body, which we have labeled sentience, but a more fundamental consciousness-a basic self that is aware and conscious but not material, a self not restricted to the impermanence of the phenomenal world.

Buddha warned his students to steer clear of identifying with the five aggregates: you are not your physical body; not your mind; not your perceptions; not your feelings; not your sensations. Those qualities, individually and in composite, are not self, he taught. There must be a self, however, able to recall the aggregates that comprise past lives. A self that exists outside and separate from the five aggregates solves the conceptual impasse. It is the nature of this self, which is not the five aggregates, that must be understood in order to make sense of the paradox.

Perhaps what was meant by "no self" was, in actuality, "not self." If one takes this view, one can see the skandhas as the "not self" while there exists that which is the self. "Self" and "not self." This interpretation escapes the outright denial of the existence of the permanent self. It leads to an understanding of the nuances of an immaterial self that provide a different version of anatta.

The task of grasping this concept, unfortunately, requires familiarity with the practical and experiential side of Buddhism; without firsthand experience, the going gets rough. Perhaps this is the reason the Buddha declined to explicate the matter for the student who pressed for an answer; perhaps this is why he left the matter in the "indeterminate" category (in his public teachings). He could find no way to explain that which had not been experienced. Words fell short. All he could say was that it was both "A" and "not A" at the same time, apparently hoping the student would press on, looking for a deeper understanding.

This history should give us pause. Any attempt at an explanation may be foolhardy; however, I believe there are those who have had experiences which provide insights into the problem. It is primarily to their attention I address this piece. Others, lacking in such experience, may still be able to draw upon intuitive resources to conjure the picture I will paint. Turning to one of the most famous of the Buddhist texts, we consider what the Tibetan Book of the Dead offers on the subject. The Book of the Dead was written as an instruction manual for monks charged with guiding the recently deceased through stages after death known as Bardos. In these stages, the deceased encounters challenging phenomena that must be understood and overcome. Success in navigating this between-lives period, it is suggested, plays an important role in the future life of the deceased. It is clear Tibetans consider a conscious individual survives body death. And yet, this raises another problem...

Those who separate from the body in near death situations report mental imagery, perceptions, sensations, feelings, and thoughts, while separate from the body.

In the Bardos, the deceased remains the effect of his mental formations, sensations, feelings, and perceptions. Though these four khandhas (or skandhas) are no longer tied to the personhood of the body, their existence continues. Near death experience accounts support this view. Those who separate from the body in near death situations report mental imagery, perceptions, sensations, feelings, and thoughts, while separate from the body. It appears the conscious being carries with it the memories (mental formations) and connections (feelings and sensations) of its past existence as well as a sense of continuity of self.

This aggregate "baggage" explains, in part, past-life recalls-the individual stream of consciousness accumulates mental forms. It is as though the individual stream of consciousness, proceeding through time, continually sums up, or integrates, its experience. In clinging to the khandhas, this stream of consciousness (or spirit) performs like a cosmic pack rat, storing tokens and reminders of the past in a giant cosmic scrapbook. Thus we stumble, quite unexpectedly, upon the concept of karma or kamma.

Karma can be described as past causes and effects exerting influence on the present. Our actions in the past will be revisited upon us in the present. That which we cause today will appear in our mirror in the future. Karma lies behind the admonition "what goes around come around." It is the idea we create our own destiny, painted with an ironic brush. Apparently karma is not the impersonal cosmic force some make it out to be. If we accept the above description of the fate of the disembodied-they cling to the accumulated mental detritus of the past-it appears karma has a personal nature. The individual stream of consciousness, toting its past, insures the laws of karma play out in a very personal way.

In our explanation of reincarnation and karma, the discussion has taken a dramatic turn away from the anatta doctrine. It appears we have a continuity of consciousness which carries the accumulated past from lifetime to lifetime, making possible the laws of karma. Apparently the anatta doctrine is false and misleading. But why would the Buddha sabotage his own teachings with an untruth? It doesn't make sense. There must be a reason...

The deceased individual, without a body, clinging to the aggregates, remains trapped in a false identity, a false self.

The deceased individual, without a body, clinging to the aggregates, remains trapped in a false identity, a false self. In this post-mortem state, that which might be considered a soul remains encumbered by its attachment to the past. The being clings to mental formations, sensations, feelings, and a false self comprised of accumulated karmic "identities" that are "not self." If so, then, even after death, the struggle to achieve enlightenment continues, which is the prominent idea in The Tibetan Book of the Dead. Perhaps the essence of the "no soul" doctrine is the warning that the "soul identity" one assumes after death is also not the true self; that, even then, the student must learn to detach from the aggregates and no longer cling to form.

The Buddha spoke not only to the lay public, but also to dedicated monks, those who, like Tibetan Buddhists, experienced states of existence separate from the body, either as a result of meditative practice or a recall of past lives. The Buddha, perhaps, taught his most experienced followers to continue their practice beyond death. He taught them to continue efforts to cease clinging to the four khandhas which are carried into the afterlife; perhaps he taught them to detach from the accumulated mental formations that code for karma.

The Buddha, perhaps, taught his most experienced followers to continue their practice beyond death.

Not only in the Tibetan Bardos, but also in the realms of Pure Land Buddhism, we find descriptions of a phenomenal realm beyond our bodily existence. It appears the conscious being, wrapped in the four aggregates, qualifies as a soul. As the anatta doctrine teaches, this soul identity is a false self which must be discarded if one is to achieve a cessation of suffering and reach the state of nirvana.

It is worth slowing up and taking another look at the snapshot just developed. In this picture, the conscious being, wrapped in the khandhas or aggregates-self-accumulated karma-suffers from a collection of past causes which, in the present, dictate the future. Buried within these karmic mental formations lies the compulsion to continue on the wheel of birth and death. The state of nirvana results when the conscious being steps outside the aggregates-the gross and the subtle-to stand free in the realm of the formless, free from the impermanent world of forms. Identification with false selves is jettisoned and the being becomes aware of self in the realm of the formless.

Carl Becker supports this analysis of the realms when he writes: "In its broadest categories, the Buddhist universe may be divided into three realms: things both immaterial and formless (arupadhatu), those with form but only subtle matter (rupadhatu), and the physical/sensual realm of form and gross matter (kamadhatu)."

The Buddha's hesitation to explain the anatta doctrine becomes clear as we explore the nature of these realms. If one's focus lies entirely within the realm of form and gross matter (kamadhatu), what chance does one have of understanding how the soul (in rupadhatu) is a "not self?" For those whose focus has moved to the next realm (the realm of subtle form, rupadhatu) the teachings become critical. The Buddha might have warned those students, "You are not yet there. Do not stop. This is not the end of the path." He might have admonished them to continue past the false self that is the soul wrapped in the aggregates, on to the realm of the immaterial and formless, the realm of the pure consciousness, on to nirvana.

As with anatta, karma, and reincarnation, the literature abounds with debate regarding nirvana. Some advance nihilistic visions and interpretations. The above description, however, appears to clarify nirvana as awareness of the immaterial and formless state (arupadhatu). The Buddha was known to have achieved nirvana, yet remained present and teaching, which puts the lie to the nihilistic argument.

Nirvana, it appears, had more to do with achieving recognition of the immaterial self, a self able to observe forms without identifying with those forms.

Nirvana, it appears, had more to do with achieving recognition of the immaterial self, a self able to observe forms without identifying with those forms. Nirvana thus appears to be a state of consciousness free from attachment to form. Free from attachment to form, the conscious being terminates the compulsion to ride the wheel of birth and death. Achieving nirvana, the being can choose to reincarnate, but does not suffer a compulsion to do so. The bonds to suffering are severed. The form suffers, but the immaterial and formless self does not suffer, except by virtue of its attachment and identification with forms.

Thus a divide separates the immaterial and formless consciousness from the world of material forms, both subtle and gross. It is here that another key Buddhist concept, emptiness, becomes relevant. "Emptiness" refers to the idea that material forms possess no substantive, independent existence. The material world is not primary; it does not stand, uncaused, on its own. All phenomena are "empty." Rupadhatu and kamadhatu do not possess independent existence. They are contingent realms. Their existence is an "illusion." Their existence issues forth from the realm of arupadhatu, the immaterial and formless. Thus, Buddhism, at its heart, is an Idealistic religious philosophy, not a philosophy based upon nihilistic materialism. ...the integral concepts of Buddhism-anatta, reincarnation, karma, emptiness, nirvana-are woven together in a seamless unity.

The paradox that motivated our analysis fades. The contradiction dis-integrates; the integral concepts of Buddhism-anatta, reincarnation, karma, emptiness, nirvana-are woven together in a seamless unity. The Buddha was not schizophrenic; his teachings are consistent from top to bottom. They make up the most profound ontological analysis of this universe ever performed. The paradox ends up illuminating the pernicious influence of our attachment to form, our identification with matter, subtle and gross. Out of this attachment and identification arises the philosophy of materialism, the celebration of form as ultimate, form as primary, form as ontological cause. That Buddhism, through mistranslation, misinterpretation, and misunder-standing, should be transformed into materialism comes as no surprise. The impulse to cling to matter weaves the veil of illusion before our eyes. In our first attempts to see, it is this veil we observe. The Buddha taught us to see beyond the veil. He taught we are not that which we observe, we are not the veil-the veil is "not self." Removing the veil does not end our sight, it frees us to see. Removing the veil does not plunge us into the darkness of nihilistic non being, it opens our eyes to the clear light of unlimited being. Those who adopt Buddhism as an antidote against a supernatural view of the universe will see my words as those of a heretic.

Those who adopt Buddhism as an antidote against a supernatural view of the universe will see my words as those of a heretic. Their use of the anatta doctrine to dismiss transcendent consciousness will not be served by my argument. While there are few among us who do not welcome the empirical soundness that is a hallmark of Buddhist studies, equating empiricism with materialism is an error. The Buddha demonstrated that an empirical route leads to the supernatural, to the transcendence of consciousness.

Bibliography

Balsys, Bodo: *Ahimsa: Buddhism and the Vegetarian Ideal,* New Delhi, Munshiram Manoharlal Publications, 2004.

Batchelor, Martine and Kerry Brown: *Buddhism and Ecology,* London, Cassell, 1992.

Bell, Sir Charles: *Portrait of a Dalai Lama: The Life and Times of the Great Thirteenth,* Boston, Wisdom Publications, 1987.

Cook, Elizabeth: *Holy Places of the Buddha,* Berkeley, Dharma Publishing, 1994.

Dargyay, Eva M.: *The Rise of Esoteric Buddhism in Tibet,* Delhi, Motilal Banarsidass, 1977.

Dayal, Har: *The Bodhisattva Doctrine in Buddhist Sanskrit Literature,* London, Kegan Paul, 1932.

Eppsteiner, Fred: *The Path of Compassion: Writings on Socially Engaged Buddhism,* Berkeley, Parallax Press, 1988.

Eppsteiner, Fred: *The Path of Compassion: Writings on Socially Engaged Buddhism,* Berkeley, Parallax Press, 1988.

Gombrich, Richard F.: *Buddhist Precept and Practice,* Delhi, Motilal Banarsidass, 1991.

Gonda, Jan: *Vedic Literature: Samhitas and Brahmanas,* Wiesbaden, 1975.

Hakeda, Yoshito S.: *Kukai, Major Works,* New York, Columbia University Press, 1972.

Haldar, J. R.: *Early Buddhist Mythology,* New Delhi, Manohar, 1977.

Jones, Ken: *Beyond Optimism: A Buddhist Political Ecology,* Oxford, Jon Carpenter, 1993.

Keown, Damien: *The Nature of Buddhist Ethics,* New York, St. Martin's Press, 1992.

Khoroche, Peter: *Once the Buddha Was a Monkey: Arya Sura's Jatakamala,* Chicago, University of Chicago Press, 1989.

Lalwani. K.C.: *Kalpa Sutra of Badrabahu Svami*, Delhi, Motilal Banarsidass. 1979.

Lamotte, Etienne: *The Suramgamasamadhi Sutra,* London, Curzon, 1998.

Mookerjee, Satkari: *Buddhist Philosophy of Universal Flux,* Delhi, Motilal Banarsidass, 1980.

Morrell, Robert: *Early Kamakura Buddhism: A Minority Report,* Berkeley, Asian Humanities Press, 1987.

Nyanatiloka, *A.: Guide through the Abhidhamma Pitaka,* Kandy, Buddhist Publication Society, 1971.

Payutto, Prayudh: *Buddhist Economics: A Middle Way for the Marketplace,* Bangkok, Buddhadhamma Foundation, 1994.

Poppe, Nicholas: *The Twelve Deeds of Buddha,* Seattle, University of Washington Press, 1967.

Powers, John: *Wisdom of Buddha: The Samdhinirmocana Sutra,* Berkeley, Dharma Publishing, 1994.

Sarkisyanz, E.: *Buddhist Backgrounds of the Burmese Revolution,* The Hague, Martinus Nijhoff, 1965.

Sotoshu Shumucho: *International Symposium: The Future of the Earth and Zen Buddhism,* Tokyo, Sotoshu Shumucho, 1991.

Sprung, Mervyn: *The Problem of Two Truths in Buddhism and Vedanta,* Boston, Reidel, 1973.

Strong, John: *The Legend of King Asoka,* Princeton, Princeton University Press, 1983.

Thomas, E. J.: *The Life of the Buddha as Legend and History,* London, Routledge & Kegan Paul, 1927.

Titmuss, Christopher: *The Green Buddha,* Devon, Insights, 1995.

Wells, Kenneth E.: *Thai Buddhism, Its Rites and Activities,* Bangkok, Christian Bookstore, 1960.

Williams, Paul: *The Reflexive Nature of Awareness,* London, Curzon, 1997.

Index

C

K

L

M

N

P

R

S

T

□□□